GAME DEVELOPMENT ESSENTIALS

GAME QA & TESTING

Luis Levy

Jeannie Novak

DELMAR
CENGAGE Learning

Australia • Brazil • Japan • Korea • Mexico • Singapore • Spain • United Kingdom • United States

Game Development Essentials:
Game QA & Testing
Luis Levy & Jeannie Novak

Vice President, Career and Professional Editorial:
  Dave Garza

Director of Learning Solutions: Sandy Clark

Senior Acquisitions Editor: Jim Gish

Managing Editor: Larry Main

Senior Product Manager: Sharon Chambliss

Editorial Assistant: Sarah Timm

Vice President Marketing Career and Professional:
  Jennifer Baker

Executive Marketing Manager: Deborah S. Yarnell

Marketing Manager: Erin Brennan

Marketing Coordinator: Jonathan Sheehan

Production Director: Wendy Troeger

Senior Content Project Manager:
  Kathryn B. Kucharek

Senior Art Director: Joy Kocsis

Technology Project Manager:
  Christopher Catalina

Production Technology Analyst: Thomas Stover

Cover Image: *Demigod* courtesy of
  Gas Powered Games

For product information and technology assistance, contact us at
Cengage Learning Customer & Sales Support, 1-800-354-9706

For permission to use material from this text or product,
submit all requests online at **www.cengage.com/permissions.**
Further permissions questions can be emailed to
permissionrequest@cengage.com

Library of Congress Control Number: 2009926201
ISBN-13: 978-1-4354-3947-4
ISBN-10: 1-4354-3947-3

Delmar
5 Maxwell Drive
Clifton Park, NY 12065-2919
USA

Cengage Learning is a leading provider of customized learning solutions with office locations around the globe, including Singapore, the United Kingdom, Australia, Mexico, Brazil, and Japan. Locate your local office at:
international.cengage.com/region

Cengage Learning products are represented in Canada by Nelson Education, Ltd.

To learn more about Delmar, visit **www.cengage.com/delmar**

Purchase any of our products at your local college store or at our preferred online store **www.ichapters.com**

Notice to the Reader

Publisher does not warrant or guarantee any of the products described herein or perform any independent analysis in connection with any of the product information contained herein. Publisher does not assume, and expressly disclaims, any obligation to obtain and include information other than that provided to it by the manufacturer. The reader is expressly warned to consider and adopt all safety precautions that might be indicated by the activities described herein and to avoid all potential hazards. By following the instructions contained herein, the reader willingly assumes all risks in connection with such instructions. The publisher makes no representations or warranties of any kind, including but not limited to, the warranties of fitness for particular purpose or merchantability, nor are any such representations implied with respect to the material set forth herein, and the publisher takes no responsibility with respect to such material. The publisher shall not be liable for any special, consequential, or exemplary damages resulting, in whole or part, from the readers' use of, or reliance upon, this material.

Printed in the United States of America
1 2 3 4 5 6 7 13 12 11 10 09

CONTENTS

Chapter 2   The Mysterious World of Testing: working conditions & demographics 27

Chapter 3 The Many Faces of Testing: the game life cycle 47

Chapter 4   Planning Your Strategy: bug categories, tools & documentation 73

Chapter 8 Surviving & Escaping the Dungeon: transcending testing

Introduction

Game QA & Testing:
the new professionals

I want to be a game tester when I grow up! Most likely, this sentence has never been uttered. Game testing is just not one of *those* professions—at least, not yet. Gamers usually want to become game designers, producers, artists, or programmers. However, consider this little known fact: Game testing is one of the best ways to break in the game industry!

When game projects staff up in May, hundreds of testers flood publishers and developers alike with the unbridled energy of hardcore gamers. However, a majority of these testers had no training whatsoever before being hired to do what is a fairly technical job. They're blamed for lacking knowledge to which they have never been exposed. When developers complain about testers, their major gripes center around a lack of professionalism— skills, appearance, attitude, education, or initiative. In this book, we will attempt to correct this. Written by industry insiders, *Game QA & Testing* is intended as an in-depth introduction to the world of game testing—from basic game development concepts to advanced testing techniques. We want to take testing to the next level—helping testers to become elite specialists in particular fields (e.g., art, audio, level design, networking, performance, compatibility, physics, artificial intelligence). This is no easy task, and no other industry moves quite as fast as the game industry. Still, *Game QA & Testing* contains enough information to swiftly change the game for would-be testers.

In this book, you will learn: the role of game testers in quality assurance (QA) departments; the difference between QA and production testing; basic and advanced testing techniques; how to avoid being put "on call"; how to get promoted; and the future of testing. As one of the few books of its kind on the market, *Game QA & Testing* is a much needed, invaluable resource for students and game developers alike.

Today, testing is seen as a necessary evil—and testers are sometimes portrayed as hardcore gamers looking for a quick buck. This will all change as testers become highly sought-after professionals with unique skills. It's all a matter of time and effort—just like mastering a game!

Luis Levy
Santa Monica, CA

Jeannie Novak
Santa Monica, CA

About the *Game Development Essentials* Series

The *Game Development Essentials* series was created to fulfill a need: to provide students and creative professionals alike with a complete education in all aspects of the game industry. As more creative professionals migrate to the game industry, and as more game degree and certificate programs are launched, the books in this series will become even more essential to game education and career development.

Not limited to the education market, this series is also appropriate for the trade market and for those who have a general interest in the game industry. Books in the series contain several unique features. All are in full-color and contain hundreds of images—including original illustrations, diagrams, game screenshots, and photos of industry professionals. They also contain a great deal of profiles, tips, and case studies from professionals in the industry who are actively developing games. Starting with an overview of all aspects of the industry—*Game Development Essentials: An Introduction*—this series focuses on topics as varied as story & character development, interface design, artificial intelligence, gameplay mechanics, level design, online game development, simulation development, and audio.

Jeannie Novak
Lead Author & Series Editor

About *Game Development Essentials: Game QA & Testing*

This book provides an overview of game quality assurance (QA) and testing—complete with historical background, techniques, strategies, and future predictions.

This book contains the following unique features:

- Key chapter questions that are clearly stated at the beginning of each chapter
- Coverage that surveys the topics of game QA and testing concepts, process, and techniques
- Thought-provoking review and study exercises at the end of each chapter suitable for students and professionals alike that help promote critical thinking and problem-solving skills
- Case studies, quotations from leading professionals, and profiles of game QA and testing professionals that feature concise tips and techniques to help readers focus on issues specific to game QA and testing
- An abundance of full-color images throughout that help illustrate the concepts and practical applications discussed in the book

There are several general themes that are emphasized throughout this book, including:

- Defining the role of the game tester and how it fits into the game development team
- Exploring technology considerations associated with game testing
- Illustrating techniques and disciplines associated with game testing
- Investigating game testing issues associated with bug reports, documentation, and tracking
- Evaluating existing games and how they've been improved through game testing

Who Should Read This Book?

This book is not limited to the education market. If you found this book on a shelf at the bookstore and picked it up out of curiosity, this book is for you too! The audience for this book includes students, industry professionals, and the general interest consumer market. The style is informal and accessible with a concentration on theory and practice—geared toward both students and professionals.

Students that might benefit from this book include:

- College students in game development, interactive design, entertainment studies, communication, and emerging technologies programs
- Art, design, programming, and production students who are taking game development courses
- Professional students in college-level programs who are taking game development courses
- Game development students at universities who are taking game testing, production, and prototyping courses

The audience of industry professionals for this book include:

- Managers, directors, and producers from other industries who are interested in becoming game development professionals
- Game art, design, programming, and production professionals who are interested in becoming game test leads and QA managers
- Professionals such as producers, designers, and programmers in other arts and entertainment media—including film, television, and music—who are interested in transferring their skills to the game development industry

How Is This Book Organized?

This book consists of three parts—focusing on the evolution of the tester within a career in game development.

Part I   Game Start—Focuses on providing a historical and conceptual context to game QA and testing. Chapters in this section include:

- **Chapter 1   QA & Testing Through the Ages: a historical background**—discusses functions, standards, platforms, advantages, and the history of game QA and testing

- **Chapter 2   The Mysterious World of Testing: working conditions & demographics**—explores misconceptions, roles, environment, and tester characteristics

- **Chapter 3   The Many Faces of Testing: the game life cycle**—definition and varieties of bugs; how game testing and QA are incorporated into a game's life cycle; and the distinction between different testing disciplines

- **Chapter 4   Planning Your Strategy: bug categories, tools & documentation**—explores bug categories, tracking tools, management roles, and documentation associated with game QA and testing

Part II   Level Up—Focuses on the details associated with both basic and advanced testing. Chapters in this section include:

- **Chapter 5   Start Your Engines! bare bones bug hunting**—discusses bug spotting tips, reports, verification, and game genres

- **Chapter 6   Race to the Finish Line: elite bug hunting**—focuses on advanced bug hunting skills, normal vs. tough bugs, testing techniques, task forces, and achieving greatness as a tester

Part III End Game—Focuses on how to get a testing job, work up the testing ladder, and future predictions. Chapters include:

- **Chapter 7 Ready, Set, Go!: entering the world of game testing**—explores the job search and application process, how to get noticed by prospective employers, and educational opportunities—along with resume, cover letter, and interviewing tips

- **Chapter 8 Surviving & Escaping the Dungeon: transcending testing**—explores getting promoted, moving laterally, avoiding common mistakes, and standing out as a tester

- **Chapter 9 Testing Future Waters: what's next & how to get there**—highlights trends, "beneficial" bugs, lifecycle overview, and future predictions related to game QA and testing

The book also contains a **Resources** section—which includes a list of game development news sources, guides, directories, conferences, articles, and books related to topics discussed in this text.

How to Use This Text

The sections that follow describe text elements found throughout the book and how they are intended to be used.

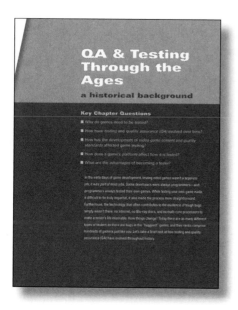

key chapter questions

Key chapter questions are learning objectives in the form of overview questions that start off each chapter. Readers should be able to answer the questions upon understanding the chapter material.

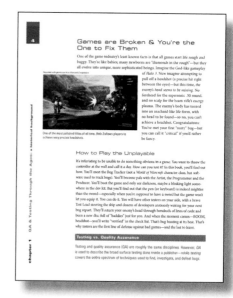

notes

Notes contain thought-provoking ideas provided by the authors that are intended to help the readers think critically about the book's topics.

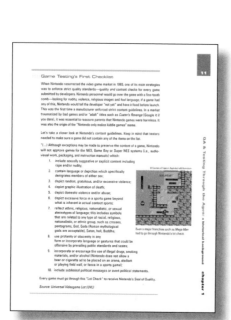

sidebars

Sidebars offer in-depth information from the authors on specific topics—accompanied by associated images.

case studies

Case studies contain anecdotes from industry professionals (accompanied by game screenshots) on their experiences developing specific game titles.

tips

Tips provide advice and inspiration from industry professionals and educators, as well as practical techniques and tips of the trade.

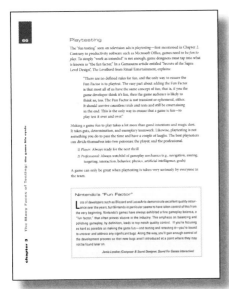

quotes

Quotes contain short, insightful thoughts from industry professionals, observers, players, and students.

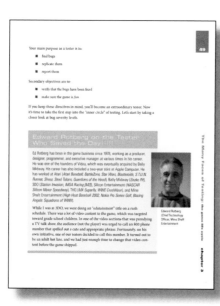

profiles

Profiles provide bios, photos, and in-depth commentary from industry professionals and educators.

chapter review

Chapter review exercises at the end of each chapter allow readers to apply what they've learned. Annotations and guidelines are included in the instructor resources, available separately (see next page).

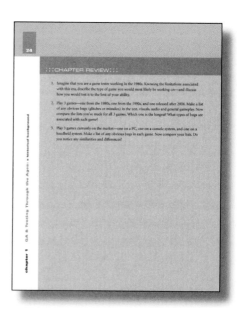

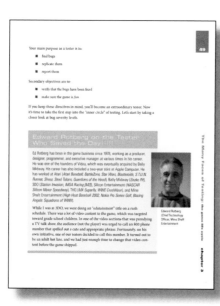

About the Companion DVD

The companion DVD contains the following media:

- Testing software: Bugzilla, DevTrack (video and link to DevTrack Web version), and TestTrack Pro (PC and Mac trial versions)

- Game engines: Torque (Windows and Mac versions 1.5.1) and Game Maker (version 7)

- Modeling and animation software: Autodesk 3ds Max (version 9) and Autodesk Maya (version 8.5 PLE)

- Game design, technical, and testing articles and documentation: Obsidian Entertainment (sample test plan), iBeta Quality Assurance (sample checklist and test plan), Gas Powered Games (Chris Taylor GDD template), Torn Space (Michael Black *Sub Hunter* GDD), NCsoft (*City of Heroes / City of Villains / Dungeon Runners / Tabula Rasa: Caves of Donn* developer diaries, *Guild Wars: Eye of the North* dungeons & quests), CCP Games (*EVE Online*), Dragon's Eye Productions (*Furcadia*), Harvey Smith/Witchboy's Cauldron (game design articles), and Barrie Ellis/One-Switch Games (game design articles)

- Game demos/trial versions: Blizzard (*Diablo II*), Firaxis (*Civilization IV, Sid Meier's Railroads!),* Stardock (*Galactic Civilizations II: Gold Edition*), THQ (*Company of Heroes*), Enemy Technology (*I of the Enemy: Ril'Cerat*), Star Mountain Studios (*Bergman, Weird Helmet, Frozen, Findolla*), GarageGames (*Marble Blast: Gold, Think Tanks, Zap!*), Max Gaming Technologies (*Dark Horizons: Lore Invasion*), Chronic Logic (*Gish*), Large Animal Games (*Rocket Bowl Plus*), 21-6 Productions (*Tube Twist, Orbz*), CDV (*City Life, Glory of the Roman Empire, War Front: Turning Point*), Last Day of Work (*Virtual Villagers, Fish Tycoon*), Hanako Games (*Cute Knight Deluxe*), Microsoft (*Zoo Tycoon 2: Marine Mania*), U.S. Army (*America's Army*), Cyan Worlds, Inc. (*Myst Online*), CCP Games (*EVE Online*), and Wizards of the Coast (*Magic: The Gathering Online*)

About the Instructor Resources

The instructor resources (available separately on DVD) was developed to assist instructors in planning and implementing their instructional programs. It includes sample syllabi, test questions, assignments, projects, PowerPoint files, and other valuable instructional resources.

Order Number: 1-4354-3946-5

About the Authors

Growing up in Sao Paulo, Brazil, Luis Levy was an extremely bright child but had trouble with his fine motor skills. His mother, a progressive psychologist, saw playing video games as the perfect remedy. She knew from early studies that games could

Photo credit: Jeannie Novak

help him fine-tune his movements in a fun and effective way—and that's precisely what she did. On Luis' ninth birthday, he received a Sega Master System as a gift from his parents. The console's pioneering 3D graphics with special LCD glasses took Luis' imagination and dexterity to a whole new level. Games such as *Phantasy Star* and *Space Harrier 3D* also taught him his first English words. Luis later created batch programs in DOS for an old PC XT and even played *Prince of Persia* on the computer's rusty green phosphor monitor. He also became a major film buff and a member of a very exclusive film club at age 16. By that time, he had become the main "movie critic" for friends and family and also an expert in both hardware and software. Luis wrote intricate short stories and shot award-winning documentaries (including a daring trip to Brasilia on a bus filled with homeless children and adults) at Brazil's renowned private film school, FAAP—where he received a B.A. in Film and Television. After working as a writer in both advertising agencies and Internet/new media corporations, Luis moved to the U.S. to pursue his true passion: video games. Months after his arrival, he became QA Tester at Activision—where he tested and troubleshot AAA titles such as *Quake 4* and *Call of Duty 2* in PC and current and next-gen consoles. Luis was also Production Tester on *Call of Duty 3* at Treyarch, where he belonged to the multiplayer team. In addition to *Game QA & Testing*, Luis is co-author of *Play the Game: The Parent's Guide to Video Games*. He is currently Assistant Account Executive at The Bohle Company—a public relations firm in Los Angeles specializing in video games and technology that has provided services to Microsoft, 3DO, Activision, Sega, Gravity Interactive, Emergent Game Technologies, and other high-profile clients.

Jeannie Novak is the founder of Indiespace—one of the first companies to promote and distribute interactive entertainment online—where she consults with creative professionals in the music, film, and television industries to help them migrate to the game industry. In addition to being lead author and series editor of the *Game Development Essentials* series, Jeannie is the co-author of *Play the Game: The Parent's Guide to Video Games* and three pioneering books on the interactive entertainment industry—including *Creating Internet Entertainment.* Jeannie is the Online Program Director for the Game Art & Design and Media Arts & Animation programs at the Art Institute of Pittsburgh – Online Division, where she is also Producer & Lead Designer on a educational business simulation game

Photo credit: Luis Levy

that is being built within the *Second Life* environment. She has also been a game instructor and curriculum development expert at UCLA Extension, Art Center College of Design, Academy of Entertainment and Technology at Santa Monica College, DeVry University, Westwood College, and ITT Technical Institute—and she has consulted for the UC Berkeley Center for New Media. Jeannie has developed or participated in game workshops and panels in association with the British Academy of Television Arts & Sciences (BAFTA), Macworld, Digital Hollywood, and iHollywood Forum. She is a member of the International Game Developers Association (IGDA) and has served on selection committees for the Academy of Interactive Arts & Sciences (AIAS) DICE Awards. Jeannie was chosen as one of the 100 most influential people in high-technology by *MicroTimes* magazine—and she has been profiled by CNN, *Billboard Magazine,* Sundance Channel, *Daily Variety,* and the *Los Angeles Times.* She received an M.A. in Communication Management from the University of Southern California (USC), where she focused on using massively multiplayer online games (MMOGs) as online distance learning applications. She received a B.A. in Mass Communication from the University of California, Los Angeles (UCLA)—graduating summa cum laude and Phi Beta Kappa. When she isn't writing and teaching, Jeannie spends most of her time recording, performing, and composing music. More information can be found at *www.jeannie.com* and *www.indiespace.com.*

Acknowledgements

The authors would like to thank the following people for their hard work and dedication to this project:

Jim Gish (Acquisitions Editor, Delmar/ Cengage Learning), for making this series happen.

Sharon Chambliss (Senior Product Manager, Delmar/Cengage Learning), for her reliability, professionalism, and management throughout the series.

Kathryn Kucharek (Senior Content Project Manager, Delmar/Cengage Learning), for her terrific help during the production phase.

Sarah Timm (Editorial Assistant, Delmar/ Cengage Learning), for her ongoing assistance throughout the series.

David Ladyman (Media Research & Permissions Specialist), for his superhuman efforts in clearing the media for this book.

IMGS, Inc., for the diligent work and prompt response during the layout and compositing phase.

Jason Bramble, for his masterful work in DVD design, authoring, and implementation.

Per Olin, for his organized and aesthetically pleasing diagrams.

Ian Robert Vasquez, for his clever and inspired illustrations.

David Koontz (Publisher, Chilton), for starting it all by introducing Jeannie Novak to Jim Gish.

:::

A big thanks also goes out to the people who provided inspiration or contributed their thoughts, ideas, and original works to this book:

Aaron Marks (On Your Mark Music Productions)

Baron R.K. Von Wolfsheild (Qtask, Inc.)

Barrie Ellis (One-Switch)

Ben Long (Noise Buffet)

Brandon Adler (Obsidian Entertainment)

Brian Reynolds (Big Huge Games)

Chris Lenhart (ITT Institute of Technology)

Chris Taylor (Gas Powered Games)

David Dawson (Snowblind Studios)

David Price (THQ, Inc.)

Edward Rotberg (Mine Shaft Entertainment)

Eric Doggett (Moondog Media)

Evan Call (iBeta)

Farhad Javadi (Central Piedmont Community College)

Floyd Billings (Sony Online Entertainment)

Frank T. Gilson (Wizards of the Coast)

Gordon Walton (BioWare Austin)

Harvey Smith (Witchboy's Cauldron)

James Owen Lowe (Icarus Studios)

Jamie Lendino (Sound For Games Interactive)

Jason Kay (RKG Games)

Jerome Strach (Sony Computer Entertainment America)

John Comes (Uber Entertainment)

Josh Bear (Twisted Pixel Games)

Justin Mette (21-6 Productions)

Michael Black (Torn Space)

Michael E. Moore (DigiPen Institute of Technology)

Nathan Madsen (Madsen Studios / NetDevil)

Richard Allan Bartle (University of Essex)

Starr Long (The Walt Disney Company)

Todd M. Fay (DemoNinja.com)

:::

Thanks to the following people and companies for their tremendous help with referrals and in securing permissions, images, and demos:

Adrian Wright (Max Gaming Technologies)

Ai Hasegawa, Hideki Yoshimoto & Janna Smith (Namco Bandai)

Alexandra Miseta (Stardock)

Apple, Inc.

Berkman Center for Internet & Society at Harvard Law

Brian Hupp (Electronic Arts)

Briar Lee Mitchell (Star Mountain Studios)

Carla Humphrey (Last Day of Work)

Chari Andrian & Angelique Blackwell (Midway Games)

Chris Parker (Obsidian Entertainment)

Chris Van Graas (Beepa)

Cindy Chau & Jerry Chu (Sega of America)

David Greenspan (THQ)

Digital Pictures

Eric Fritz (GarageGames)

Estela Lemus & Theresa Pascual (Capcom)

Evan Call (iBeta Quality Assurance)

Evil Avatar

Game Developers Conference

Genevieve Waldman (Microsoft Corporation)

Georgina Okerson (Hanako Games)

Gravity Interactive

James Montgomery Flagg

Janna Bureson (NCsoft)

Jocelyn Portacio & Rivka Dahan (Ubisoft)

Josiah Pisciotta (Chronic Logic)

Kevin Saunders (Obsidian Entertainment)

LinkedIn

Mario Kroll (CDV Software)

Mark Overmars, Sandy Duncan & Sophie Russell (YoYo Games)

Mark Temple (Enemy Technology)

Megan Wallace (Blizzard Entertainment)

Mellisa Andrade (Think Services)

Mod DB

Myrna Anderson & Karine LaMareille (Atari, Inc.)

nahtanoj on flickr (Wikipedia Commons)

Neversoft

Nintendo

Paul Unterberg & Jeff Johnstone (TechExcel)

Pete Hines & Grif Lesher (Bethesda Softworks)

Peter Murray (Firaxis)

Ray Schnell & Paul Cunningham (Creative Heads)

Rich Weil (Cartoon Network)

Robert Taylor (Activision)

Ryan & Justin Mette (21-6 Productions)

Sandra Lew (Foundation 9 Entertainment; Shiny)

Sarah Wigser (Seapine Software)

Scott Fisher & Charlotte Riffey (University of Southern California)

Steve Nix (id Software)

Susan Nguyen (Game Institute)

Swtpc6800 (Wikipedia Commons)

Take-Two Interactive Software

Terri Perkins (Funcom)

Thomas Donohoe (The Art Institute of Pittsburgh - Online Division)

Tony Fryman (Cyan)

Twitter

Vikki Vega (Sony Computer Entertainment America)

Virgin Games

Wade Tinney & Andrea Meyer (Large Animal Games)

Wendy Zaas (Rogers & Cowan)

Wgungfu (Wikipedia Commons)

Questions & Feedback

We welcome your questions and feedback. If you have suggestions that you think others would benefit from, please let us know and we will try to include them in the next edition.

To send us your questions and/or feedback, you can contact the publisher at:

Delmar Learning
Executive Woods
5 Maxwell Drive
Clifton Park, NY 12065
Attn: Graphic Arts Team
(800) 998-7498

Or the series editor at:

Jeannie Novak
Founder & CEO
INDIESPACE
P.O. Box 5458
Santa Monica, CA 90409
jeannie@indiespace.com

DEDICATION

To Jeannie, who has successfully debugged me.

—*Luis*

To Luis, the hunter who skillfully tracked me down.

—*Jeannie*

Part I:
Game Start

CHAPTER

1

QA & Testing Through the Ages

a historical background

Key Chapter Questions

- Why do games need to be *tested*?

- How have *testing* and *quality assurance (QA)* evolved over time?

- How has the development of *video game content and quality standards* affected game testing?

- How does a game's *platform* affect how it is tested?

- What are the *advantages* of becoming a tester?

In the early days of game development, testing video games wasn't a separate job; it was *part* of most jobs. Game developers were always programmers—and programmers always tested their own games. While testing your own game made it difficult to be truly impartial, it also made the process more straightforward. Furthermore, the technology that often contributes to the existence of tough bugs simply wasn't there: no Internet, no Blu-ray discs, and no multi-core processors to make a tester's life miserable. How things change! Today there are as many different types of testers as there are bugs in the "buggiest" games, and their ranks comprise hundreds of gamers *just like you.* Let's take a brief look at how testing and quality assurance (QA) have evolved throughout history.

Games are Broken & You're the One to Fix Them

One of the game industry's least known facts is that all games start life rough and buggy. They're like babies; many newborns are "diamonds in the rough"—but they all evolve into unique, more sophisticated beings. Imagine the God-like gameplay

Reprinted with permission from Microsoft Corporation

One of the most polished titles of all time, *Halo 3* allows players to achieve very precise headshots.

of *Halo 3*. Now imagine attempting to pull off a headshot (a precise hit right between the eyes)—but this time, *the enemy's head seems to be missing.* No forehead for the supersonic .50 round, and no scalp for the beam rifle's energy plasma. The enemy's body has turned into an arachnid-like life-form, with no head to be found—so no, you can't achieve a headshot. Congratulations: You've met your first "nasty" bug—but you can call it "critical" if you'd rather be fancy.

How to Play the Unplayable

It's infuriating to be unable to do something obvious in a game. You want to throw the controller at the wall and call it a day. How can you test it? In this book, you'll find out how. You'll meet the Bug Tracker (not a *World of Warcraft* character class, but software used to track bugs). You'll become pals with the Artist, the Programmer and the Producer. You'll boot the game and only see darkness, maybe a blinking light somewhere in the dev kit. But you'll find out that the pen (or keyboard) is indeed mightier than the sword—especially when you're *supposed* to have a sword but the game won't let you equip it. You can do it. You will have other testers on your side, with a brave Test Lead steering the ship and dozens of developers anxiously waiting for your next bug report. They'll return your enemy's head through hundreds of lines of code and burn a new disc full of "baddies" just for you. And when the moment comes—BOOM, headshot—you'll write "verified" in the check list. That's bug hunting at its best. That's why testers are the first line of defense against bad games—and the last to leave.

Testing vs. Quality Assurance

Testing and quality assurance (QA) are roughly the same disciplines. However, *QA* is used to describe the broad surface testing done inside a publisher—while *testing* covers the entire spectrum of techniques used to find, investigate, and defeat bugs.

The Industry Needs You

A little known fact is that the game industry absolutely *needs* testers. The industry depends on people like you. Developers don't have enough time to test the games they're making. They need production, QA, and compatibility testers; they need *hundreds* of you. Testers spot invisible walls, deformed characters, sloppy net code, missing textures, unbalanced weapons, map holes, long loading times, and lethargic controls. They spot all these "bugs," report them broken, and later report them fixed—"verified." They're part of a complex hierarchy that starts with testers and ends with studio heads and executive producers. Without testers, developers and publishers have no game to speak of—and nothing to put on store shelves.

Painting by James Montgomery Flagg

Game QA & Testing will show you how to:

- break into the game industry through testing
- survive life as a tester
- turn testing into an express freeway to a salaried position at the developer or publisher of your dreams

However, before we can tell you about all of the above, we need to go back in time—back to when the Atari 2600 was a next-gen console and *Charlie's Angels* ruled the airwaves.

Basic History

Looking back, it's hard not to gasp in shock at how primitive computing really was at the inception of the game industry. An Apple II was a multimedia, number-crunching monster compared to Commodore's PET. The Sega Genesis was a "next-gen" system. Keep in mind that computers had to start *somewhere*. If you grasp the basics, you'll stand a better chance of understanding multi-core leviathans such as the Xbox 360.

The Primordial Bits

In the early days of game development, memory was a rare commodity. In 1974, $338 bought you an Altair 8800 with an Intel 8080 and a whopping 4 kilobytes of RAM. Game consoles were more akin to calculators, not computers, so they had far less processing power.

Courtesy of Swtpc6800 (Wikipedia Commons)

Courtesy of Wgungfu (Wikipedia Commons)

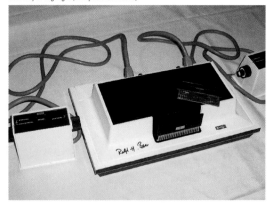

In 1974, $338 bought you an Altair 8800 with an Intel 8080 and a whopping 4 kilobytes of RAM.

Early systems such as the Magnavox Odyssey had no programmable hardware.

The truth is that there was simply no way of actually playing more than one game on the extremely under-powered consoles of the time. (*Pong*, we're looking at you!) This was the age of *non-programmable hardware* such as the Magnavox Odyssey and the aforementioned Atari *Pong*. Even if a cartridge was present, it had no *ROM* (read-only memory) to speak of—only simple switches that told the CPU what kind of game to play. You ended up playing variations of the same game—even if they were named *Tennis*, *Hockey*, and *Shooting Gallery*.

In the scenario we just described, the one person who developed the game was naturally the one to test it. A few hours of testing every night were more than enough, right? Like the Lone Ranger, the Lone Developer tested his own games in his own time. This, in essence, was the whole QA process during most of the 1970s. There simply wasn't a real need for a testing team.

Then, with the advent of the Fairchild Channel F in 1976, everything changed. Consoles now could play more than one game; they could, in fact, play an unlimited number of them if enough development houses put their minds to it. This freed consoles to provide gamers with all the entertainment they could pay for and brought forth the variety that games so desperately needed.

Courtesy of Wgungfu (Wikipedia Commons)

The Fairchild Channel F introduced the possibility of multiple games on a single system.

As cartridges became the dominant form of storage—ROM memory got cheaper— more complex games started being developed. For the very first time, consoles could display characters, backgrounds, and enemies. Sound evolved from "non-existent" to joyful *bleeps* and *blips*.

However, even if your game took all of 4K in ROM, there's still not a lot you could do with it. It's not like you could go off-road in *Enduro* or buy Pitfall Harry a new hat. *Pitfall* was regarded as "huge" at the time, but it was still straightforward to test. *Vanguard* was much more sophisticated than *Space Invaders*. Still, add one tester, a few hours every night, free coffee—and you'd get "mission accomplished" every time!

SNK Playmore USA

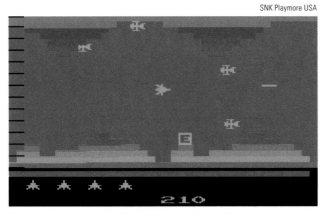

Vanguard took console shooters to a whole new level.

The Dark Ages

To understand the transformation games went through in the 1980s—which explains why teams of zero testers evolved into teams of three—you need to grind through *the darkest time in game history*. Remember the early 1980s, when games were "The Next Big Thing"? Well, maybe you don't, but your parents sure do. It was the time of *Pac-Man* and *Galaga*, *Starsky & Hutch*, Ronald Reagan, and George H. W. Bush. In just a few years, video games went from "The Next Big Thing" to "Fading Craze." This may seem a bit sudden and rather unlikely, especially now that games are growing an average of 50% per year (according to the Entertainment Software Association)—but this actually happened. The official name of this period is "The Video Game Crash of 1983." In short, since games were making publishers so much money, low-quality, low-brow, shameless opportunists began to flood the market with a massive wave of *shovelware* (cheaply developed software sold at bargain prices). Then as the number of (bad) products grew exponentially, it became more and more difficult for quality titles to differentiate themselves. First, sales dwindled, quickly followed by stock prices—and while some lost money, others lost everything. (Some fervently believe that the culprit was *E.T.*—killing off the game industry with a single tap of its glowing, heavily-pixilated finger. Rumors, we say.)

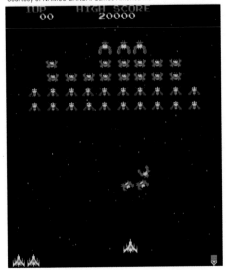

Courtesy of NAMCO BANDAI Games America Inc.

In the early 1980s, games such as *Galaga* were "The Next Big Thing."

The Chosen One

The "old" game industry did in fact die. As the Atari 2600 and 5200, Bally Astrocade, and Mattel Intellivision (among countless others) drew their last breaths, a new generation was coming: bigger, better, *boxier*. Enter the NES. . . .

A fact that few ever mention is that the Great Horrible Video Game Crash of 1983—guess what?—only took place in the U.S. That's right: Japan, the *other* big video game market at the time, survived unscathed. The NES (Nintendo Entertainment System) started life as the Famicom—"Family Computer." Released in 1983, the Famicom came equipped with keyboard and disk drive. The reason was that personal computers such as the Commodore 64 were aggressively targeting the console market and Nintendo knew that one of the reasons the "West" was going downhill was due to the "Personal Computer Revolution." So they made the Famicom more like a computer—effectively adding value to an already unique product.

Nintendo

Nintendo

Nintendo's Famicom (left) took off in Japan, but it didn't succeed in North America until it became the Nintendo Entertainment System (NES; right).

The Famicom was not a big seller at first—a motherboard manufacturing defect scared off early adopters—but a revised motherboard soon hit the market, and sales took off. With a game library composed initially of arcade ports such as *Donkey Kong* and *Popeye*, the Famicom proved to be a respected force in the Japanese market—while the U.S. game industry crashed and burned.

"Arcade ports" appears in the above paragraph, and we guess that nobody flinched. Today, arcade ports are a dime a dozen and "arcade perfect" means nothing. But back in 1983, "arcade perfect" was a big, big deal. Take a look at the accompanying screenshot from *Donkey Kong*: Can you imagine the shock of those who grew up dreaming of a home console version of *Donkey Kong*, now realizing a proper arcade port was on the way?

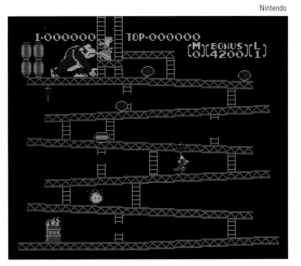

Nintendo

Donkey Kong was faithfully ported to the NES.

The lure of the Famicom (and later NES) wasn't the bright red color of its case or its innovative controllers; it was technically light-years ahead of anything in the market. The Famicom/NES was a huge generational jump that not only revived the U.S. market but led the way toward sophisticated, more complex games. And complex games need testers. So you can thank Nintendo for single-handedly bringing back joy to U.S. shores *and* giving origin to the first Game Testers.

A New Dawn

Eight out of 10 gamers who are old enough to remember have warm and fuzzy feelings when they think of the 1980s and 1990s. They recall lazy Saturday afternoons sipping lemonade in their friends' houses while playing *Super Mario Bros.* They see Sonic The Hedgehog for the first time, running toward a loop faster than anything before it—a blue-ish blur ripping through the scenery. They picture *F-Zero's* Mute City in all of its Mode 7 glory.

Nintendo

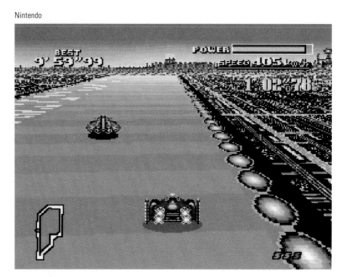

Players who remember the 1980s and 1990s can still picture *F-Zero* in all of its Mode 7 glory.

Those games were so far ahead of anything in the late 1970s that they actually *needed* to be tested. Game developers could no longer improvise on the testing and call it "bug free" themselves. For the first time, there was a real need for professional video game testers. As publishers became more powerful, having a minimum standard of quality was also rapidly gaining ground. That's precisely what Nintendo did with its Seal of Quality, which paved the way for *compliance testing* (done specifically by the hardware manufacturers prior to shipping). Very suddenly, Nintendo needed testers—and developers needed *their* testers if they wanted to be ready for Nintendo's feared "Lot Check" (a type of compliance testing). Computer game development teams didn't have to worry about it—but in a market still wounded, and a boom on the horizon, it was safer to abide by Nintendo's rules. (See the accompanying sidebar for an in-depth explanation of Nintendo's Seal of Quality.)

:::::Game Testing's First Checklist

When Nintendo resurrected the video game market in 1985, one of its main strategies was to enforce strict quality standards—quality *and* content checks for every game submitted by developers. Nintendo personnel would go over the game with a fine-tooth comb—looking for nudity, violence, religious images and foul language; if a game had any of this, Nintendo would tell the developer "not yet" and have it fixed before launch. This was the first time a manufacturer enforced strict content guidelines. In a market traumatized by bad games and/or "adult" titles such as *Custer's Revenge* (Google it if you dare), it was essential to reassure parents that Nintendo games were harmless. It was also the origin of the "Nintendo only makes kiddie games" meme.

Let's take a closer look at Nintendo's content guidelines. Keep in mind that testers needed to make sure a game did not contain any of the items on the list.

"(...) Although exceptions may be made to preserve the content of a game, Nintendo will not approve games for the NES, Game Boy or Super NES systems (i.e., audio-visual work, packaging, and instruction manuals) which:

1. include sexually suggestive or explicit content including rape and/or nudity;

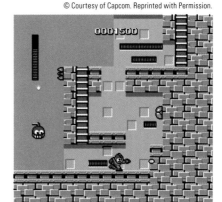

© Courtesy of Capcom. Reprinted with Permission.

2. contain language or depiction which specifically denigrates members of either sex;

3. depict random, gratuitous, and/or excessive violence;

4. depict graphic illustration of death;

5. depict domestic violence and/or abuse;

6. depict excessive force in a sports game beyond what is inherent in actual contact sports;

7. reflect ethnic, religious, nationalistic, or sexual stereotypes of language; this includes symbols that are related to any type of racial, religious, nationalistic, or ethnic group, such as crosses, pentagrams, God, Gods (Roman mythological gods are acceptable), Satan, hell, Buddha;

Even a major franchise such as *Mega Man* had to go through Nintendo's lot check.

8. use profanity or obscenity in any form or incorporate language or gestures that could be offensive by prevailing public standards and tastes;

9. incorporate or encourage the use of illegal drugs, smoking materials, and/or alcohol (Nintendo does not allow a beer or cigarette ad to be placed on an arena, stadium or playing field wall, or fence in a sports game);

10. include subliminal political messages or overt political statements.

Every game must go through this "Lot Check" to receive Nintendo's Seal of Quality.

Source: Universal Videogame List (UVL)

QA & Testing Through the Ages: a historical background   chapter 1

The accompanying diagram shows an average ten-fold increase in maximum addressable memory (storage capacity) from 8-bit to 16-bit. The conclusion is that more sophisticated 16-bit games might require up to five testers while most 8-bit games could be completed with one or two testers max, or *without testers at all.* Also, 16-bit systems lasted much longer than 8-bit thanks to add-ons and special chips such as the Sega Virtua Processor (SVP) and Nintendo's Super FX/FX2. If you think about it, 16-bit systems would only fade from the game world around 1995 or 1996—well into the 32-bit revolution.

Diagram by Per Olin

Maximum Cartridge Sizes

Platform	Mb (megabits)	KB (kilobytes) / MB (megabytes)
SMS	4Mb	512KB
NES	8Mb	1MB
SNES	32Mb	4MB
Genesis	40Mb	5MB

Cartridge capacities increased dramatically during the evolution from 8-bit to 16-bit systems.

The eight-year lifespan from 1988 to 1996 resulted in wildly different testing challenges. While *Altered Beast* could be beat in 30 minutes and had five linear, short levels, *Donkey Kong Country* could take well over six hours—even days for some. There is also an obvious gap between 2D games such as *Earthworm Jim* and early 3D games such as *Hard Drivin'.* A new dimension means that much more can go wrong, and it translates into more testers or more testing time needed.

Nintendo

While *Altered Beast* (left) could be completed in 30 minutes and had five linear, short levels, *Donkey Kong Country* (right) could take well over six hours—even days for some.

Courtesy of Midway Games, Inc.

Courtesy of Double Helix

3D games such as *Hard Drivin'* (left) introduced many more elements that could go wrong than in a 2D game such as *Earthworm Jim* (right).

Referring to the accompanying diagram, if you look at the team sizes in an early 16-bit title such as *Altered Beast* and compare it with *Sonic 3*—released late in the Genesis lifespan—you'll notice that teams had to balloon in order keep up with increased expectations of quality and content. The hardware might be the same, but expectations grow as platforms mature.

Diagram by Per Olin

Team Sizes

Game Title	Year	Dev Team*	Tester Sub-Team
Comix Zone	1995	40+	19
Sonic 3	1994	90+	41
Donkey Kong Country	1994	40+	9
Golden Axe 2	1991	16	6
Altered Beast	1989	6	0

* including tester sub-team

Team sizes grew exponentially as 16-bit platforms evolved.

Bigger cartridges meant bigger teams. The early development in storage can be blamed for the rapid increase in team size, yet this was nothing compared to the seismic change brought by optical media.

All the Space in the Universe

In 1988, NEC changed the face of the video game industry by adding a CD-ROM to its successful PC engine. The $399 add-on would revolutionize the way games are made—including the amount of testers needed on any given project. You may have grown up using CD-ROMs. Do you know how large the average hard disk was in 1988? Around 40 MB. Compare that with CD-ROM technology, in which the very first models were introduced at 550 MB. The difference in storage capacity was staggering—and frankly, developers didn't know what to do with it. Titles utilizing *full motion video (FMV;* full-screen, 15 frames per second or higher) primarily focused on grainy video and CD-quality audio—sacrificing gameplay. While some games attempted to become interactive movies—such as *Night Trap*—others relied on video to provide detailed, "moving" backgrounds.

Digital Pictures, Inc.

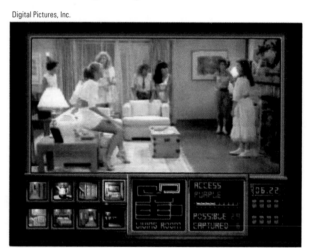

Night Trap, one of the first games that utilized full motion video (FMV), was an early attempt at an interactive movie.

Though the CD-ROM made a showing in the 16-bit era, the technology would only be fully exploited by 32-bit powerhouses—the 5th generation of home consoles. Computers had been offering games in CD-ROM format since the early 1990s (e.g., *Myst* and *The 7th Guest*), but consoles took a while to fully make use of half a gigabyte of data.

Proper games in CD-ROM format demand considerably more from testers. In this case, size does matter; levels can be much more expansive when loaded from a disc—and sound, which was traditionally overlooked in older systems, assumes a much larger role. Suddenly, "impossibles" such as lengthy introductions and orchestral soundtracks became commonplace and game budgets ballooned from $20,000 to almost $1 million per title.

Myst (left) and *The 7ᵗʰ Guest* (right) were among the first computer games to make full use of the space available on a CD-ROM.

With greater storage capacity comes greater testing complexity. It sounds like a line from *Spiderman*, and it means something similar: Testing games with large amounts of data takes considerably more skill and effort from a testing team. The potential of games in CD-ROM format would only be glimpsed with the introduction of the 3DO and fully realized by the Sony PlayStation in 1994.

Nintendo vs. Sony

The "Multimedia Revolution" changed everything. However, Nintendo's journey to multimedia had a nasty mini-boss: Sony. After a failed deal with the electronics powerhouse, Nintendo ditched its CD-ROM add-on due to legal fears and decided to go instead with a high-capacity cartridge. This was the origin of the Nintendo 64 (N64) and the reason for its greatest weakness: extremely limited storage capacity. N64 games contained about 96 megabits, certainly more than the 40 megabits of the Genesis but far from 600 mega*bytes* (MB).

Nintendo

While most of the information in this section can be applied to N64 titles, cartridge games could never achieve the level of detail found in CD-ROM based titles. This is the primary reason why the N64 didn't perform as expected. N64 games were more expensive to manufacture and purchase, lacked CD-quality soundtracks, and often included low-resolution textures.

Playful Worlds

The Sony PlayStation sold well over 100 million units. The console is regarded as one of the most successful in history. Before we move on to the next wave, we should stop and think about two firsts associated with Sony's innovative white console.

First Known Consumer Dev Kit

In 1997, Sony released the Net Yaroze. This consumer-focused development kit allowed anyone to develop their games for the PlayStation. At a cost of $750, it came with the following bag of goodies (according to Gamespot).

- 1 Net Yaroze PlayStation console (black matte texture)
- 2 PlayStation controllers (black matte texture)
- 1 AC power cord
- 1 AV cable
- 1 Net Yaroze boot disc (greenish PlayStation CD-ROM)
- 1 Net Yaroze software development disc (CD-ROM containing development tools for a PC)
- 1 access card (black dongle resembling a memory card, required for booting in remote-controlled mode)
- 1 communications cable (serial cable used to link the console and the computer)
- 1 "Start Up Guide" manual
- 1 "Library Reference" manual
- 1 "User Guide" manual

Many amateur games were developed in this "console." More than just a dev kit, the Net Yaroze was a token of faith in Sony's fans and a prelude of the days of Microsoft's XNA and user-created mods. It also gave gamers a brief (and expensive) look behind the curtain of game development.

chapter 1

First Fully Realized Open-World Games

We owe the PlayStation for the origin of console-based full virtual worlds. Initially, PlayStation games consisted of traditional 3D platformers—but this soon shifted to sprawling 3D worlds. An example of this type of game is *Driver*. Almost forgotten after *Grand Theft Auto 3* stole its thunder in 2001, *Driver* was one the first games that allowed the player to drive around existing cities for miles and miles on end. This degree of freedom was exhilarating and contributed greatly to *Driver*'s success in 1997. Where once driving games felt simplistic and limited, the cities in *Driver* had a sense of continuity—"being there" versus "playing that."

Driver (left) and its successor *Grand Theft Auto* (*GTA 3*, right) allow the player the freedom to drive around existing cities for miles and miles.

From a testing standpoint, things got *a lot more complicated* with open-world, free-roaming games (i.e., sandbox games). In a game such as *Spiderman 2*, another *GTA* wannabe, the amount of detail in each individual street is mind-boggling. Testing a game such as this requires dozens of testers and the division of the city into different zones. It's a huge undertaking!

With the emergence of sandbox-style, open world games, testing became a very serious business. As 32-bit matured, games moved from level-based 2D romps to entire 3D worlds filled with seemingly living things. This transition took games to a whole new level and made testing truly an essential phase of game development.

Two Black Boxes

As the original PlayStation was ready to step out of the spotlight, Sega released the Dreamcast—which was different than anything ever seen in the console world; it came equipped with a 56 K modem for online play, ran Windows CE as its operating system, and had special memory cards that doubled as portable gaming systems.

Courtesy of NAMCO BANDAI Games America Inc.

© Sega. All Rights Reserved.

SoulCalibur (left), ported to the Dreamcast (right) in 1999, left everyone who saw it in action speechless and hungry for more.

The Dreamcast was very innovative—and games for the system looked amazing. From the blurry N64 graphics to the trembling textures found in PlayStation games, nothing could prepare gamers for the beauty of the Dreamcast's graphics. Sega's white console not only allowed for anti-aliasing, but it also sported a very powerful video card (NEC PowerVR2) and a lot of storage space—thanks to Sega's proprietary *GD-ROM* technology (giga disk read-only memory; a disc with roughly 1 GB of data). *SoulCalibur*—ported to the Dreamcast in 1999—left everyone that saw it in movement speechless.

Yet this section is not entitled "Sega's Amazing New Console." We are going to talk about two black boxes—Sony's PlayStation 2 (PS2) and Microsoft's Xbox. The Dreamcast survived for roughly two years before Sega pulled the plug; its downfall could have been avoided if publishers and developers worldwide hadn't immediately jumped into PS2 development.

Every game development professional knows that the PS2 is a complex and sophisticated machine—and guess what? It's a challenging testing platform as well. Sony's devkits are large, to say the least. The Dreamcast, on the other hand, was very much a Microsoft animal and friendlier to code and test. This explains why for two long years, PS2 games were somewhat buggier than their Dreamcast counterparts.

Our second black box, the Microsoft Xbox, is really the spiritual successor to the Dreamcast. Released in 2002, the Xbox ran a lightweight version of Windows and had Microsoft's famous tools and tech support in the "plusses" column. In fact, the Xbox was really a PC crammed into a console case—including a then-powerful Pentium III processor and whopping 64 MB of RAM (double that of the PS2). Also, many games born on the Dreamcast found their way to the Xbox after Microsoft's console proved to be very popular with hardcore gamers and Sega loyalists. Just as the PS2 was a more complex programming environment, it was also more difficult for testing teams to handle. The ease with which PC games were ported to Xbox is a testament to Microsoft's more user-focused approach.

Sony Computer Entertainment America   Reprinted with permission from Microsoft Corporation

Where testing PS2 games was more complex (left), Xbox was fairly friendly (right).

The PS2 and Xbox, 128-bit and 256-bit respectively, brought the power of computers to games. Both of these next-gen consoles had network ports, hard drives, and surround sound. The PS2 played DVDs from the box, and the Xbox was the first console to bring 5.1 Dolby Digital surround sound to the masses. These technical capabilities also made testing each console a very complex ordeal, since network ports meant built-in "online play" and hard drives meant "big games with complicated loading and saving."

Modern Times

Support for the Xbox by Microsoft has greatly diminished in favor of the Xbox 360, but the PS2 is still going strong—particularly with independent games and Japanese titles that have never before been seen in the U.S. The PS2 is still wildly popular, and you might even have to test games on it. Chances are, though, that no more major titles will be released on the PS2—so if you stick to Sony games, you'll get to deal with the highly complex PlayStation 3 (PS3). Like the PS2, the PS3 breaks from the traditional architecture commonly seen in game consoles. On the Microsoft side, the Xbox 360 is an evolution of the original Xbox; however, it ditches the Intel chipset for a custom triple-core IBM CPU. So the Xbox 360 is not as straightforward as the original, but it's still fairly friendly to develop for and to test.

Sony Computer Entertainment America   Reprinted with permission from Microsoft Corporation

Sony's PS3 (left) and Microsoft's Xbox 360 (right) introduced HD gaming.

The PS3 and Xbox 360 introduced HD gaming to the world, and the many resolutions available could very well make your testing existence a nightmare. It gets more complicated: Full OSs are utilized (Xbox 360 and PS3), but developers rarely mess with them. You won't have to worry about most of the technical backbone in both consoles, but some of the online features will be problematic. Features such as adding friends, starting games, and muting annoying players need to be tested and are often found broken in pre-release; almost every game now includes multiplayer mode, so these are very common bugs.

You won't have to worry about backwards compatibility, but networking will always be a major pain in the neck. It's also harder to keep a steady frame rate with the adoption of high resolutions like 720p and 1080p, which demand considerable processing power. Most games start at 10-15 frames per second (fps) due to non-optimized code. Careful testing and reporting are necessary to help them hit 30 or 60 fps.

PC vs. Console

Testing games for the PC is completely different than testing for a console. Let's start with a list of unique PC game testing elements:

■ Mouse/keyboard interface

■ Need for install

■ Multiple OSs

■ Minimum requirements

■ Video card issues

■ Connection issues

BigStockPhoto

These six items make testing PC games a whole new challenge—even for experienced console testers. For starters, every time there's a new version of the game—a new build—you need to uninstall it and then install the new one. This usually means spending 20 minutes staring at the computer screen.

Testing games for the PC is completely different than testing for a console due to unique testing elements such as the mouse/keyboard interface.

Some testers also have to live with the *minimum requirements* machine, which is the slowest computer in the room. They have to make sure the game runs on this kind of computer; 15 frames per second is a common occurrence in the low-end side of PC specs. Needless to say, this kind of frame rate can be headache inducing. PC games also introduce their share of video card problems. Video drivers need to be downloaded and tested. Multiple machines in the room have all kinds of different Nvidia and ATI video cards. You're lucky if you get a good one; those testing stations are highly sought after.

What used to be a major difference with consoles is now more of a "familiarity." The network connection in PCs is very delicate, and a bad update or an OS mixup can cut your Internet connection. PC testers need to ensure that network settings are strong, and must monitor how much bandwidth the game is taking for itself—especially since all games are designed for a minimum broadband standard (around 400 bits per second [bps]).

We'll go into detail in Chapter 4 on all basic procedures for testing PC games. For now, suffice it to say that only elite testers get to work on PC games, since so much can go wrong. On the other hand, you can browse the web on PCs if things are slow or if the game is being installed. With consoles, you either talk to your fellow testers, stare at a blank TV screen . . . or read a book!

It's Your Choice

Why become a tester? Why work like a lunatic for up to 18 hours a day, six days a week, for very little pay? There are many answers to this question.

- *"I hate 'normal' jobs, but I love playing games":* Some think "Hey, I already spend my days playing games; I might as well get paid for it." However, this is a miscalculation: You don't choose the games you test, and you don't choose who you "play" with. You'll be testing the same game, day after day, until you can't stand it. You will have to play with people that might not necessarily "like" you. Also, testers who subscribe to this strategy usually don't take the job very seriously—and are not taken seriously in return.

- *"I can do it during summer break":* Some are "summer testers"—showing up when the school year ends and disappearing once classes start. This is not a good idea either; you join the project with everyone but then leave just when things start to get interesting. Those who quit at the end of summer miss out on all the cool things that happen to the surviving testers—those who make it to the very end of the project.

- *"I want to make games":* This is a good one. Testing can lead to permanent positions at the developer—if you're a production tester, that is. If you're doing QA work at a publisher, you might become an assistant producer or a marketing intern in the best-case scenario. However, most of the time, QA testers rarely rise; production testers have a better shot at getting full-time jobs.

All these choices are valid, but some are smarter than others. What matters most is that you know *what* you're doing and *where* you're going when you start work as a tester. Think about your goals, resilience, and "love of the game." Face the challenge of crunch early on—then look deep into yourself and ask the following question:

Will I play this game almost every day, for the next nine months, with a smile on my face, sharp eyes and ears, faithfully reporting every bug I see? If you answered "yes," you just might make it as a professional video game tester.

In this chapter, we showed you that early games were very simple and didn't need to be tested. This was the case until the NES came to market and Nintendo enforced strict quality and content standards. With the 16-bit revolution, a ten-fold increase in storage capacity made games much more complicated—and required testing was born. We also discussed the basic differences between testing on game consoles versus computers. You now know how PCs pose a very different testing challenge—and why PC testers are the very best testers in the business. Finally, you answered "yes" to the question on the previous page—which means you're ready for Chapter 2, where we explore the amazing (and frustrating) world of game testers.

:::CHAPTER REVIEW:::

1. Imagine that you are a game tester working in the 1980s. Knowing the limitations associated with this era, describe the type of game you would most likely be working on—and discuss how you would test it to the best of your ability.

2. Play 3 games—one from the 1980s, one from the 1990s, and one released after 2004. Make a list of any obvious bugs (glitches or mistakes) in the text, visuals, audio and general gameplay. Now compare the lists you've made for all 3 games. Which one is the longest? What types of bugs are associated with each game?

3. Play 3 games currently on the market—one on a PC, one on a console system, and one on a handheld system. Make a list of any obvious bugs in each game. Now compare your lists. Do you notice any similarities and differences?

2

The Mysterious World of Testing

working conditions & demographics

Key Chapter Questions

- What are some *misconceptions* about game testing?

- What are the *daily responsibilities* of a QA tester and production tester?

- What are the *working conditions* associated with a testing team?

- What are some tester *types*, and how can they be described as game characters?

- What are some *demographics* associated with testers?

In this chapter, we'll shatter some common misconceptions and unveil the mysterious world of testing. You'll learn about what a typical day in testing looks like for both QA testers and production testers. We'll introduce you to the testing ecosystem—working conditions and the environment you should expect as you enter this career. Finally, we'll also take a look at tester demographics from an informal survey—along with tester "types" that will give you an introduction to your future co-workers. Perhaps you'll recognize your own traits among these fun characterizations!

A Tall Tale

Testing games is great. You work from home, playing games all day long, making a few grand a month without leaving the couch. They send you the coolest games in the mail—like Netflix—and all you have to do is send them your opinion via email. On top of that, you get the latest consoles for free!

No! The above is an unrealistic fantasy world propagated by a few misleading television ads. Let's take a look at the myths from both ends of the spectrum.

"Game Testing Sucks!"

When you're testing video games, you often play the same game level over and over again for months on end. You have blisters on your hands and a headache from looking at a tiny screen 10 hours a day. When you come home and try to play games "just for fun," you start noticing all kinds of peculiar little things in games—things you never saw before. Like the characters in Stuart Gordon's Lovecraft-based horror flick, *From Beyond*, you realize those hideous "bugs" have always been there—but you didn't notice them before you became a tester. Thanks to an untrained eye and a short attention span, you were content. Now you're on the other side—a member of the "behind the scenes" elite who *know*. The hard truth is that, sometimes testing games is not fun at all—and it can leak into your recreational gaming experience. Why? Because testing games is—you'll never guess it—eye opening . . . and a lot of *work*.

"Game Testing Is Awesome!"

On the bright side, for every eight hours of suffering, there's at least two of the sheer joy of working on a game. There's always the moment when you realize you're actually making money *while* playing video games. This is a fleeting thought—but satisfying nonetheless. The more testers get involved in the game, the more pleasure they get from it. You can read previews of the game you're working on and play multiplayer matches with journalists and PR representatives. And once you hit *gold* and the game is ready to for launch, you get to check Game Rankings (gamerankings.com) for all the reviews you can read in one sitting. You even get to play the game *you* worked on with a bunch of people in Xbox Live. Nothing can top *that*!

The two statements we've explored—"game testing sucks" and "game testing is awesome"—are two sides of the same truth: *Game testing is sometimes boring, sometimes fun—but always cool!* Game testing is a job. Like all jobs, sometimes you love it and sometimes you hate it. Testing comes complete with a routine, hierarchy, and even "office politics." When you start working as a tester, you take the very first step toward becoming a full-fledged game developer. Game testing is a path, not an easy one, to become an industry professional—and to see all games in a "professional" light, whether you love them or hate them!

The Tester Path

Becoming a tester is like becoming a superhero; no comic book character spends years in "super school," chooses a major in Heroics, graduates, and suddenly gets work as . . . an intern-hero. No. They find out they have superpowers and go save the world. In real life, improv makes for a lousy testing technique. We want to change that; we want testers to be able to learn their craft, practice, and make mistakes. But we also want testers to be at the top of their game—literally. Right now, practically *anyone* can be a tester—so publishers are forced to babysit would-be testers instead of counting on their expertise. The journey from wanna-be tester to pro is a difficult one, but many have proven that taking game testing seriously from the beginning makes for a promising start.

iStockphoto

The journey from wanna-be tester to pro is a difficult one.

Orientation

When you begin working as a tester, the first thing you do is to go through "game tester boot camp." This is a one-day orientation program that's supposed to teach you everything you need to know about testing in a few short hours. If you end your first day knowing what a bug is and can define at least three different bug varieties, consider yourself lucky. There's a reason why most prospective testers zone out during training or spend precious time kidding around and making jokes. Often, these orientation sessions don't cover the reality of the testing experience. This is one area that needs much improvement in order to make the field more professional. Testers often find that testing has a technical side *after* they get the job—and they realize only too late that they're simply not up to the task.

The Split

When everybody shows up for work the very next day, managers are ready to split them into different teams. It's a normal, corporate triage process. By now, the person leading the orientation has a pretty good idea of who's there to work (and who's there to play)—and advises managers to put the best in PC testing and the worst in portables, usually Nintendo DS and Sony PSP. Everybody else goes to game consoles—Nintendo Wii, Sony PS3, and/or Xbox 360. We've observed this process in at least one (major) publisher; other publishers and/or developers might have different methodologies, but the logic behind this process still applies: PC is the most difficult platform to test on, while consoles are less difficult (and portables are often fairly simple), so it makes more sense to send the best to the PC team.

Diagram by Per Olin

Platform & Difficulty Level

	PC	Console	Portable
Hardware	Variable	Standard	Standard
Resolution	Variable	Standard	Fixed
External Controllers	Mouse/keyboard or joystick	Standard	None (built-in)
Networking Issues	Common	Common	Occasional
Driver Issues	Common	N/A	N/A
CPU/GPU/OS	Variable	Fixed	Variable
Development Kit	N/A	Required	Required
Difficulty	HARD	MEDIUM	EASY

PC is the most difficult platform to test on, while consoles are less difficult (and portables are often fairly simple).

A Typical Day in Testing: QA Edition

9:00am   You arrive at the publisher. Your keycard gives you access to the QA department, and you punch your time *in*.

9:15am   Your lead gives you a lengthy checklist. You start from the top.

10:15am   15 minute break. Ping pong time!

10:30am   Back to work. Better get cracking on that checklist.

12:00pm	Break for lunch. Some testers eat, others play *Street Fighter Alpha* with their oversized arcade controllers.
1:00pm	Lunch break over. The checklist awaits.
4:30pm	15 minute break. What about some pool?
4:45pm	Break is over. How about that checklist?
5:30pm	The lead allows some cool multiplayer action.
6:00pm	Punch your time *out*.

What we just described is an eight-hour day. It looks fairly fun—even with that nasty checklist continuously rearing its head. But this schedule applies only to non-crunch periods. When crunching, your day would be *very far* from what we just described.

Normal days in testing are similar to a "9-to-5" type of job. You arrive at 9:00am and leave at 6:00pm, and you have a one-hour break for lunch. However, 90% of all games go into what we call *crunch mode* (or *crunch time*)—an extension of working hours that allows the game to be finished on time. There's a point in production when producers realize that they need more than eight hours of work from developers and testers—and usually an extra day to boot. So a decision is made, and your 40-hour week instantly becomes a 72-hour week—12 hours a day, six days a week. This is sometimes called *light crunch*, and there's nothing a tester can do about it. Most developers try to avoid crunch mode, but they rarely succeed. It turns out that planning a game properly is an uncommon skill—and more often than not, games get delayed and testers and developers alike get shafted. However, if you think 72-hour weeks are bad, wait until you hear about *heavy crunch*. That's getting in a little later (at least 10:00am) and leave *when you're told to* (which can be 10:00pm, 2:00am, 4:00am, 6:00am . . . you get the idea—whatever is necessary to keep the game on track). Some go to work seven days a week and end up logging 90 hours when close to launch.

Crunching the Quality of Life

Heavy crunch got a very bad rep when *EA_spouse* went public with the plight of her husband, an Electronic Arts employee who worked so much overtime that he never got to see his family (or sunlight). In response, the International Game Developers Association (IGDA) formed a "Quality of Life" committee and released an associated whitepaper. Now publishers and developers try their very best to avoid heavy crunch, with limited success.

A Typical Day in Testing: Production Testing Edition

While QA testing definitely has a very specific routine, production testing doesn't. In production testing, every day is a surprise *since the game is still being made* and work is done side-by-side with the developers. Production testers are introduced to the game in late alpha while QA testers might start with beta or late beta. It's only a difference of 2-3 months, but production testers see the newest code and the heinous bugs that come with it. Once QA testers put their hands on the game, major bugs are usually gone and the game is now fairly stable—and thus easier to test.

10:00am	No daily timecard required. Production testers can submit weekly timecards.
10:10am	The producer stops by for a chat. Twenty-minute *Batman* vs. *Spiderman* discussion ensues.
11:00am	The lead splits the team in two or three sub-teams.
12:00pm	Lunch. Some browse the web; others play games.
1:00pm	Back to work. A networking issue has everybody working as a single team now.
4:00pm	Still hard at work. It's a tough one.
6:30pm	Someone has a breakthrough. A programmer is called. He is now working on it.
7:00pm	Dinner break. Dinner is catered . . . and free.
7:40pm	The programmer has a fix. He starts burning a new build.
8:10pm	The new build and multiple copies are done. The team starts all over again.
8:50pm	Someone has replicated the issue. Whoopee.
9:20pm	The team finally has "steps." The programmer is called. Again.
11:00pm	New build.
12:30am	Nobody can replicate it this time. The team tries for an hour and a half. The bug has been fixed.
1:00am	Everybody is allowed to go home.

This schedule probably freaked you out. It's a nightmare scenario: a complicated bug and the excruciating *test-retest-fix-burn-verify* sequence. Unfortunately, this is a good chunk of production testing. On the other hand, the rest absolutely makes up for it.

Playtesting: When Testing is *Fun*!

Just when we were on our way to simultaneously ruining your dreams *and* boring you to death, playtesting comes to the rescue. The objective in *playtesting* is to assess how fun and/or efficient the game is in various different departments. The accompanying diagram shows which factors are taken into consideration for different game genres.

Diagram by Per Olin

You're probably thinking, "Hey, aren't these the same standards by which games are reviewed?" The answer is a resounding *yes*. However, playtesting involves "reviewing" the game before the press gets its hands on it—while the game is still in production, in fact. It's a way to try all gameplay possibilities, explore all exploits, choose all characters, and race all tracks. With playtesting, developers are able to fine-tune gameplay and extract fun out of cold C++.

When you playtest, you're not looking for bugs. You're looking for killjoys and unfair rules, unbalanced weapons and overly complicated maps. You're making sure the game is really fun to play, the elusive "fun factor" mentioned in so many reviews. Bar none, this is the best type of testing. Still, if your game is single-player only—a soon-to-be extinct species—playtesting won't be that much different than doing a playthrough during normal testing.

Genre & Balance

First-Person Shooter
- Weapons balance
- Map balance
- AI skill
- Difficulty level
- Controller layout

Racing
- Driving dynamics
- 3D models
- Track design
- Opponent AI
- Difficulty level

Fighting
- Character balance
- Arena design
- Backgrounds
- Special moves
- Sound effects

::::: Blizzard Energy: Testing *Warcraft III*

Courtesy of Blizzard Entertainment, Inc.

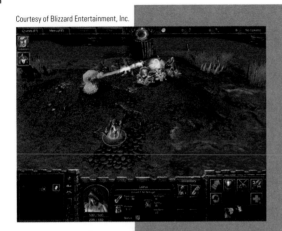

When I was at Blizzard, it was a lot of fun. But come on, how could it not be? We were working *Warcraft III*—the follow-up to one of the greatest games of all time. The office was clean and organized, which helps. But more important was the sheer energy present at that place. Here were some of the greatest creative minds in the game industry. You'd walk into the office everyday and see the trophy case filled with all sorts of wacky consumer products from Korea bearing Blizzard names—such as *StarCraft* sneakers and sodas! It was exciting.

Todd M. Fay (Owner, DemoNinja.com)

The Ecosystem of Testing

Only the strong survive. Just like it was in high school, only your intelligence and skills can save you from a horrible fate. Merely showing up is not enough. You need to lead. You need to find and verify the most severe bugs. And you need to do that every . . . single . . . day. We're going to share a real nightmarish scenario with you. Fortunately, conditions have improved at most companies since the days of the Dungeon and the Freezer. If you find yourself in a similar situation, you may want to look elsewhere!

Welcome to the Dungeon . . .

Most of the time (but not always, as you'll see from some of the industry tips in this chapter), testers are put in the least comfortable, coldest, most unloved offices. This is because testers are seen as "dispensable" and easy to hire. There's no such thing as catering to testers! At a large publisher, the "corporate" upper floors were chock full of executives, producers, and the marketing team—in contrast to what became known on the QA team as "the Dungeon." As you may have guessed, the Dungeon was underground; no windows, no sun, no fun—just a bunch of cubicles surrounded by an outer ring of cold, sterile rooms. The offices destined for the team were also very crowded. Console testers were crammed into small spaces so that their desk areas were the size of their televisions—usually only 13" monitors! Imagine 20 people in a room full of wires, consoles, old televisions, and action figures. That's what a testing room can look like. Oh, and cell phones didn't work in the Dungeon. Just a little detail, of course, since members of the QA team apparently *didn't have lives!* All the team could do was laugh about it—and rush up to ground level on breaks in case a conversation with a spouse or significant other was needed.

. . . And the Freezer

The Dungeon was cold, but not as cold as "the Freezer"—which was *really* cold because it was once a server room (and computers don't like heat very much). Of course, nobody gave it a second thought when assigning that room to other human beings. Many team members got sick working down there. The cold air from the A/C system would blow from all angles, no matter where you sat. It was impossible to take a nap during breaks; cold air hitting you from the bottom makes for quite unpleasant sleep. It was summer in California, 80° F outside, and all the game testers were freezing at 58° or 60° F in "the Freezer." This same publisher had proper offices for a few testing teams, but this was an exception: The only reason why one lucky QA team ever got a nice meeting room/testing chamber was because the company ran out of space downstairs. Marketing execs would give the QA team quizzical looks as they crossed the 2nd floor to go the restroom!

The accompanying diagram shows how PC testing is definitely much more comfortable than either console or portable testing. The environment for portable testing can be a nightmare due to having to look at that little screen 8-12 hours a day; needless to say, this has given testers *epic* headaches.

Diagram by Per Olin

Platform & Quality of Environment

	PC	Console	Portable
Desk	Medium (or large shared meeting table)	Small desk	None
Chair	Office chair	Office chair	Couch
Equipment	PC; 15" monitor	Console; 13" monitor	Console (monitor N/A)
Environment	GOOD	AVERAGE	FAIR

Fortunately, most working conditions have been changing for the better. This shift is accompanied by the growth of professionalism and a higher value being placed on testing and QA teams. In the next few pages, we'll take a look at a few positive reports from the front.

Positive Working Conditions for Testers

Obsidian treats its testers very well. It tries to integrate its testers into the game development process, something that is pretty rare in the industry. For example, I did design work on *Mask of the Betrayer*—and one of my *Storm of Zehir* testers, Megan Parks, created environmental art for that game. The hours can be grueling if the project is in crunch mode—but this is a normal situation for everyone on the project, not just QA, and it's something that everyone in the industry has to get used to. Obsidian tries to make it up to its employees when not in crunch, though. Movie days, game nights every Wednesday, and a relaxed atmosphere really help relieve the stress and make you feel like a valued employee.

Brandon Adler (Quality Assurance Lead, Obsidian Entertainment)

Sony Computer Entertainment values quality assurance and provides a clean, professional environment that fosters exceptional work. Additionally, many of the full-time staff members have significant tenure—which is very rare in QA. Typically, QA is often viewed as a quick stepping stone into the industry, but much pride is fostered in the work that is performed within Format QA, as employees strongly believe the success of the platforms depends on the diversity of the software, as well as the stability of its performance.

Jerome Strach (Quality Assurance Manager, Sony Computer Entertainment America)

Our testers are in heaven . . . no, really! They can work anywhere, at any time—and they often do not have to test the same thing every single hour and day. The developers respect them, depend on them, and help them. One of our testers that came from Activision, which is actually pretty good to testers, says that this is the best job he has ever had. The reason we can do this is because we use a social collaborative tool—which means we don't have to watch the clock, but rather, the testers can simply test, and log their time to the actual issue. Since the whole team can see the results, it makes for an open and transparent process.

Baron R.K. Von Wolfsheild (Chief Software Architect, Qtask, Inc.)

The environment is casual, with opportunity for testers to have some fun. But don't take that for a lack of professionalism. Our testers are very passionate about video games and they take their role very seriously.

Evan Call (Business Development, iBeta)

Our testers have a large office space of their own that provides little distractions. They have many testing kits for all platforms.

David Dawson (Environmental Artist, Snowblind Studios)

> **W**e have a good boss and a production team in place that understands that quality assurance is not an enemy, and that we are simply trying to put forth the best game possible. It has been a real blast working with this group of people.
>
> *Floyd Billings (Assistant Quality Assurance Lead, Sony Online Entertainment)*

> **T**he testers at my company are critical to the continued development and overall success of the project. While most quality assurance positions are entry level, we do our best to make testers feel valued and integral to the team—because they are!
>
> *Nathan Madsen (Composer & Sound Designer, Madsen Studios / NetDevil)*

Into the Wild: Gamers vs. Testers

It's time to dispel another common misconception—that all hardcore gamers are testers. Not so: "Every tester is a hardcore gamer, but not all hardcore gamers are testers." Being a gamer, even a hardcore gamer, is just not enough to become a tester. Even those who spend 12 hours a day maxing their stats in *World of Warcraft* might be unfit for game testing. Game testing requires discipline. You have to be able to switch to a different "mode," one where your main objective is *not to have fun*. This is more difficult than it seems. Have you ever tried not having fun on purpose? Did you ever play a horrible game just for kicks—10 hours straight?

It takes courage to play an unfinished game. This is where maturity is needed—along with perseverance. When you face the challenge

Diagram by Per Olin

Gamer vs. Tester

	Gamer	Tester
Purpose	Fun	Mastery
Exploration	No	Yes
Genres	Limited	No preference
Focus	Play speed / accuracy	Skill / achievements
Avoids	Bad games	Nothing

of playing a boring or broken game for hours on end, you do it because you have a higher objective. You want to find all that is wrong, fix it, and come back another day. This is why testers are officially named QA Analysts or Junior Engineers and not "Game Testers." You have to think like an engineer working on the construction of a 100-floor building. You have to look for flaws in the structure and make sure it can handle an earthquake and a tornado—*at the same time*. Do you know many gamers with this mentality? These are the ones fit for testing. Fun lovers and casual gamers cannot handle the stress and frustration of playing an unfinished game.

Testers as Game Characters

It's fitting that most testers resemble characters in some of the games they play. In this section, we reveal some interesting characteristics of game testers in a humorous (yet no less truthful) way.

Illustration by Ian Robert Vasquez

Blank

The Blank is just like the character at the beginning of a traditional role-playing game (RPG). This character has no memories, skills, knowledge, or equipment. This is the tester who likes to play games and, following a friend's "advice," applied for a game testing position. Most of the time, Blanks are not even technically minded; an iPod is too complicated for them.

Prognosis: Blanks can either learn from the best and become pros, or resign themselves to boredom and sleep on the job. Just like in a game, the only way a Blank becomes good is on that rare occasion when some undiscovered talent is revealed that turns out to be immensely helpful.

Illustration by Ian Robert Vasquez

Technician

Technicians are … technical. They often have attended at least one technical school, and they might even be programmers already. They know and love "the machine." Most are interested in moving to the tech team at some point.

Prognosis: Lacking observational skills, the Technician doesn't have the best "eye"—and can't hear that well either. Technicians can, however, break through the toughest bugs. Their analytical skills and knowledge of code are huge assets to the team. Technicians eat programming bugs for breakfast.

Artist

Artists love film and music and are usually able to draw and paint. They are plugged in, edgy, and always ready to pick a fight if their favorite movie gets trashed for being "too complicated." Most are interested in moving to the art team at some point.

Illustration by Ian Robert Vasquez

Prognosis: Artists have amazing eyes. They can see every single visual bug—even the smallest ones. They spot *z-fighting* (when textures seem to "fight" with each other; discussed further in Chapter 4), texture seams, and floating pixels without any effort. Artists usually have good ears as well, so they easily notice audio bugs. On the other hand, Artists might lack analytical thinking; this can make their job very difficult if a bug is more elaborate—something that involves 12 testers, for example. Artists might give up if they feel that their opinions are not respected or if the lead doesn't appreciate their penchant for visual bugs.

Hybrid

A Hybrid has the soul of an Artist and the skills of a Technician—often someone with a programming background, but who enjoys drawing on the side. Hybrids will talk about parallel programming at one point and then suddenly switch to Fellini's body of work and the reasons why David Lynch's *Twin Peaks* is the best television show ever made.

Illustration by Ian Robert Vasquez

Prognosis: Hybrids can be maddening. Sometimes their skill levels are simply not high enough for them to actually crack a bug's steps. They *almost* get it right and *almost* understand the truth behind invisible players and/or teleporting tanks. On the other hand, Hybrids can also be fast thinkers, and they are able to switch modes in the blink of an eye. Hybrids might also turn out to be leaders, suddenly becoming very valuable to developers.

Illustration by Ian Robert Vasquez

Stone

Stones are not game characters, but game props or objects. Known for not speaking and not moving, Stones just sit and wait until the elements turns them into little particles that one day will be carried by a mighty wind. Stones are either always "under the influence" of a substance or always sleeping.

Prognosis: Most Stones are useless but, again, some hidden talent might shine under all that immobility. Sometimes, Stones are excellent at full-on *speedruns* (playing through the game really fast) because their concentration skills are unmatched. On the other hand, they might not be the best communicators—and neither care about nor follow hierarchy.

Berzerker

Berzerkers . . . berserk. They are always angry at something or someone. Efficient at fighting, arguing, and complaining, Berzerkers seem to thrive on chaos and may actually *fear* a peaceful work environment.

Illustration by Ian Robert Vasquez

Prognosis: A Berzerker might team up with an inept lead and act like an "attack dog." We've seen this one up close, and it wasn't a hulking figure with a Mohawk haircut; it was a short, stubby Emo figure. Berzerkers might be good at testing, maybe even phenomenal, but they make everything personal and more difficult than it has to be. The only way to deal with them is to be extremely professional and let them know that any Viking-like behavior will be reported to the QA lead.

Mini-Boss

Mini-Bosses tend to be frustrated Artist or Technician types—and most of the time they are older than other testers. Just like the in-game mini-bosses, weaker types who serve as mere bumps to the next level, Mini Bosses think they have power—but they're testers just like everyone else.

Illustration by Ian Robert Vasquez

Prognosis: Mini-Bosses want to be in control. Barking orders and taking names: that's what they do. They see themselves on the fast track to a leadership position and as peers to the lead tester. Even if Mini-Bosses indeed have talent, their poor social skills annihilate any chances of promotion.

Elf

The Elf likes to look good. Elves are all about image and reputation. They don't go to work as game testers because they see it as a career; no, Elves test games because it's *cool*.

Illustration by Ian Robert Vasquez

Prognosis: The Elf is a rare type in testing. However, just because they are hard to find, it doesn't mean that their influence is null. Elves can drive a lead crazy with the most absurd theories. They also like to speak up to Executive Producers in the middle of do-or-die team meetings.

Even if you don't fit any of the above categories, you just might find yourself becoming one of these types (or meeting several) once you get a job in game testing!

Those Who Test: Demographics

Demographics consist of statistical information associated with a particular population (e.g., testers). In this section, we'll discuss some of the assumed tester demographics in the categories of gender, age range, social strata, education, and lifestyle. We'll then compare these assumptions with the results of an informal survey we conducted with respondents consisting of game QA/testing managers and other game professionals who have managed teams (e.g., producers, directors, leads). Here are the assumptions:

- The vast majority of testers are males; although female testers exist, they are rare.
- Many testers are currently in high school—and it's rare to find testers over the age of 21.
- Although some testers are of college age (between 18 and 21), they do not currently go to school—and it's rare for testers to have college degrees.

Let's take a look at the survey results.

Gender

It is widely assumed that testers are mostly male. It doesn't mean that females are "missing in action" from development studios; they are present but most often in other departments such as art (e.g., texturer, modeler, animator), human resources, marketing, and management (e.g., producer). Our survey results showed that for 70% of the respondents, 10% of testers in recent projects were female. Other respondents indicated that 20-40% of testers on recent projects were female. Significant findings indicate that:

- each testing team included at least one female member
- as many as 40% of team members were female

Although the majority of respondents indicated that only 10% of team members on recent teams were females, these results show that the gender demographics of the tester population are indeed shifting. According to *Game Developer Magazine*'s 8th Annual Salary Survey (April 2009), the number of female testers more than doubled from 2007 to 2008 throughout the US, Canada, and Europe.

Age Range

Another common assumption is that it's rare for testers to be in their 30s; by this age, there's a real need for money in one's life—and game testing doesn't really provide this. This assumption about age demographics is not necessarily a stereotype—which is most likely because of the entry-level pay associated with most testing positions. Our survey results showed that for 62% of the respondents, most testers in recent projects were between the ages of 22 and 25. Other respondents indicated that most testers on recent projects were either 18-21 (15%) or 26-29 (23%). Significant findings indicate that:

- although no testers were 30 or older, none were under 18
- the vast majority of testers were over 21

Although the majority of respondents indicated that most testers on recent teams were in their early 20s, these results show that the use of teenagers to test games as a summer diversion might be fading in favor of grooming testers for promotions and other positions within a game company.

Big Stock Photo

The results of our survey showed that there's a rise in testers who are female and/or over 21 years of age.

Social Strata

By and large, the general assumption is that you're not going to find testers from upper-class families. Testing is often seen as a "fun, but meaningless" job, and those with better resources tend to seek out more "adult" jobs. Still, once in a while you'll meet people who could be working a serious job or not working at all, hammering away at a broken game. They are testing games because: a) they can afford it; or b) they take game development seriously, want to pay their dues, and move up. Other than that, game testers are mostly middle-class or lower middle-class—often from families of blue collar workers and small business owners. Our survey results supported this assumption. All testers were either middle class (54%) or lower-middle class (46%).

Psychographics

Not traditionally included in demographics, lifestyle choices are part of what is known as *psychographics* (consisting of lifestyle, behaviors, attitudes, and values). People who have "alternative lifestyles" and convey this in their appearance (e.g., piercings, Goth makeup, multicolored hair) may embrace testing because it's a safer, less threatening, and more accepting environment than other entry-level jobs—and game testing offers a path to a full-time position in game development.

Education

Game testers are not known for having PhDs. First, testing doesn't even require a college-level education. Second, it's next to impossible to go to school and test at the same time (unless you're working only part-time). It's a common assumption that testers are not college educated—and that, although most have finished high school, they often join a testing team to "take a break" from their current education path. Imagine our surprise when 38% of survey respondents indicated that most testers had Bachelor's degrees! Although 23% of survey respondents indicated that testers were high school graduates without any college experience, the same percentage indicated that most testers had taken college courses in the past. A dramatic shift in the educational background of testers is clearly taking place; this is being supported by colleges and universities currently offering game industry degrees and game testing courses (discussed further in Chapters 7 and 9).

: :

This chapter has revealed what being a tester entails, along with the many interesting individuals you'll meet once you apply for that testing job. You have learned about overtime, typical days and not-so-typical ones. In the next chapter, we'll reveal all the different testing disciplines and how to become a pro at each of them. Get ready for the challenge of a lifetime: making sure unfinished games hit their quality and performance targets, while having fun at the same time!

:::CHAPTER REVIEW:::

1. Why do you think that the orientation being used to train testers at some game companies is ineffective? Based on what you now know about a typical day in testing, working conditions, and tester demographics, discuss how you might set up an informative and engaging orientation session for either QA or production testers.

2. Why aren't all hardcore gamers automatically well-suited for positions on the testing team? Discuss the difference between gamers and testers, and use examples in your analysis.

3. List the current demographics of testers that resulted from the authors' survey. Do you feel that there's a beneficial reason why the current demographics are so specific? What do you think would need to happen to widen these demographics in the future?

The Many Faces of Testing

the game life cycle

Key Chapter Questions

- What is the definition of a *bug*?

- What are the primary *severity levels* associated with bugs?

- What are the *phases* in the standard life cycle of a game?

- What is the distinction between *closed* and *open beta*?

- What are the distinctions between different testing *disciplines*?

Game testing might seem simple and self-contained, but the truth is that testing is akin to engineering and programming. No wonder the official title for game testers is sometimes "Jr. Engineer"! Some of you will actually need programming skills to succeed at testing. Others will need an eye for detail—or the succinct prose of a journalist. In this chapter, we'll uncover the world of bugs. We'll also tackle definitions and severity levels, and examine how testing relates to the life cycle of a game—while looking at various testing methodologies.

Bugs Defined

Let's hear it for the dictionary definition! According to Merriam-Webster, a bug can be many things:

1. a) an insect or other creeping or crawling invertebrate (as a spider or centipede)

   b) any of several insects (as the bedbug or cockroach) commonly considered obnoxious

   c) any of an order (Hemiptera and especially its suborder Heteroptera) of insects that have sucking mouthparts, forewings thickened at the base, and incomplete metamorphosis and are often economic pests—called also true bug

2. an unexpected defect, fault, flaw, or imperfection (the software was full of bugs)

3. a) a germ or microorganism especially when causing disease

   b) an unspecified or nonspecific sickness usually presumed due to a bug

4. a sudden enthusiasm

5. enthusiast (a camera bug)

6. a prominent person

7. a crazy person

8. a concealed listening device

9. a weight allowance given to apprentice jockeys

Definition #2 is the winner here; since a video game is a form of software, it fits like a glove. Let's take a closer look at this definition:

- *unexpected:* No one creates bugs on purpose; if it seems like it was done on purpose, it's an Easter egg—a different animal altogether.

- *defect, fault, flaw, or imperfection:* Something is wrong; it makes the game worse, ugly, or unplayable.

In games, every element that does not enhance the game but detracts from it is a bug. Sometimes a bug is almost impossible to see—and sometimes it's right in your face, taking up the entire screen. Or maybe it's an audio bug and you'll hear it if the 5.1 surround sound is at full volume, shaking the whole building. When you're a game tester, it's your job to locate all the bugs you can, replicate them—make them occur again, at will—and write a report for the developers. You are the eyes and ears for the game they are making.

Your main purpose as a tester is to:

- find bugs
- replicate them
- report them

Secondary objectives are to:

- verify that the bugs have been fixed
- make sure the game is *fun*

If you keep these directives in mind, you'll become an extraordinary tester. Now it's time to take the first step into the "inner circle" of testing. Let's start by taking a closer look at bug severity levels.

Edward Rotberg on the Tester Who Saved the Day :::::

Ed Rotberg has been in the game business since 1978, working as a producer, designer, programmer, and executive manager at various times in his career. He was one of the founders of Videa, which was eventually acquired by Bally Midway. His career has also included a two-year stint at Apple Computer. He has worked at Atari (*Atari Baseball, BattleZone, Star Wars, Blasteroids, S.T.U.N. Runner, Shuuz, Steel Talons, Guardians of the Hood*), Bally Midway (*Snake Pit*), 3DO (*Station Invasion, IMSA Racing [M2]*), Silicon Entertainment (*NASCAR Silicon Motor Speedway*), THQ (*MX Superfly, WWE CrushHour*), and Mine Shaft Entertainment (*High Heat Baseball 2002, Nokia Pro Series Golf, Blazing Angels: Squadrons of WWII*).

Edward Rotberg
(Chief Technology
Officer, Mine Shaft
Entertainment

While I was at 3DO, we were doing an "edutainment" title on a rush schedule. There was a lot of video content to the game, which was targeted toward grade school children. In one of the video sections that was parodying a TV talk show, the audience (not the player) was urged to call an 800 phone number that spelled out a cute and appropriate phrase. Fortunately, on his own initiative, one of our testers decided to call this number. It turned out to be an adult hot line, and we had just enough time to change that video content before the game shipped.

Bug Severity Levels

To get things going, let's first learn about the four different *severity levels* associated with bugs. The nomenclature may differ from developer to developer, but respective meanings are virtually identical.

Diagram by Per Olin

Bug Severity Levels

	Low	Medium	High	Critical
Description	Do not impact game flow or perception	Annoying without affecting gameplay	Seriously affect gameplay	Interrupt gameplay
Examples	Rare graphical glitches; short sound distortions; user interface typo	Sticky spot; frequent graphical glitches; missing some sound effects; title screen typo	Stuck spot; no sound effects; missing dialogue; can't open door that ends level; can't change weapons	Crashes; freezes; data corruption
Action	Can be fixed later; may never be fixed	Should be fixed soon	Must be fixed soon	Demand immediate attention; if spotted during certification, game is sent back to developer

Low Priority Bugs

Low priority bugs (or *low bugs*) hardly matter; in fact, it often makes no difference to the development team whether they are fixed or not. Examples of low bugs are minor graphical glitches, a short sound distortion here and there, some small error in the user interface (including a typo, which would personally frustrate us!)—any "error" that does not impact the flow or the way the game is perceived in a major way. Low bugs abound in every single game you've played, from low-budget to AAA; they are sometimes ignored in favor of more serious bugs—the ones that *do* make a difference.

Medium Priority Bugs

Medium priority bugs (or *medium bugs*) should be fixed. They occur more often than low bugs—and they can almost always be counted on to happen. So if a visual bug happens often, instead of rarely, it might be upgraded to medium. At the same time, a bug can be categorized as low if it occurs deep in the user interface; the same bug might be a medium bug if it occurs on the title screen. Another example is a bug that would annoy a player, but not affect gameplay.

High Priority Bugs

High priority bugs (or *high bugs*) must be fixed. A game that ships with high bugs is either a bad game or it has been rushed to market. High bugs seriously affect gameplay; they make everything stop in its tracks. If you can't open a door and that same door ends the level, you got yourself a high bug. If you can't change weapons, that's a high bug. If the frame rate drops to 20 fps instead of the usual 60, guess what? It's a high bug.

Bugs That Won't Die

The longevity of some bugs amazes me. I've had players of *MUD2* complain about some strange but obscure goings on which, when I finally tracked them down, were in major pieces of code that have been executed tens of thousands of times a second for 15 years. It's astounding that the program ever worked at all, let alone that it managed to do so robustly for so long. This isn't an isolated incident, either; it's happened at least half a dozen times. I look at the code and think, "Why didn't it instantly crash?!"—but this somehow managed to be avoided.

Dr. Richard Allen Bartle (Visiting Professor in Computer Game Design, University of Essex)

Critical Bugs

Critical bugs are very special. A critical bug demands immediate attention from the developers. Nobody goes home—and if they're already home, they better come running back. Critical bugs are responsible for "the sky is falling" 2:00am phone calls and other general chaos! But what is a critical bug, really? Critical bugs cause "disasters" such as crashes, freezes, and data corruption. If you ever had a 50-hour saved game corrupted in one sweep, you know what we mean. Critical bugs must be fixed at all costs—and if the publisher spots a critical bug during *compliance testing* (discussed later in this chapter), the game is sent back to the developer.

Testing at Every Stage

Testing is a critical component to the process. In fact, you should test at *every* stage of development. At NCsoft, QA worked directly inside our *Scrum* process teams (which meet frequently and quickly to address problems and update everyone on progress) and tested content as it was being created before we even sent the game on to publishing QA.

Starr Long (Executive Producer, The Walt Disney Company)

Testing & the Game Life Cycle

For further reading on this topic, please see *Game Project Management* (Hight/Novak)— part of the *Game Development Essentials* series.

Games are living, breathing pieces of software. They all begin with a seminal idea that evolves into a prototype. If well-fed, this prototype grows and grows—soon becoming a pre-production game. As the game matures inside the developer's belly, it's eventually ready to go out in the world—usually with a big "push" from the marketing and PR departments.

Concept / Design

In the *concept* phase, the designer, producer, or other "vision" person heading the project has an idea for a game. A short concept document is written that describes the idea to other developers. Concept art is often also supplied that focuses on a few characters, interior/exterior environments, props, and structures. If proof of concept is successful, the concept document will usually evolve into the *game design document (GDD)*. The development of this document occurs during the *design* phase of a project.

Production / Prototype

Once an internal *production* green light is given, the developer works on a *prototype* of the game. The prototype is very rough and not really a game at all, but it contains a sample of the gameplay. If a publishing deal is not yet in place, the prototype will be shopped around to publishers and prospective investors—a process that sometimes condemns a prospective game to years in "limbo." It's essential that the prototype contains the gold in the game—that shining gameplay mechanic/story hook that can make a game financially successful.

Alpha

The *alpha* phase comprises a game's first major milestone, which is usually written into the contract (i.e., developers don't get paid if certain requisites are not met). The alpha phase demands feature completion, which includes a full *playthrough* (play a game from beginning to end) but often includes placeholder and temporary assets. Contrary to what some may think, the alpha phase is more about locking in the features than having a bug-free game.

> We are in the process of cross-training our QA people to also do network monitoring and administration. This will prepare them to run more "live" games such as *Webkinz* that we expect to become more commonplace.
>
> *Jason Kay (Chief Operating Officer, RKG Games)*

Beta

The *beta* phase is perhaps *the* most important milestone; it is roughly the time when all assets are in place and the game is virtually finished. A game doesn't fully hit the beta phase until all assets are permanent and all high bugs have been addressed;

therefore, the days before beta can be terrifying—especially if you take into consideration that a big chunk of the developer's funding is conditional on hitting the beta phase on time. After hitting beta, developers are able to embark on something the industry calls *polishing*.

> Testing is essential to presenting the game or milestone to the publisher for review. If we cannot get this right, then what kind of product will we be giving our customers who spend their hard-earned money to buy our game?
>
> *David Dawson (Environmental Artist, Snowblind Studios)*

Gold

When a game hits the *gold* phase, it's ready for market. Bear in mind, we didn't say "done"—but it still can be shipped. Today, with consoles perennially connected to the Internet, games are regularly released in "almost ready" state and then fixed up though downloadable updates (or *patches*). Unfortunately, this doesn't result in better games. (Remember *Test Drive Unlimited*—which was unfinished when it hit the streets and would only be really finished about six months after launch?) Even so, gold is still seen as the time when a game has fully matured.

Time Management During the Development Cycle

Invariably the most challenging testing-related experience is proper time management as it relates to the development cycle. Project managers and producers need to ensure that milestones are adhered to and that the QA schedule not be viewed as a buffer that can be easily squeezed at the end of the process. Far too often, we see this attitude permeate developers—and ultimately the most successful products that launch are those that are given adequate resources and are simply managed well. Executive management will frequently make decisions that are not in the best interest of the consumer. While it must be recognized that the bottom line needs to be considered, a product's shelf life and longevity ultimately comes down to word-of-mouth and reviews. Companies such as id Software and Blizzard recognize that quality comes first and they are not beholden to deadlines; very few companies, however, have this luxury. But there is something to be said about that mindset and the importance they place on quality product.

Jerome Strach (QA Manager, Sony Computer Entertainment America)

Beta Testing in Detail

Besides being a major milestone, beta testing can be divided into two varieties: closed and open. Closed betas are used to protect a game from the general public, while still involving a very high number of testers. If a closed beta is successful, a developer might opt to move into an open beta.

Closed Beta

Closed beta (sometimes known as *internal beta*) means that no one outside the developer and publisher has access to the game. Most games go though beta quietly, rushing to make the release date. Beta testing, in this case, is very private.

Courtesy of Gravity Interactive

Requiem: Bloodymare had a very successful closed beta process.

Some developers spend time polishing the game during closed beta. Now that the game is feature complete and feature locked, developers can ensure that all aspects of the game work as intended—and that gameplay is much more fun. *Requiem: Bloodymare* is a title that did exactly that: Gravity used closed beta to fine-tune the gameplay and get rid of networking bugs, preparing the game for a successful launch. Even the best features can mean nothing if the implementation is faulty.

Open Beta

Open beta (also known as *public* or *external beta*) is often utilized for the rising number of games that have online components. Some genres such as MMOGs (or MMOs; massively multiplayer online games) are built on the online component. Connectivity and network issues can be paramount to an MMO's success. With the game growing exponentially, production testers and QA are simply not able to test the whole game—even if you have 1,000 testers on hand. External help is needed— and these external beta testers take part in open beta. External testers are not paid for their work; playing an early copy of the game for free is seen as enough of a reward. Open beta is used to *stress test* servers (push the servers to the limit with an extreme number of users), balance gameplay, find low and high bugs, and make sure the game runs properly when thousands of players are trying to "kill and maim" at the same time. Some closed betas are highly sought after (e.g., *Age of Conan*), while others have trouble gathering enough players—with adverse consequences once the game hits stores.

Funcom

Entry to the *Age of Conan* closed beta was in high demand.

James Owen Lowe on QA Integration :::::

James Lowe is a content designer and writer for Icarus Studios working on the post-apocalyptic MMO *Fallen Earth*. He has a BA in Communication & Culture from Indiana University and a BS in Game Art & Design from the Art Institute of Pittsburgh–Online Division (formerly the Art Institute Online). He lives in the Triangle area of North Carolina with his wife Mandy and daughter Nora.

James Owen Lowe
(Content Designer & Writer, Icarus Studios)

From the point of view of a writer and content designer, I feel that one of the best things we've been able to do in the development of *Fallen Earth* is to integrate multi-disciplinary teams, including QA, into the content development process. Our content development teams are primarily composed of writers and content designers, world builders, scripters, and QA. As a new major content unit is being built, such as a town or level, QA is able to check the world area for art-related issues (such as collision, bad textures, etc.) while the writing and scripting teams prepare missions and other interactive content. As the events and missions are being implemented, QA is right behind—testing missions, finding oversights, and providing near-immediate feedback. This allows for faster iterations in the content development—providing greater, more focused polish over a shorter period of time than if we turned over a completed content unit for QA to test. As content development teams move on to other tasks, the QA team keeps going back over major content units, along with all other systems—continually providing feedback and discovering bugs, doing team and multiplayer testing, and assessing the whole "fun factor."

Jerome Strach on QA Collaboration :::::

Jerome Strach
(QA Manager,
Sony Computer
Entertainment America)

As an active gamer for over 30 years and a working professional in the game industry for over 20 years, Jerome Strach has witnessed much growth and technological advancements. He earned money from his paper route to buy his first Atari 400 in 1980, and he recently was honored to participate in the final QA approval for *Metal Gear Solid 4* and *Grand Theft Auto IV*. Working for companies such as Atari, Digital Pictures, Pixar Animation Studios, and Sony, Jerome was given a chance to explore many facets of game development—everything from quality assurance to programming to producing, which included working alongside some amazingly talented individuals. Believing life is a continual education process, he is now committed to delving deeper into information technology and network administration to hone his skills as the industry increasingly utilizes online connectivity and incorporates both social networking and casual interaction into games.

First-party development (companies such as Sony, Microsoft, and Nintendo—which are hardware manufacturers, publishers, *and* developers) has a large quality assurance (QA) department—and as with any company, that department is critical for providing valuable feedback. Fortunately, Sony values QA—and this support originates from Japan. It should be noted that QA departments cannot inject quality into bad designs or poor concepts. Quality titles that are fun to play remain the sole responsibility of the game designers and producers to work out prior to getting far long the road of development. *Focus groups* (assembled by the publisher's marketing department to elicit feedback from a game's target audience provide feedback on a game's level of difficulty and fun, among other elements) should always be utilized early *and* often. Equally important is the need for developers to remember that the QA team is your ally and not your enemy. The interaction between the groups should be supportive and not combative. This is easier said than done when people are functioning on little sleep and living off energy drinks—but it needs to be said regardless. Collaboration will always make for a better product—but at the very least, the proper utilization of the skills and talent provided within the QA department can tremendously improve the success rate when looming manufacturing deadlines near and street dates haunt your dreams.

Production Testing & QA

On the surface, "QA" sounds like the basic quality assurance process that every product undergoes—whether it's HDTVs or toothbrushes. Before a product hits the market, it's essential that certain quality markers are met, if not surpassed. QA assures that. In games, QA works as a double- or even triple-check process, where a game goes though a very fine-tooth comb. Certain areas of the game are verified by more than one tester, and a rotation prevents anyone from getting used to a level and thus numb to possible bugs. QA is known a game's last line of defense.

Production testing is far from the last line of testing defense. Infantry is more like it! As a production tester, you will never get stable code. The game might not boot at all. Production testing is the process of making a build stable enough for QA *and* make sure that the game is fun to play. Therefore, a production tester must balance these two somewhat opposed objectives daily—being aware of technical issues and gameplay simultaneously. The bugs you will find as a production tester will be much more complicated than the bugs found by a QA team—that is, if you're doing your job right. The QA team is not supposed to stumble on bugs that should be found by production testers, in part because the sheer volume of a QA team (which can be upwards of 900 testers) makes QA expensive! A broken build results in money down the drain and happy testers playing ping-pong.

Testers & the Development Pipeline

Testers not only help us with the general problem of "removing bugs from the game," but they also help us prevent problems in the development pipeline—preventing developers from getting stuck with buggy builds of tools (or the game on their systems, unable to make any progress).

Brian Reynolds (Founder & Creative Director, Big Huge Games)

The QA-Testing Partnership

QA and testing go hand in hand with the larger game development process. You cannot have one without the other. QA is very important in getting out a game or expansion that is fun, bug free, and challenging all at the same time. The QA team does not create the game, but it can determine if the feel or vibe of a particular system is as intended from the dev side—as well as detect and report the bugs found. Others understand this and are more than willing (eager in fact) to cooperate with us to make sure their work is the best that it can be.

Floyd Billings (Assistant QA Lead, Sony Online Entertainment)

Testing Disciplines

As you learned in Chapter 1, testing started as a couple of people making sure the game worked. From there, it evolved into an essential part of a game's lifecycle—the "be all, end all" of a solid title. If your game had shoddy QA, sales would soon nose-dive—and retailers wouldn't be happy. The *testing disciplines* listed in this section are areas of knowledge *within* testing—in contrast to testing techniques (which will be discussed in Chapter 6).

Balance Testing

Balance testing ensures that gameplay is fair to both the human and AI player alike. If one is too powerful, there's something wrong. In single-player games, balancing involves making sure that the "easy" level is not too easy, "hard" is not too hard—and "medium" offers a nice, gradual rise in difficulty. Multiplayer games need to be balanced as well. Maps need to be neutral in their design, weapons must be equal in power (if not, the characters wielding them should be), and spawn points need to be placed fairly. The truth is that without balance, all matches are skewed and no victory is fair—or fun. This is so important that developers sometimes spend months balancing the gameplay!

Funcom

It is crucial that multiplayer games like *Age of Conan* are balanced.

Balance testing demands acute attention to detail. At the end of the day, it's the feel of the game (and your notes) that will help the developer fine-tune the gameplay. It's a fun job—exhilarating sometimes, but a very serious task nonetheless.

How to Balance a Game

Here are some guidelines for balancing a game during the testing process:

- Make sure the code is stable. Crashes and freezes will make balancing impossible.

- Enlist an equal number of testers for each side. Make sure their skill levels are matched by members of the opposite team.

- To balance weapons, load a neutral map. To balance a map, have everyone equip weapons of the same class.

- Play for at least one hour, making notes on the strengths and weaknesses of each weapon class. Write down the score as well, if a scoring system has been implemented.

- When the hour is up, have everyone switch teams. Do the same with the new set of weapons.

- Start an impromptu discussion. Write down opinions, observations, and final scores.

- You should have a hypothesis now. Check with the lead to see if you have enough time to investigate your hypothesis. If the lead suggests it, arrange everyone into different task forces and test it. (Task forces will be discussed in more detail in Chapter 6.)

- Chances are, you now have a good idea of how each weapon feels. Communicate your findings to the lead in written form.

Once developers come up with a new build, you'll have to do this all over again. In *Call of Duty 3*, the producers tasked the team with playing a lot of *Halo 2* at home for balancing. After this was done, the devs changed all weapon values in the game to *Halo 2* levels. Gameplay became arcade-ish, with several hits before someone died. Once the entire team despised the new values, the devs interceded again and brought them closer to *CoD* levels—not quite like *CoD2* but closer than *Halo*! The result was a game easier to play than *CoD2*, but not as forgiving as *Halo*—which made it *fun*. Ultimately, this is the purpose of all balance testing. If you see players describing your game as "fun" on the Internet, it's a job well done!

Compatibility Testing

Exclusive to PC, *compatibility testing* is the process by which the game is tested with multiple hardware configurations. The objective is to make sure the game is fully compatible with parts and peripherals found on the market. Testers need to be proficient in PC assembly and troubleshooting, since the job consists of installing multiple pieces of hardware and seeing how the game runs with each one of them. Compatibility testing is much more technically demanding than balance testing.

Installing *GPUs* (graphics processing units, the high-performance video cards used for 3D games) and RAM modules is not for the faint of heart. Even background applications can have an impact on how a game runs. Knowing how to perform compatibility testing is a somewhat rare skill, and most testers will never need to learn it. However, in order to advance your career, you might have to tackle compatibility testing before moving on to other things.

> Most games made by Blizzard (e.g., *Diablo, Diablo II, World of Warcraft, StarCraft*) are virtually bug-free because Blizzard does not mind pushing a launch back six months in order to present a polished product.
>
> *Floyd Billings*
> *(Assistant QA Lead, Sony Online Entertainment)*

Audio Compatibility Testing for Mobile Games

In particular, music and sound for cell phone games present a challenge because every phone has a different instrument set. What sounds good on one phone can sound horrible on another. Our phone game projects require testing on a lot of devices to ensure the greatest level of accuracy.

Eric Doggett (Owner, Moondog Media)

I am currently working on a 14-game project for one company. The games will be ported to over 15 different mobile phones, each with their own audio file types, size limits, and speakers. I had to audition each phone and build my own playback system comprising two ½-inch speakers configured to play back directly from my workstation. When speakers are this small, much of the bass and treble are stripped away and the sound is extremely distorted. There is a lot of work involved in testing these devices and making them sound good!

Ben Long (Composer & Sound Designer, Noise Buffet)

Soaking

"Soaking" sounds like cooking—and in a way, it is. In game development, soaking is a sub-discipline of testing—one where the tester doesn't really do anything but leaves the console or computer running for extended lengths of time. For example, a tester might leave the game on the title screen for three days and then verify whether it crashed or not. Soaking is necessary because sometimes memory leaks or rounding errors might hurt the game's stability in the long run—which would be undetectable during normal testing. Soaking testing is usually done by a lead tester.

Compliance Testing

Compliance testing is the one testing variety everybody seems to hate. But what gives compliance testing such a bad rap? Before a game is sold in the market, it first needs to go though *certification*; this process is conducted by the hardware developers themselves (such as Sony, Microsoft or Nintendo), who need to be absolutely sure that a game follows established guidelines before it is allowed to be sold on store shelves:

- Sony has what is called *TRC (Technical Requirements Checklist)*.

- Microsoft's is similar, but not the same: *TCR (Technical Certification Requirements)*.

- Nintendo uses the same term it did for *Super Mario Bros.* in the 1980s: *Lot Check*. (See Chapter 1 for more details.)

> Nintendo has a really good reputation for having games that appear to be bug-free. *Super Mario Galaxy* on the Wii was not only a great game, but it also showed tremendous polish and a dedication to making sure a weird bug never took you out of the experience.
>
> *Josh Bear (Chief Creative Officer, Twisted Pixel Games)*

::::: *RocketBowl* Microsoft Certification

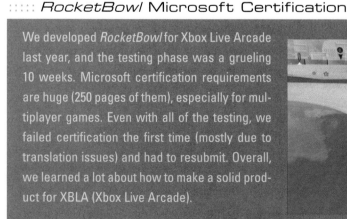

We developed *RocketBowl* for Xbox Live Arcade last year, and the testing phase was a grueling 10 weeks. Microsoft certification requirements are huge (250 pages of them), especially for multiplayer games. Even with all of the testing, we failed certification the first time (mostly due to translation issues) and had to resubmit. Overall, we learned a lot about how to make a solid product for XBLA (Xbox Live Arcade).

Justin Mette (President, 21-6 Productions)

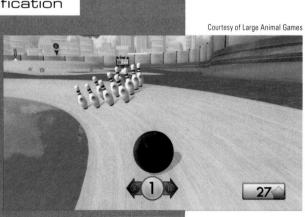

Courtesy of Large Animal Games

::::: *Grand Theft Auto IV:*
The Rockstar of Compliance Testing

Rockstar Games and
Take-Two Interactive Software, Inc.

Rockstar's *Grand Theft Auto IV* was a very clean *Format QA* [another term for *compliance testing*] submission from the beginning. This high-profile title had its release date slip—which most likely contributed to the developer's ability to ensure that bugs were minimized and that features were thoroughly tested in-house. Additionally, it should not be overlooked that the large budget most likely played a key role in ensuring that project management could devote necessary resources to do the work—and do it right. Finally, with a simultaneous multi-platform release date, this increased total headcount—and I'm positive more eyes were working the product as a result of this marketing strategy. In conclusion, it cannot be stressed enough that top notch software engineers and supportive project management undoubtedly played the single most important role in this title's tremendous success.

Jerome Strach (QA Manager, Sony Computer Entertainment America)

Each compliance checklist is composed of several different basic categories, such as the warning that flashes on the screen if you don't have enough storage space. This warning must follow certain guidelines or the game will fail once it reaches the console manufacturer (which we usually refer to as "first party").

Other common compliance requirements:

- The game must not display any religious images
- The game should pause once the controllers are not attached
- Before formatting a memory card or a hard drive, a message warns the user that all the data will be erased
- All copyrighted brands or names are acompanied by their respective copyright or trademark signs
- If data gets corrupted, the game warns the user and suggests reformatting the memory card or hard drive

Sony Computer Entertainment America

Compliance testing helps to ensure that the game actually saves when you select "OK" (*Gran Turismo 4* shown).

Testing for compliance gets repetitive quite easily. Can you imagine testing a PS2 memory card for two hours, following *very specific* instructions? There's simply no playing involved in something like this; it's hard work—that's all. Combing the game for these items is very difficult; very few testers are actually able to go though the hardware manufacturer's requirements and find all the compliance bugs. Compliance testing is a unique skill and one developers and publishers are known to seek out in new hires.

Compliance Testing for *Gun*

Luis was once selected among a large group of testers to learn compliance testing. This happened in the lull between two projects. Each one of the testers was provided with old *builds* (preliminary versions) of *Gun* and we would spend days going though the compliance checklists, trying to get the hang of it. While some of the items were fairly simple (e.g., "the game must go to pause mode once the controller is disconnected"), others could have been classified as "hardcore" (such as the PS2 network adaptor, which required a CD driver)!

Courtesy of Neversoft

Localization Testing

Localization testing is a reality because we live in a global economy. "Localization" involves converting a game from one region to another, and it usually includes translation. A game might be made in China with the help of Irish and Australian developers—or maybe it was made by someone in Los Angeles, but it was exported worldwide. More commonly, games are made in Japan and Korea and end up on American shores. For example, Konami and Capcom are famous Japanese developers, and Gravity Interactive is a name brand in South Korea. Many of Nintendo's core games first see life in Japan, and then they are localized for North America. Once these games get exported overseas, they need to be translated. However, these translation jobs are sometimes full of mistakes. This is a bad sign for a foreign game, especially if the game in question is striving for some kind of dramatic impact.

> On the PC side, Blizzard rules the roost on polish. *Diablo, Warcraft, Starcraft, World of Warcraft*: All of those games were polished to an incredible level for the PC.
>
> *Starr Long (Executive Producer, The Walt Disney Company)*

::::: Localization Testing in *Call of Duty 2*

Activision

Usually, games are tested once they arrive in the US, but Luis had to do localization testing on *Call of Duty 2* once it went to China and Japan. His character would have to keep dying, over and over again, so that Luis could compare the "death quotes" on the screen with the correct Chinese or Japanese characters. This was pure torture—and he's glad he never had to do that again! Still, it's a job that must be done—and there's always *somebody* that enjoys this kind of task. Currently, Korean MMOs are the ones that must go through careful localization—since mainstream Japanese games rarely have this problem anymore.

:::::"All Your Base are Belong to Us": *Zero Wing*'s Claim to Fame?

The most famous example of bad translation can be found in *Zero Wing*. "All Your Base Are Belong to Us"—a line from the intro of the Sega Genesis game—inspired a slew of media homages (including techno dance tracks, t-shirts, and April Fool's jokes). Even YouTube posted the phrase "ALL YOUR VIDEO ARE BELONG TO US" when it was taken down temporarily for maintenance.

As an example, here is the full dialogue seen in the game's intro:

Narrator: In A.D. 2101, war was beginning.

Captain: What happen?

Mechanic: Somebody set up us the bomb.

Operator: We get signal.

Captain: What!

Operator: Main screen turn on.

Captain: It's you!!

CATS: How are you gentlemen!!

CATS: All your base are belong to us.

CATS: You are on the way to destruction.

Captain: What you say !!

CATS: You have no chance to survive make your time.

CATS: Ha Ha Ha Ha ....

Operator: Captain!!

Captain: Take off every 'ZIG' !!

Captain: You know what you doing.

Captain: Move 'ZIG'.

Captain: For great justice.

Playtesting

The "fun testing" seen on television ads is *playtesting*—first mentioned in Chapter 2. Contrary to productivity software such as Microsoft Office, games need to be *fun to play*. To simply "work as intended" is not enough; game designers must tap into what is known as "the fun factor." In a Gamasutra article entitled "Secrets of the Sages: Level Design", The Levellord from Ritual Entertainment, explains:

> "There are no defined rules for fun, and the only way to ensure the Fun Factor is to playtest. The easy part about adding the Fun Factor is that most all of us have the same concept of fun; that is, if you the game developer think it's fun, then the game audience is likely to think so, too. The Fun Factor is not transient or ephemeral, either. It should survive countless trials and tests and still be entertaining in the end. This is the only way to ensure that a game is fun—to play test it over and over."

Making a game fun to play takes a lot more than good intentions and magic dust. It takes guts, determination, and exemplary teamwork. Likewise, playtesting is not something you do to pass the time and have a couple of laughs. The best playtesters can divide themselves into two personas: the player, and the professional.

1) *Player:* Always ready for the next thrill

2) *Professional:* Always watchful of gameplay mechanics (e.g., navigation, aiming, targeting, interaction, behavior, physics, artificial intelligence, goals)

A game can only be great when playtesting is taken very seriously by everyone in the team.

Nintendo's "Fun Factor"

Lots of developers such as Blizzard and LucasArts demonstrate excellent quality assurance over the years, but Nintendo in particular seems to have taken control of this from the very beginning. Nintendo's games have always exhibited a fine gameplay balance, a "fun factor," that often proves elusive in the industry. This emphasis on balancing and polishing gameplay, by definition, leads to top-notch quality control. If you're focusing as hard as possible on making the game fun—and testing and retesting it—you're bound to uncover and address any significant bugs. Along the way, you'll gain enough control of the development process so that new bugs aren't introduced at a point where they may not be found later on.

Jamie Lendino (Composer & Sound Designer, Sound For Games Interactive)

:::::Playtesting in *Call of Duty 3*: Get that Bike Right!

Playtesting involves going over all possible varieties of play and making sure all of them are fun. This is serious work: All it takes is for one faulty game sub-system to ruin the whole experience. We'll give an example of *Call of Duty 3*, a game in which Luis worked as a production tester. *Call of Duty 3* changed the *CoD* series forever with the introduction of vehicles. Until *CoD3*, all the vehicles in a level were mere decoration—accessories for the level design. With *CoD3*, jeeps, bikes, and tanks became not only drivable but essential strategy elements.

Activision

However, adding vehicles to a first-person shooter (FPS) is more complex than it might seem at first. When you drive a jeep in *CoD3*, the last thing you want to be is a sitting duck. With a bike, you want to avoid becoming a sluggish moving target—and the tank must be maneuverable enough to cram through tight European villages such as Poissons.

When fine-tuning the bikes, Luis decided he'd do everything he could to make the bikes fun. (Luis is a racing game fanatic, so he figured he was the one for the job.) There were two different bikes for the US and Germany. At first, they were both quite slow—and their handling was sub par. In order for the bikes to be effective strategically, they first needed to be drivable—offering a degree of control to the rider. Bike crashes in real life are deadly, but bike crashes in-game can bring defeat and certain humiliation.

As a production tester, Luis would spend a lot of time driving the bikes fast, jumping, hitting obstacles, and attempting to run his enemies over. When a big problem was spotted, he'd write to the producers in detail—explaining why the current suspension setup was ineffective or "boring." Soon enough, the programmers made the bikes faster. Later on, they made drifting possible—with a tail-happy rear-end. These two touches of gameplay allowed the bikes to be effective *and* fun, pushing the fun factor way up.

Usability Testing

Usability testing is a fairly recent advance in software testing—surprisingly so, considering its importance in the player's satisfaction. Microsoft is a big fan of usability testing—having learned the hard way after users kept complaining about how Windows machines were so much harder to use than a similar Macintosh system.

Electronic Arts, Inc.

Usability testing in *Jane's AH-64D Longbow* included checks for how well the PC cockpit matched a real AH-64D cockpit.

Usable means "easy to use"—not "easy" as in difficulty level, but intuitive to interact with other characters, use items, find your way, or drive vehicles. If a certain mechanism in the game makes no sense at all (e.g., you can't aim and move at the same time), this could be written as a usability bug. Perhaps the game was designed that way and nothing is really broken. It doesn't matter: Gameplay mechanisms need to *make sense* and be easy to use. You should worry about beating the game, not the control scheme. Energy spent otherwise takes away from the fun you might be having otherwise. Since it is responsible for visual control and feedback schemes, a game's visual *interface* is scrutinized during the usability testing process. Although uncommon for QA (which is used to catch more superficial bugs), all testers end up having to deal with usability issues. You may have even had to deal with them yourself—in games you've purchased!

We've discussed several areas of knowledge within testing that are considered "disciplines"—including balance, compatibility, compliance, localization, playtesting, and usability testing. Understanding these disciplines will help you become a well-rounded tester. As you become more skilled as a tester, you will be able to apply advanced techniques (discussed in Chapter 6) to each of these disciplines.

:::

As you can see, game testing is many times more complex than the brainless ads on television might suggest. While testing a game is a skill easily learned, understanding the game industry and how it relates to each variety of testing is a much bigger challenge. Where QA testing has a "brute force" aspect to it (after all, you're banking on a large number of bodies), production testing might be almost Jedi-like—with a couple of ace testers that are the only ones capable of cracking tough networking bugs. In the next chapter, we'll learn what steps need to be taken *before* you begin testing.

:::CHAPTER REVIEW:::

1. Play a game for at least 4 hours—taking notes on the various bugs you find. Categorize each bug with an appropriate severity level (low, medium, high, or critical). What sorts of bugs seem to be higher priority than others? Is there a pattern associated with severity level (e.g., location in the game, discipline, frequency)?

2. Go to BetaWatcher.com and join an open beta test for an upcoming game. Maintain a journal during your testing experience and report your weekly progress. When the test has completed, discuss what you learned during the process.

3. What are the testing varieties discussed in this chapter, and how do they differ? Selecting one of these varieties, and then test an existing game based on that variety's criteria. Provide a list of improvements that should be made to this game based on the variety you chose.

CHAPTER

Planning Your Strategy

bug categories, tools & documentation

Key Chapter Questions

■ What are the *roles and responsibilities* of managers who make decisions before testing begins?

■ What are the primary bug *categories* and associated examples?

■ What types of *documentation* are used in a game project that are relevant to testing?

■ How are bug *tracking tools* used in the testing process?

■ What are the possible *status* designations associated with a bug?

Just like everything else in life, game testing requires a certain amount of *preparation*; without it, you can't expect great results. When you take the time to choose your applications and work on your best laid plan, success will be at hand. In this chapter, we'll focus on the roles and responsibilities of QA and testing leads and management personnel. We'll also take a look at various bug categories so you can hunt them more effectively. Finally, we will examine documentation and tools that are widely used to help game QA and testing teams get the job done.

The Decision Makers

Long before the "lightning strikes" and testing begins, some important decisions must be made. Let's take a closer look at *who* usually makes these decisions. Kermit the Frog famously said "It's not easy being green." Well, it's not easy being the boss either. In this section, we'll attempt to describe the roles of producer, QA manager, lead tester, and floor lead. As the game industry lunges forward, sometimes it's hard to keep track of *who's* doing *what*.

NCsoft

QA testers at NCsoft

QA in the Planning Process

Quality assurance (QA) plays a pretty large role at Obsidian. The developers attempt to include QA in the planning process as much as possible, and this really helps us in our own planning. Getting to see any potential problems and voice our opinions has been invaluable in the projects that I have worked on. QA also holds the most important role in my eyes; we have to determine if a game is fun. I have seen lots of game designs change based on QA feedback; testers don't usually realize it, but this can be the most important job that they perform.

Brandon Adler (QA Lead, Obsidian Entertainment)

Producer

The *producer* oversees the game after months (perhaps even years) of development. "Keeper of the Calendar" and "Master of the Budget," the producer will be the first to defend the studio from a greedy publisher and the first to *fire* the same studio if it fails to deliver. When the game is finally ready for testing, the producer reaches out to the QA manager and gets the ball rolling.

QA Manager

When the game is ready for testing, the producer on a project turns to the *QA manager*—who most likely has been recently hired or was moved from another project. The QA manager assesses the situation and considers several questions:

- *How big is the game?* The "size" of the game—next-gen or portable, console or PC—will help the QA manager determine what kind of production testing will be needed and how large the QA team should be later in the project.

- *How much time do we have?* The time remaining, or how many months to launch, will help the QA manager devise a schedule, inhuman or not. The QA manager can plan testing based on this information, focusing on each milestone.

- *How much money do we have?* Without money, no testers can be hired. In an MMO, no money might mean no open-beta testing. In a next-gen title, especially one that is large and multiplayer-focused like *Halo*, it might mean less time and manpower to polish the game.

- *What platforms are to be tested?* If the game is console-only, compatibility testing can be avoided. If the game is a multi-platform title (e.g., released on DS, PSP, Xbox 360, PS3 and PC), then *large* teams are needed. The QA manager then usually finds a lead tester for each platform.

QA managers don't live rock star lives; they're the unsung heroes of QA, the "wizards" hiding away from the limelight. If you take the time to talk to them, you'll find out they know *a lot* about testing.

"Cheap Soda Never Hurts": QA Manager Responsibilities

As QA Manager, my primary responsibility is to provide an environment that enables my staff to perform with excellence. Fostering communication and the ability for people to feel comfortable in approaching management with concerns or issues is vital when ensuring a department's success. Trying to recognize personal growth and successes keeps motivation high and morale strong; nothing will bring a department to its knees faster than gossip or poor morale. Finally, it's important to keep senior people active participants in the sub-management of the department and to ensure that training for all staff and contractors keeps the department functioning smoothly. Cheap soda never hurts either!

Jerome Strach (QA Manager, Sony Computer Entertainment America)

Lead Tester

The *lead tester* may help build the team from previous foot soldiers and is usually one of the most talented and most experienced. Lead testers do most of the work necessary to start testing and are also responsible for any builds burned or in use—which can be quite large in number depending on the size of the team. Although it's possible for the game to be copied to a hard drive in modern systems, there comes a time when actual discs are required. At this point, your skills as a lead will be tested; how will you manage all those copies that are lying around while keeping other testers in check? Lead testers are usually experienced testers from other departments. Once a team is assembled, the lead tester might decide to pick a floor lead in order to help with the work load—since larger teams will automatically require more supervision.

> We have our QA integrated into the development process. A feature or addition is not "done" until the owner of that feature and the QA lead have signed off on it.
>
> *Gordon Walton*
> *(Vice President & Studio Co-Director, BioWare Austin)*

Assistant Lead Responsibilities

As Assistant QA Lead, I am responsible for reviewing all bugs submitted by my team to make sure they contain all the information they should and are very easy to understand—and to route the bug with the appropriate level of urgency. I am also resposible for many reports that I submit to my immediate superiors as well as back at corporate headquarters. I attend multiple meetings a day for many different aspects of the game. I am also resposible for tasking my testers with their daily schedules and items to test. We also test every hot fix, expansion, and change to any of the games I am working on. Last but not least, I also do a large amount of testing myself!

Floyd Billings (Assistant QA Lead, Sony Online Entertainment)

Floor Lead

The *floor lead* is the "unofficial" lead tester, a possible replacement if things go bad, and/or an assistant of sorts if everything is running well. On some projects, there may be several floor leads—like in a multi-platform game where Xbox, PlayStation, and Wii versions are being tested simultaneously. Floor leads have no real authority and are sometimes temp employees. What they *do* have is experience and a deeper understanding of the development process. Since floor leads help with the evaluation of each tester, getting along with them might save your job. Another thing to keep in mind is that the job seems very easy and straightforward at first—but this couldn't be further from the truth. To be an efficient floor lead, you'll have to develop not only technical but social skills. You'll be the first line of defense against relationship conflicts and personal issues within the team, so make sure you can handle it.

Bug Categories

Bugs come in many shapes and sizes. When you spot a bug, the first thing you do is write about it. So if you see a tank flying through the air—and leaving floating tracks, no less—write it down. When you fully understand the bug, it's then time to put everything in the database. This is when you classify the bug severity (low, medium, high, or critical) and category. It is essential to categorize a bug properly; if you categorize a bug incorrectly, you send developers on a "wild goose chase"—ruining planning and causing unnecessary delays.

In the accompanying diagram, we've divided bugs into eight main categories: visual, audio, level design, artificial intelligence, physics, stability, performance, networking, and compatibility. Several different varieties of bugs are listed for each category. Let's take a detailed look all these categories and associated examples.

Diagram by Per Olin

Bug Categories

Visual	Clipping	Z-fighting	Screen-tearing	Missing texture	Visible artifacts
Audio	Audio drops	Skipping	Distortion	Missing sound fx	Volume too low / too high (bad mix)
Level Design	Stuck spot	Sticky spot	Map hole	Invisible wall	Missing geometry (opposite of invisible wall; you can see it, but you can't walk through it)
Artificial Intelligence	Stuck (unable to move correctly through path)	Don't move	Die too often	Fail to follow	Can't open doors
Physics	Object floats when it's not supposed to	Object doesn't break	Object doesn't stop moving after being touched	Unrealistic gravity	Impossible to pile objects on top of one another
Stability	Freeze	Crash (black screen)	Crash to desktop (PC)	Can't load level	Unresponsive
Performance	Low frame rate	Levels take too much time to load	Minimum spec machine can't run the game (PC)	Game takes too long to install	Game pauses frequently to load data
Networking	Can't connect / dropped connection	Can't join invite	Lag	Invisible players	Scoring errors
Compatibility	Game crashes on ATI videocards	Logitech controller doesn't work	Game doesn't run on Windows ME	Bluetooth headset only outputs mono	Game is not compatible with Windows Vista 64 bit

Visual

Visual bugs are errors that affect a game's graphics. They can range from barely noticeable flickering to glaring texture issues that stick out like sore spots. Examples of visual bugs include clipping, z-fighting, screen tearing, missing textures, and visible artifacts. Let's take a closer look at each of these bugs.

Electronic Arts, Inc.

The highly detailed world of *Dead Space* demanded keen sets of eyes during the testing phase.

Clipping

Clipping is when a polygon overlays or penetrates another polygon. A classic example is a soldier standing behind a closed door with his weapon going *through* the door. This happened a lot in *GoldenEye 007* (N64). Clipping is also an issue with vehicles. A character's legs should *not* stick out of a jeep, for example!

Z-Fighting

In programming, the Z coordinate corresponds to depth. If there's a problem, textures in different depths might overlap and *fight*. (This is where the name comes from.) During QA testing in *Quake 4*, it was common to see z-fighting on the elevator command boxes. Usually, either the elevator door or wall texture would end up in a violent conflict with the original, correct texture.

Using Movement to Spot Z-Fighting

The best way to spot z-fighting is to have your character move forward and backward with the target in sight; your movement will uncover the bug by making it active and *extremely* visible.

Screen Tearing

A "classic" visual bug, *screen tearing* occurs when the graphics processing unit (GPU) can't draw a frame fast enough—resulting in a distracting "tearing" effect. Usually, the origins of this bug are performance-related—perhaps due to lack of time or because it's especially difficult to program for the platform. If screen-tearing becomes too noticeable, developers might cap the frame rate at 30 fps instead of the usual 60—a "quick-and-dirty" fix.

Missing Textures

When you encounter *missing textures*, all you see is flat white or placeholders (images that "fill in" once the engine notices that textures are missing). The problem is that missing textures are forgotten, and near-gold code often still contains some. Although a missing texture is usually a low-priority bug, it can be classified as "medium" if you spot it in an especially visible place. If you ever find a temp texture in late beta, enter it as a high priority bug. It's *that* serious.

Visible Artifact

Graphic bugs might be low priority, but that doesn't mean they can't be strange and annoying. A *visible artifact* is usually one of many little bits and pieces scattered on the screen that are not connected to anyone or anything. They are just *there*—sometimes floating, sometimes in a corner.

"Stray Pixels"

Luis caught some visible artifacts floating near his character in *Quake 4* in a well-lit hangar. He named them "stray pixels" at the time, since that's exactly how they looked. Just so you understand how complicated these artifacts can be: When Luis moved his character to the *other side* of the stray pixels, they disappeared. Heady stuff!

Testing Within the Game World

As an environmental artist, I create full scenes or objects for the game world. As with any asset made for the game, you must test it within the game world itself to ensure you don't miss something that could cause a crash.

David Dawson (Environmental Artist, Snowblind Studios)

Clipping, z-fighting, screen-tearing, missing textures, and visible artifacts are just a few art-related bugs you might see during a QA testing session. Most testers can detect visual bugs more easily than audio bugs, because most people can see discrepancies more easily than they can hear them; for this reason, audio bugs can be more of a challenge to track down.

Audio

Audio bugs can range from volume differences to complete audio meltdowns. Examples of audio bugs include audio drops, skipping, distortion, missing sound effects, and volume level. Let's take a closer look at each of these bugs.

Courtesy of Rockstar Games and Take-Two Interactive Software, Inc.

The audio in *Grand Theft Auto IV* is a feast for the senses.

Audio Drop

An *audio drop* might remind you of what happens during a conversation on a bad cell phone connection. It's like taking the word "love" out of "I love you." You end up with "I ____ you", which might as well mean "I HATE you!" Now, leaving failed relationships behind, audio drops are easily noticeable and very annoying. You might miss important dialogue, a telling gunshot sound effect, or your favorite line in a song. However, sometimes drops occur among a cacophony of sound effects, so it becomes more difficult to identify. Those are the tough ones.

Skipping

Just like a scratched audio CD, *skipping* is easily identifiable. In games, though, skipping usually follows a frame rate "hiccup." This is a good indication it might be performance-related, not asset-related. If it's indeed a performance problem, your only solution is to write it up as "performance." (See a discussion of performance bugs later in this chapter.) There is, however, a chance that the sound effect/music track in question is actually damaged.

Distortion

Let's say you just captured the enemy flag—but instead of hearing "Good one, Commander," the line sounds more like a duck with a British accent being strangled. This is a *distortion* bug. Like skipping, audio distortion might also be performance related—especially if the CPU "hangs" right in the middle of playback.

Audio Testing in Game Music & Sound Design

I'm the manager of the audio department, and I work closely with the QA dept to ensure that all audio content is performing as intended. When a bug report comes in, I first check to see if the source of the bug is coming from something my department created. If it is, we fix the error, then test the bug. If the problem is resolved, we can close the bug. If the problem is outside my department, then we work with each related team to help track down the problem and address it.

Nathan Madsen (Composer & Sound Designer, Madsen Studios/NetDevil)

As a composer and sound designer, I'm usually involved in a game fairly late in the process. Not only does this allow me to create audio that complements the characters, environments, and gameplay—but it puts me in the unique position of game tester. Since I spend so much time creating and testing sounds in the actual game, I typically run across bugs as part of the process and make it a point to document and report these to my contact. While I'm not actually hired to test a game, as part of the team, I'd be incredibly remiss if I didn't.

Aaron Marks (Composer & Sound Designer, On Your Mark Music Productions)

My role is to create original music, sound, and voice for games. These audio files must be tested for playback on a variety of destinations. The speaker system in a coin-op arcade game has completely different specs than those in a mobile phone—and the audio must be tested accordingly. Console games must sound great through tiny TV speakers as well as a surround theatre system!

Ben Long (Composer & Sound Designer, Noise Buffet)

Audio can be a tough beast. Many sound effects and other audio assets are added late in the development process, even if the audio group was involved early on—particularly with newer, lower-budget platforms. As a result, things that are taken for granted on top-end consoles (smooth transitions, having enough audio channels, track and instrument assignments, seamless ambient loops) rear their ugly heads once again on the Nintendo DS, web, and mobile devices. On these platforms, it's 1989 all over again--so testing becomes even more important!

Jamie Lendino (Composer & Sound Designer, Sound For Games Interactive)

Missing Sound Effect

A *missing sound effect* is similar to a missing texture, with one big difference: usually no placeholders are used. If a sound effect is missing, you will hear silence and that's it. A missing sound effect is ultimately the responsibility of the programming and/or the audio team.

Volume Level

If a game has volume sliders for every game element—like "engine," "road noise," "opponents," and "track music"—that's not a bug. However, if the game is mixed a certain way—and you can't change it in the Options Screen—a sound effect that's too faint or music that's overbearing can be classified as a *volume level* bug.

Aaron Marks & Jamie Lendino on Game Audio Testing :::::

Aaron Marks
(Composer & Sound
Designer,
On Your Mark Music
Productions)

Practically falling into the game industry almost 10 years ago, Aaron Marks has amassed music and sound design credits on touchscreen arcade games, class II video bingo/slot machines, computer games, console games—and over 70 online casino games. Aaron has also written for *Game Developer Magazine*, Gamasutra.com, Music4Games.net, and the Society of Composers and Lyrists. He is the author of *The Complete Guide to Game Audio*, an expansive book on all aspects of audio for video games, and of *Game Audio Development*, part of the *Game Development Essentials* series. He wrote an accredited college course on game audio for the Art Institute Online, is a member of the AES Technical Committee for Games, was on the launch committee for the Game Audio Network Guild (G.A.N.G.), and is the owner of On Your Mark Music Productions—where he continues his pursuit of the ultimate soundscape, creating music and sound for a multitude of projects.

From an audio standpoint, testing takes a bit more discipline in order to be effective. Great games have the tendency to suck you in and make you forget the purpose of 'playing' in the first place. But once you get past that idea, it's important to listen. Not only are you checking that the proper sound is triggered and that the sounds sync to the animations, but you are also listening to how everything in the soundscape fits together and whether the sounds are appropriate. One or two testers not liking a sound isn't a big deal, but a dozen who all complain about a particular sound are significant and usually make it worth fixing. As long as everyone remains open to critique of 'creative' assets, a game will be the better for it.

Jamie Lendino is an independent sound designer and music composer with 10 years of experience in the game industry. He has created audio for over 30 games, including *Monopoly: Here & Now, SpongeBob's Atlantis SquarePantis: Atlantis Treasures, Elder Scrolls IV: Oblivion, Zoo Tycoon 2: Endangered Species, Mage Knight: Apocalypse,* and the mobile version of *True Crime: New York City.* When he's not creating alien sound effects or working out drum parts for his next composition, he is busy indulging his other passions: writing, reading (both fiction and non-fiction), fast cars, and astronomy.

Jamie Lendino
(Composer
& Sound Designer,
Sound For Games
Interactive)

As part of a contract audio company, I often have to take the initiative in testing and QA areas. If I want to be involved in the QA and testing process, lend my "professional ear," so to speak, and offer to improve and polish assets that are already delivered, I usually have to speak up. For example, I love to hear that a client says something I created sounds great and accepts it—but I also want to make sure that the assets I submit benefit the game as much as possible (whether that means fine-tuning audio files or even lowering or removing them entirely). Large companies have this process fully fleshed out with excellent on-staff audio departments, so it's not a problem there. They know what they need from me and are very specific. But newer, smaller studios appreciate it when you go the extra mile in helping to make sure audio assets are integrated, balanced, and mixed properly—which can be a challenge if you're working remotely, as is often the case with game audio.

We do a lot of asset testing before even submitting anything. This includes balancing levels, tuning EQ, and mixing/mastering all assets as part of a group as well as individually. Once they're in the current game build, we could easily go back and fine tune. Everything is multitracked, separated into folders, named, time-stamped, and versioned so that at any point we can return to any iteration of an audio asset. All audio tracks are printed to digital files as well; this way as we move from old workstations to new ones and can easily pull up work we did for an older project even if the old plug-ins aren't installed. New versions of plug-ins can kill settings made with older versions, no matter how meticulous you think you are—so this is another important step.

Audio drops, skipping, distortion, missing sound effects, and volume level are just a few audio-related bugs you might see during a QA testing session. A tester with a discriminating pair of ears may easily detect audio bugs, but level design bugs can only be hunted down by testers who have the perseverance to focus on a more sophisticated "gameplay" testing process.

Level Design

When a level is badly constructed, you might end up with a hole in the ground or even an invisible wall. When things don't make a lot of sense *spatially*, this is a good indicator that you've encountered a *level design* bug. Examples of level design bugs include stuck spots, sticky spots, map holes, invisible walls, and missing geometry. Let's take a closer look at each of these bugs.

Courtesy of Rockstar Games and Take-Two Interactive Software, Inc.

The Darkness has amazingly detailed levels.

Stuck Spot

Oh, the *stuck spot*—a classic name for a classic bug. You might remember the very first 3D platformers, such as *Super Mario 64* and *Banjo-Kazooie*. It was fun to jump all over the place, except if you landed between three trees and got "stuck." In many cases, the culprit is the level designer. Bad geometry is preventing your character from moving. However, stuck spots are also common in first-person shooters (FPSs); you will find them around corners and in between boxes. If you get caught in one, at best you can load an earlier save; at worst, you need to restart/reboot. Stuck bugs are high-priority bugs because they can bring gameplay to a halt.

Sticky Spot

A *sticky spot* is the stuck spot's "ugly stepsister." These bugs are medium priority and, yes—you *can* get out; it just takes time and effort. A sticky spot might evolve into a stuck spot if the level designer makes some particularly bad decisions after your bug report. On the other hand, a stuck spot might be downgraded to a sticky spot by a skilled developer.

Invisible Wall

An *invisible wall* is basically extra geometry without the art that would make it visible. Chances are the "wall" is leftover geometry from an earlier version of the map.

However, sometimes invisible walls are "by design," which means the developers *wanted* to have them there as some kind of border. This is the age-old technique that attempts to trick players into thinking that the level is larger than it seems.

Don't Get NAB'd!

Make sure to investigate invisible walls very closely to avoid being NAB'd (when a developer re-classifies your "bug" as "Not a Bug"). By the way, this also implies you don't know how to do your job! ("NAB" and other bug status designations are discussed in more detail later in this chapter.)

Map Hole

A *map hole* is somewhat fun, but very serious. If a player falls through one, the illusion is destroyed immediately. Worse, some map holes are somewhat shallow and allow players to cheat by shooting others *from under* the map. (This was the case in some of the downloadable maps for *Call of Duty 3*. There was a huge map hole in the level, so many of the testers would drop there on purpose to headshot at will.) The only way to find all map holes is to walk on every single square foot of the map. There's no other way. This is why sometimes game testing is more about disciplined, repetitive actions than skill.

Missing Geometry

Missing geometry is the opposite of the invisible wall. If the art is present but there's no wall or barrier to your movement, some geometry is missing. The most common variety of this bug is that "secret passage" right between the walls of the castle. (This one was found by Luis in *Call of Duty 3*, in the Merville map. What's funny is that the missing geometry was right behind one of the flags, so capturing it became that much easier.)

> ### Testers as "Über" Players: Working with the Design Team
>
> As Creative Director and Lead Designer, I often work with the testing departments to get feedback on balance changes and new features. Testers are usually the best at finding exploits and imbalances. There are always one or two testers I highly covet as my 'über' players!
>
> *John Comes (Creative Director, Uber Entertainment)*

Stuck spots, sticky spots, map holes, invisible walls, and missing geometry are just a few level-design bugs you might see during a QA testing session. They do involve a lot of gameplay during the testing process—but artificial intelligence bugs require even more detail work.

Artificial Intelligence

The expression "artificial intelligence" can lead you to believe that game characters always behave intelligently. Not really. When characters do something completely illogical—such as staring at a wall for five minutes—you can bet there's something wrong with the AI code. Examples of *artificial intelligence (AI)* bugs include pathfinding and non-player character behavior. Let's take a closer look at both of these bugs.

Take-Two Interactive Software, Inc.

In *BioShock*, each Big Daddy intelligently defends its Little Sister.

Pathfinding

If there are *pathfinding* issues, and a computer-controlled character can't find its way around the map, there are three possible explanations:

1) An invisible wall is blocking the character's path.

2) A map hole is breaking the script.

3) The AI is faulty.

With an AI bug, sometimes you have to eliminate all the other possibilities before pinning it on the AI.

Non-Player Character Behavior

When AI works, the *non-player character (NPC) behavior* should be so convincing that you almost believe that real humans are playing the game with you. When AI fails, you know for sure that the character is being played by a computer. It's not enough to merely complain about this bug; you need to explain to the developers why a particular behavior (e.g., facing the wrong door in an elevator) takes away from the game. If you build a strong case, the developers will look into your bug seriously and attempt to fix it. NPC behavior might also affect balance; if you depend on your NPC team to kill swarm after swarm of enemies, a bad performance on their part will make the game too difficult. On the other hand, overzealous (and overqualified) NPC teammates will make the game too easy.

AI bugs will become more common as games attempt to replicate real intelligence—such as learned behaviors. Seeing an NPC character being stuck in an elevator might be amusing—but what will your reaction be when the final boss says he can't handle the pressure and decides to quit being evil?!

Physics

Looking for *physics* bugs is now part of a tester's daily tasks, since physics *APIs (application programming interfaces)* have recently been added to game development engines and tools. Physics in games is a whole subsystem—and a powerful one at that. Both gameplay and animation are directly affected by the physics code, since they take "input" from the physics engine/subsystem. Knowing how to spot physics bugs is a very desirable skill. Examples of physics bugs include breakables and dynamic behavior. Let's take a closer look at both of these bugs.

Electronic Arts, Inc.

Half-Life 2 brought physics-based gameplay to a mainstream audience.

Breakables

A common feature of modern games is *breakable* geometry. In *Gears of War*, this is called "destructible cover," and it allows players to protect themselves against enemy fire *up to a point*. When the damage is too extensive, the cover breaks down in pieces (i.e., "destructible objects"). Now imagine what would happen if objects didn't break at all—or did so and *then* started floating toward the sky; these are two possible bugs related to breakables.

> The most challenging testing experience I've had was while working with the Havok engine creating breakables for a game we were developing. I had to test the breakables many times to make sure they performed correctly in game.
>
> *David Dawson*
> *(Environmental Artist, Snowblind Studios)*

Real Physics vs. Fake Physics

Before computers were able to easily run physics simulations, the solution was to "fake" them in code. The idea was to trick the player into thinking that "real" physics laws were at work. However, as GPUs became more sophisticated and multi-core processors entered the fray, it was suddenly possible to have an actual physics engine supporting gameplay instead of fake, hard-coded behaviors. A physics engine can be tuned for more "playful" results, but it will always be far more realistic than the alternative. Commonly used physics engines today are Intel's Havok and Nvidia's PhysX.

Dynamic Behavior

Objects don't have to be breakable to "misbehave" physics-wise. In *Quake 4*, the fake physics used to govern metal and wooden crates would constantly over-extend themselves, resulting in the wrong dynamic behavior. For example, let's say your character hits a metal box at high speed; the box should move for a certain amount of time, then stop. But in *Quake 4*, the box would sometimes keep moving. This is a clear indicator that something in the physics code is very wrong, fake physics or not.

Physics bugs will play an even larger part in game testing in the near future. Newer titles such as LucasArt's *Fracture* make extensive use of physics. The *Half-Life* franchise practically depends on it. A clear understanding of high-school physics and a decent degree of attention to detail are essential to spot them—and point the developers in the right direction.

:::::: *BioShock:* Putting It All Together

Take-Two Interactive Software, Inc.

BioShock really blew me away. Any time a company gets a great backstory together, builds an amazing environment, and takes the time to make sure the game is virtually bug free instead of rushing to the shelves, I'm sold.

Chris Lenhart
(Instructor, ITT Institute of Technology)

Stability

Stability refers to the predictability of the code—whether or not it behaves according to the development team's intentions. Examples of stability bugs include freezes, crashes, and loading bugs. Let's take a closer look at each of these examples.

Sony Computer Entertainment America

The Gran Turismo franchise is virtually free of stability bugs (*Gran Turismo 5: Prologue*, shown).

Freeze

You've seen it before. One minute, everything is going well—and then everything stops, and your screen freezes. It's like the screen is stuck in time, almost like a snapshot. A *freeze* takes away any control you might have over a game character, since the system becomes unresponsive. This is the main reason why freezes are *critical* bugs. When you spot a freeze, make sure to copy/write down any debug information available. Whatever you have will be a lifesaver for the poor programmer responsible for fixing it.

Crash

A *crash* is different than a freeze for one easily explainable reason: the screen goes dark. Like a freeze, the player loses input—but the display is gone as well. Crashes are equally bad, being classified as critical bugs.

Crash to Desktop

A *crash to desktop* is a PC-only bug. It differs from other crashes in two ways:

1. When the game crashes, it crashes back to desktop.
2. The player might lose input inside the game itself, but the operating system still works fine.

While usually less serious than other crash bugs, a crash to desktop is also a critical bug.

Loading

Game levels take up several megabytes in the console's memory. When a level is being loaded, data gets read at lightning speed from the game disc. Since the loading process is fairly complex, any bugs in the code might halt it. A *loading* bug might be caused by all kinds of issues, from missing assets to a script break. It's regarded as a high bug.

Freezes, crashes, and loading bugs are just a few stability-related bugs you might see during a QA testing session. Hunting for stability bugs may require more of a programmer's approach—similar to performance bugs, which we'll discuss next.

Performance

Performance refers to the speed with which the hardware processes the code. Examples of performance bugs include frame rate, load time, minimum requirements machine, and installation time bugs. Let's take a closer look at each of these bugs.

Reprinted with permission from Microsoft Corporation

Gears of War 2 has a rock-solid frame rate.

Frame Rate

When a game is being made, developers set frame rate goals—target frame rates for the title. In the early days of the PlayStation 3, developers aimed for 30 frames per second (fps), while most Xbox 360 games ran at 60 fps. A low frame rate is a number *below* the targeted frame rate. So if your target is 30 fps and the game dips into the teens, it's a low-priority *frame rate* bug. Most of the time, developers don't worry too much about performance until well after the beta phase. They reason that first it's necessary to build the game and *then* assess performance. The problem with that approach is that serious performance issues might be too complex to be fixed in the last two months of production. That's why some studios keep the target frame rate throughout production, making sure any performance glitch is caught early on.

Load Time

Although the exact number may vary between each game (or platform), long load-ing times will always be an issue. While developers avoid tinkering with the code if everything else works (the "live and let live" mentality), hardware manufacturers might force them to fix the issue before launch. *Load time* bug testing can be awfully tedious. You will be asked to load all levels of the game multiple times, marking the time down in your notebook. Another characteristic of load time bugs is their sheer randomness; they can be among the toughest bugs to crack.

Minimum Requirements Machine

PC game requirements include minimum requirements (a.k.a. "min spec") machines—the lowest denominator machine on which the game must run. A *minimum requirements machine* bug is found when the game won't run properly on that machine. This is actually a contractual obligation; when the developer delivers the game, it must make sure the game runs on minimum requirements machines. That's the only way to include millions of possible buyers who have no access to a heftier gaming rig. Most of the time, minimum requirements machines either have a low-end GPU, a low-end CPU, or very little RAM. Some unfortunate testers might end up with minimum requirements machines playing an FPS such as *Quake* at 12 fps!

Installation Time

An *installation time* bug is a type of performance bug because it most likely results from a problem with the installer itself. As games have increased in size, develop-ers have moved from delivering their games on 1.44 MB floppies to a single 50GB Blu-ray disc. Games always take a while to install—about 20 minutes, in general. However, if a title actually goes beyond that, something's up. It's simply not normal to experience such a long installation time.

Performance bugs are, in a way, among the easiest to spot and the hardest to fix. You can't avoid noticing that the game is running at 15 frames per second. You can't close your eyes to the fact that 200 mph looks like 35 mph on a quiet street. Fixing these bugs is another story; developers will have a difficult time trying to figure out a fix—and if the problem is serious enough, it might *never* get fixed.

Frame rate, load time, minimum requirements machines, and installation time are just a few performance-related bugs you might see during a QA testing session. Now let's take a look at bugs that specifically relate to the game platform.

Compatibility

Compatibility bugs specifically relate to how a game runs on certain hardware. Examples of compatibility bugs include video card, controller, operating system, and standards bugs. Let's take a closer look at each of these examples. (Most testers will never deal with these bugs, since compatibility is a separate type of testing; still, it's good to be familiar with compatibility issues—especially since QA testers have been known to get *promoted* to compatibility testing teams.)

Reprinted with permission from Microsoft Corporation

Halo: Combat Evolved for PC required compatibility testing, while the Xbox version did not.

Video Card

The *video card* compatibility bug was very common during *Quake 4* QA testing. ATI's drivers made the game constantly crash to desktop. In a testing team, different testers have PCs equipped with Nvidia and ATI cards to spot bugs such as these. Bear in mind that only *supported* hardware is tested; as a rule, onboard video cards such as Intel's GMA 3100 are *not* supported, so don't expect to see these in the testing lab.

Controller

A *controller* compatibility bug is important to detect because it's always difficult to ensure that every single controller brand works with a game. Most of the hard work is done by the operating system, yet some effort is left to the game's programmers. When a controller that *should work* (i.e., it's supported) doesn't, you need to write a bug about it.

Operating System

The *operating system* failure is a very common bug. Always make sure you're writing about a supported operating system; it's common to see beta testers complaining about Vista 64 compatibility when Vista 64 is simply *not* supported. Still, sometimes the operating system *is* supported and the game still doesn't run; this would certainly be defined as a bug.

Standards

Always make sure that standards such as USB and Bluetooth are supported. If you're hearing mono instead of stereo while using a Bluetooth headset, the culprit could be mechanical (e.g., a wiring problem) or related to Bluetooth compatibility. Before writing this bug up, be sure to test the hardware on another computer or console.

Compatibility bugs are often associated with either video cards, controllers, operating systems, or standards. Now let's move on to the "tough guys": the networking bugs.

::::: *Assassin's Creed:* Stylish Polish

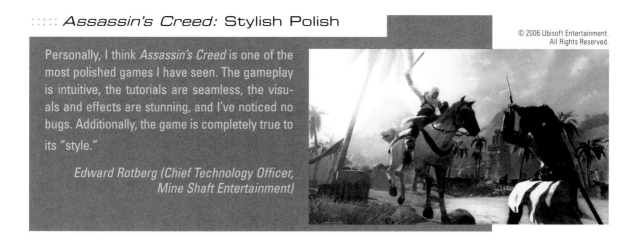

Personally, I think *Assassin's Creed* is one of the most polished games I have seen. The gameplay is intuitive, the tutorials are seamless, the visuals and effects are stunning, and I've noticed no bugs. Additionally, the game is completely true to its "style."

Edward Rotberg (Chief Technology Officer, Mine Shaft Entertainment)

Networking

Networking bugs specifically relate to server-client connectivity and bandwidth issues. These bugs include failed connections, dropped connections, unaccepted invitations, lags, invisible players, and scoring errors. Let's take a closer look at each of these bugs.

Reprinted with permission from Microsoft Corporation

Halo 3 has outstanding network code.

Failed Connection

A *failed connection* is a classic bug in Xbox Live. The message on the screen might differ (e.g., "connection failed," "failed to connect," "no connection," "dropped connection"), but the meaning is always the same: Your console can't "see" or "hear" other consoles. This bug might vary between "always happens" and "happens sometimes"—and this is important information, so write it down!

Dropped Connection

Let's say that your console was able to connect but you experience a *dropped connection* anyway. There *is* a difference between the two. Of course, if you have played several sessions with no connection problems and suddenly the connection drops, you'll have no trouble identifying the bug. The problem is when you experience a drop *right after* connecting. Some might say they "can't connect," but now you know better!

Unaccepted Invitation

The *unaccepted invitation* bug only affects systems that allow "game invites." Let's say a peer tester tries to invite you to a game. You see the prompt and choose "accept." However, you end up facing the title screen and *not* your friend's game. These bugs can become very tricky as production nears beta, since most test leads don't really pay attention to them because they're not part of the game itself. Always be on the lookout for those botched game invites!

Lag

Everyone knows *lag*. It's the irritating feeling of firing your weapon and seeing the muzzle flash half-a-second later. Lag is really a symptom of much more serious networking issues, such as dropped packets or excessive bandwidth usage. It's important to write a very detailed report when you spot lag: Was it always this laggy? When did it start? Does it end when a new game begins? Are you behind a firewall?

Invisible Player

If you cannot see another player's character or a non-player character (NPC), you have met the *invisible player* bug—a symptom of serious networking issues. Invisible player bugs might be among the most challenging bugs to investigate because it's often difficult to repeat and track; imagine having to count all the players during every session to make sure they're all present! Like lag, the "invisible player" bug should be heavily documented. Write down everything out of the ordinary and compare notes with your colleagues. It's not rare to see a game ship with these kinds of bugs—only to be fixed with a patch a couple months after launch.

Scoring Error

The scoring section in FPSs is traditionally done last, since scores are less important than "seeing stuff on screen." Even then, it's not unusual to see inaccurate scores in a game that is near completion. Since scores are low priority, sometimes nasty bugs manage to stay hidden in the scoring system. The lesson here is simple: Don't ignore potential bugs just because they might be low priority.

Failed connections, dropped connections, unaccepted invitations, lags, invisible players, and scoring errors are just a few performance-related bugs you might see during a QA testing session. It's important to always keep performance in mind when you test. Even a "perfect" game can be hurt by low performance.

> Online gaming quite often requires network bandwidth configuration and shaping; LANForge works well for this purpose. Packet sniffing is important from a QA perspective when debugging connectivity issues—and WireShark is a good utility offering value at a great price.
>
> *Jerome Strach (QA Manager,*
> *Sony Computer Entertainment America)*

Our examples of visual, audio, level design, artificial intelligence, physics, stability, performance, compatibility, and networking bugs comprise just a brief sampling of the many different types of bugs you'll encounter while testing games. While it's impossible to list all the bugs in existence, this chapter has provided you with a solid basis for the future. Knowing the basic types of bugs and how to spot them will make your life a lot easier once you stumble on an undiscovered bug of sorts—a "Nessie" of bugs, if you will.

Documentation

All testing must be done in an organized fashion. For this, documents are needed to guide you through the game. Let's take a look at the documentation that is particularly important and useful to testers and test managers.

Game Design Document (GDD)

We mentioned the *game design document (GDD)* in Chapter 3. As a tester, you will probably never see the actual GDD. Lead testers might, though, so that they become familiar with the game. The GDD describes all the creative aspects of the game and serves all teams on a project (including design, art, tech, and audio). A typical GDD consists of story/character, gameplay, interface, and level descriptions.

Critical QA Documentation

The game design document (GDD)—which all developers should work diligently to keep current for the sake of everyone associated with the title's development cycle—becomes a critical component to successful QA when authoring test cases. This area is grossly neglected in the industry—and until this problem is addressed, the industry will continue to struggle with meeting street dates and ensuring that titles are released with all desired features intact. . . . Tips for testing games might include the following mantra: "Every game released has defects and bugs—and no software is flawless." The stable products merely have masked the bugs so well they're difficult to find. The best thing testers can do is utilize the supplied materials from the developers as best they can. These materials and (if provided) a GDD should be utilized to author test cases to ensure appropriate coverage of the game. How those test cases are executed now depends on two important factors: 1) time, and 2) resources.

Jerome Strach (QA Manager, Sony Computer Entertainment America)

Art Style Guide

Where the GDD describes with words what the game must achieve, the *art style guide* (sometimes known as the "art bible" but always distinct from the "game bible," discussed in the next subsection) illustrates this with pictures and references. If the GDD mentions a church in a small French town, the art style guide will contain several pictures of quaint European churches. In racing games, the art style guide will include descriptions of all the cars included in the game with pictures and specs; in an FPS, it will illustrate each class and the weapons that may be used.

Game Bible

The *game bible* is a document put together by either the QA manager or the lead tester. Its purpose is to function as a knowledge source for new hires; it will list map names, abbreviations, how severity level will be classified within the project, and basic rules. Today, game bibles are often uploaded to *Wikis* where they become "living documents."

Checklists

Checklists are spreadsheets (usually Excel docs) that contain a collection of *test cases* covering a certain area of the game. Maybe you'll spend your day trying to die in different ways—from a checklist of different weapons. Maybe you'll be responsible for checking the saving/loading functionality. Maybe the checklist will tell you to play the game from beginning to end without saving *at all*. Most of the time, each tester (or a small group if the team is large enough) gets a different checklist; for example, you might be checking all the weapons while your coworker is taking care of map holes.

iBeta Quality Assurance

FPS MODE	Single Player			
Test	Results - 360	Results - PC	Bug #	Notes/Comments
Text	Fail	Fail	10007, 10206	
Audio	Fail	Fail	10007	
Graphics	Fail	Fail	10132, 10151	
Collision	Fail	Fail	10132, 10151	
Animations	Fail	Fail		
Main Weapon	Fail	Fail		
Secondary Weapon	Fail	Fail		
Vehicles	Fail	Fail	10186	
Particle Effects	Fail	Fail		
Interact - object	Fail	Fail		
Interact - AI	N/A	N/A		No interactable AI.
AI - animation	Fail	Fail		
AI - spawn	N/A	N/A		No AI enemies spawn.
AI - combat	Fail	Fail		
Triggers	Fail	Fail		
Ressurect	Fail	Fail		
Gameplay	Fail	Fail	10207	
Functionality	Fail	Fail		
Frame rate	Fail	Fail		
Cut Scene	Fail	Fail	10281	
Save	Pass	Pass		
Load	Fail	Fail		

Sample game testing checklist for Xbox 360 title

The idea is to have the whole team testing the game at the same time, with each person focusing on a different area. A single tester will work on several different checklists per week—returning them to the lead tester or floor lead when finished. Remember: Just as you complete one checklist, you'll receive another one!

Test Plan

Soon after starting work on a new project, the lead tester begins to assemble the "master of all checklists"—the *test plan*. This document contains all the checklists used in the game. The test plans used by QA are usually initially provided by the production testing team, since production has been working on the game for several months by the time QA joins the fray. The test plan should include the following sections:

- Game description
- Features to be tested
- Features *not* to be tested (if applicable)
- Techniques used (see Chapter 6)
- Disciplines used (see Chapter 3)
- Severity level definitions
- Pass/fail criteria (standard put in place by the hardware manufacturer)
- Test deliverables & milestones
- Testing tasks
- Technology & environmental needs (e.g., hardware, software, labs)
- Responsibilities
- Staffing & training needs
- Schedule (should correspond with production plan)
- Risks & contingencies
- Approval process

The Right Tool for the Job

When making a game, developers need a tool to track the progress of tasks and also one to track bugs. We call the latter "bug trackers." Let's take a closer look at three industry standard tools: DevTrack, Bugzilla, and TestTrack Pro.

DevTrack

TechExcel's *DevTrack* is used by publishers and developers such as Activision and Treyarch. First created in 1997, DevTrack allows developers to track every single bug in a game by managing a central database through a web interface. DevTrack is especially useful because it includes advanced sorting functionality that makes searching for bugs a walk in the park.

Courtesy of TechExcel Inc.

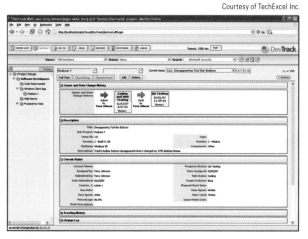

DevTrack allows developers to track every single bug in a game.

Bugzilla

Bugzilla is an open source, web-based bug tracker developed by Mozilla Foundation in 1998. Bugzilla is somewhat similar to DevTrack—but while DevTrack can be quite expensive (running with proprietary, paid software), Bugzilla is essentially free to use. This makes it a good low-budget replacement for DevTrack, with the advantage that Bugzilla is fairly well-regarded as well.

Courtesy of Bugzilla

Bugzilla is an open source, web-based bug tracker.

TestTrack

Developed by Seapine Software, TestTrack Pro is a professional bug-tracking tool extensively used in game development. Similar to DevTrack, TestTrack Pro is used by developers and publishers such as 2K Games, Atari, Epic Games, and Sega. Some find this program particularly convenient because it allows leads and assistants to pull a number of widely varied reports easily.

Courtesy of Seapine Software

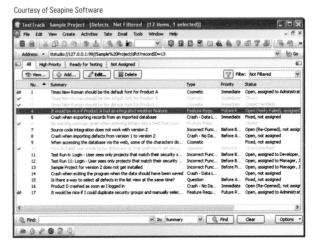

TestTrack Pro is a professional bug-tracking tool that is used extensively in game development.

Three Features of an Ideal Testing Tool

Here are three features that should ideally be incorporated into one tool:

- **Issue tracking:** A way to specifically log each separate issue, and assign it to the person who needs to fix it.

- **Wiki:** A place to throw ideas on the wall, and let everyone see them, change them, and change them again when they don't work. This same system is used as the "memory," to create things like a test plan that will be updated every time someone runs through it.

- **Forum:** A place to talk openly with the whole team, or focus just on the people who need to be deal with a specific issue.

We, of course, live in our own tool (Qtask)--which is designed especially for this very concept.

Baron R.K. Von Wolfsheild (Chief Software Architect, Qtask, Inc.)

> ## "Painless" Bug Trackers
>
> A good bug tracking system is essential. There are a number of them out there, and I've used four or five different systems at this point. The most important thing in such a system is that it is painless for the users. If no one likes to use the system, it *won't* get used.
>
> *Edward Rotberg (Chief Technology Officer, Mine Shaft Entertainment)*
>
> Much of the software we use is proprietary, but the functionality is very similar to third-party applications. We need to know when and where in the game the bug occurred and how to reproduce it. We usually supply any relevant information in the form of an automated log that can better assist teams assigned the bug.
>
> *Nathan Madsen (Composer & Sound Designer, Madsen Studios/NetDevil)*

How to Use Bug Trackers

Once you join a project, the lead tester will provide all the information pertinent to the bug tracker; project number, login and password; and anything else needed to start the process. Hold onto this information with a passion, since forgetting the basics automatically grants you the dreaded "noob" status. Let's go through a mini-tutorial, using DevTrack as an example.

Before Entering a Bug

The most important thing to remember before entering a bug into a database is that you should have already taken detailed notes about the bug you found. Most of the time, there's a very limited number of PCs in the testing lab. You will not have time to sit there and think, so be ready with detailed notes so that you can input your bug quickly.

While Entering a Bug

Here is a list of short-hand steps for entering a bug into DevTrack:

1. Access your PC account using your login and password.
2. Select the appropriate project.
3. *Search for similar bugs.* This step is essential. You have to make sure you're entering something new.
4. Add all the required information (e.g., bug title, severity, description).
5. Upload any appropriate files.
6. Make sure your bug has been saved in the system.

In the next chapter, we'll go into more detail on each of the above steps—explaining exactly how each section should be filled.

After Entering a Bug

Once your bug has been added, it still needs to be approved by the lead tester in order to filter out badly written bugs, repeats, and joke entries. As your bug gets approved, it starts a pilgrimage through the developer's systems until it finds its true owner—the lead (e.g., art, design, tech, audio) in the appropriate department, who forwards it to the responsible developer. Let's take a look at how a bug changes in status as it moves through this system.

Open

An "open" bug is one that has been recently entered in the system by the tester. The bug remains open even after it has been approved by the lead.

Assigned

A bug is "assigned" once a developer takes possession of it. The bug is assigned to that developer by the lead on that particular team.

Resolved / Fixed

When the developer in charge fixes a bug, the developer sets the status to "resolved" or "fixed."

Verified

Once a bug has been resolved or fixed, testers need to make sure that the bug is no longer in existence. Usually, testers verify their own bugs, but it's the lead who actually changes the status.

End Results

You should always aim to have your bugs closed in a single try. The back-and-forth between tester and developers—often caused by badly worded bug reports—is ill-regarded by the industry. Good testers are like "fire and forget" missiles: they get the job done, and that's it. Let's take a look at some more status designations associated with a bug's "final destination."

Closed

A *closed* bug is one that has been fixed. This is the end of the line.

Will Not Fix (WNF)

Will not fix (WNF) means that your bug is not important enough to be fixed. This is usually the case with low bugs. Developers simply don't have enough time to fix everything that gets submitted, so they focus on medium bugs and above.

Not a Bug (NAB)

As discussed earlier in this chapter, being "NAB'd" is an experience to remember. If you see *not a bug (NAB)* in your bug entry, the developers don't consider what you found a bug. To add insult to injury, they will also write down "as designed" in the notes section. Too many NABs mean you're not doing your job right.

Duplicate

If you don't do a good job searching for similar bugs before you submit, you'll end up submitting a *duplicate*. Needless to say, if your bug report reaches the developers, they will either get immediately irritated or waste their time fixing something twice in a row. The only way to avoid duplicates is to diligently search for similar issues before submitting.

Tracking software has the power to keep you sane. It all seems a bit stiff at first, but soon you'll realize how terrible it would be to track everything via email. (Some developers actually do this, with grisly consequences.) Learning the nuts and bolts of the tracking software will allow you to break away from the crowd and get noticed—in a good way.

:::

In this chapter, you learned about relevant documentation and the basic tools available to game testers—as well as the several different categories of bugs you'll encounter when testing. In the next chapter, we'll move into the actual testing process—looking for easy-to-spot bugs. You'll learn how to properly write bug reports, from spelling to titles and descriptions. Game testing is akin to an investigation; the smallest detail might help you solve the whole case!

:::CHAPTER REVIEW:::

1. Play a game for at least 4 hours—taking notes on the various bugs you find. Categorize each bug by category (e.g., visual, audio) and identify each bug based on examples discussed in the chapter (e.g., clipping, skipping). How would you prioritize these bugs?

2. Review the testing documentation included on the companion DVD for this book. Begin to write a rough test plan of your own for an original game idea. How will you ensure that your game will be tested thoroughly and accurately?

3. Open Bugzilla, DevTrack or TestTrack (included on the companion DVD for this book). Begin to familiarize yourself with the software by conducting a preliminary, rough test of a game currently in release. How do you feel the software might streamline the bug tracking process?

Part II:
Level Up

CHAPTER

5

Start Your Engines!

bare bones bug hunting

Key Chapter Questions

- What are some *bug spotting* tips?

- How are *game genres* related to specific types of bugs?

- What are the contents of a *bug report*?

- Why are *version* and *repeatability* essential for bug reports?

- What is the bug *verification* process?

Testing a new game is like starting a new relationship. You don't know what to expect, yet you're curious and excited. This has to be your frame of mind when you begin to test a game. You need to challenge *the game* to challenge *you*—while having fun in the process. This chapter explores the bug spotting process, the relationship between specific bugs and genres, bug report drafting and submission, and bug verification.

Bug Spotting

As we've mentioned many times before: *Testing a game is very different from playing it*. If you really want to spot bugs, you need to do so willingly. Merely playing a game *will* grant you a number of "finds" over time—but you will merely *stumble* upon them. Pure accident (not technique) will dictate your performance. If you're a game tester, you'll want to discover bugs at will. You'll need to have all of your testing skills on tap.

Game Genres & Bugs

As discussed in Chapter 4, bugs are software flaws that make themselves noticeable to players. If a bug exists, but can never be found, it's essentially the same as not being there. Therefore, you will only be able to spot bugs that manifest themselves as visual, audio, or gameplay flaws. If you look at different genres, it will become clear to you that bugs are genre-specific. Furthermore, the techniques you may use to spot a bug in a first-person shooter (FPS) may be vastly different than the techniques in a simulation game. While you need to verify absolutely *everything* to do a good job as a tester, some genres have "weak spots" that should always receive a healthy dose of attention.

> Subject matter knowledge is incredibly important. Your game will be better tested by testers who are extremely familiar with that type of game.
>
> Frank T. Gilson (Senior Producer, Wizards of the Coast)

2D Platformers

One of the oldest game genres, *2D platformers* started life in late 1970s arcades and took a leap forward with *Super Mario Bros.* When testing platformers, your main focus will be on gameplay. Since these games are fairly simple (even with its landmark time shifting, *Braid* is still categorized as a platformer), visual and audio bugs will be clear from the onset—while any lack of precision in player movement might be more difficult to pinpoint. You will also want to ensure that enemy behavior makes sense; it's easy for artificial intelligence (AI) bugs to slip by, making enemies behave a little "loopy."

Reprinted with permission from Microsoft Corporation

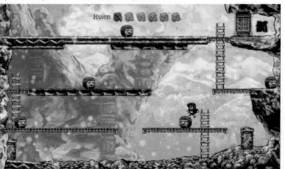

Even with its landmark time shifting, *Braid* is still categorized and tested as a 2D platformer.

3D Platformers

As platformers moved to the 3D space, the complexity of each game skyrocketed. The main issues with *3D platformers* are player control, graphics, and camera. (If you have ever played *Conker: Live and Reloaded*, you know what we mean.) *Player control* is essential in 3D platformers, so pay lots of attention to it. Similarly, 3D

Reprinted with permission from Microsoft Corporation

graphics become exponentially more complicated than the 2D background found on the platformers of old; visual bugs such as z-fighting, missing textures, and screen tearing abound.

Finally, the *camera* can sink a game even if everything else is spot perfect. Make it your mission in life to report on the camera—which can never be allowed to interfere with gameplay. If players have to constantly worry about this, they might give up playing altogether.

Player control is essential in 3D platformers such as *Conker: Live & Reloaded*, so give it plenty of attention.

Shoot 'Em Ups

While most of you might deem *shoot 'em ups* dead, the truth is that they still have a hardcore fan base. *Ikaruga* sold exceedingly well on Xbox Live Arcade, and every physical arcade in the world still pays it respect. The Achilles' heels of shoot 'em ups are difficulty level and player control. Since this genre is closely associated with the hardcore crowd, it's simply too easy to miscalculate and make a game that's impossible to enjoy. You should always monitor the *difficulty level* in multiple settings—easy, medium, hard, and "insane." You *must* make sure these settings are perfectly tuned, or the game will fail.

Player control is also an issue. While easy to implement, it's important to make sure that vehicle speeds are easily understood and that screen boundaries work well with the rest of the design. This includes *collision detection*. There can be no mistake here; shoot 'em ups live and die by the shooting mechanics and vehicle control.

Courtesy of Atari Europe SASU.

Shoot 'em ups such as *Ikaruga* live and die by the shooting mechanics and ship control.

First-Person Shooters (Single-Player)

Single-player first-person shooters (FPSs) are always sophisticated. Massive levels, hundreds of enemies on screen at the same time, and shiny graphics are not only anticipated, but *required*. While many things can go wrong in an FPS, weapon feel and level design can be especially sore spots. "Weapon feel" includes the perception of weight and other essential aspects of weapons—such as how they look, fire, and sound. You'll never be able to fix bad design, but you can make sure good design is not affected by bugs. In *Quake 4*, Luis was able to "protect" the machine gun from a crippling audio bug by paying careful, prolonged attention to it! Remember: Always care for the weapons in an FPS, more than anything.

You should also pay attention to the *level design* in a single-player FPS. In single-player mode, level design must *never* be confusing and/or labyrinthine. The last thing developers want is for players to get lost. By playing the game over and over again, you will find out which areas "flow," and which areas don't. Finally, make sure to alert developers if you keep getting lost; if a tester gets lost, imagine what will happen when "civilians" play the game!

Used by permission from id Software, Inc.

Weapon feel is a significant element in an FPS such as *Quake 4*.

First-Person Shooters (Multiplayer)

Multiplayer first-person shooters (FPSs) differ from the single-player variety due to the sheer number of connectivity issues. If you remember the days of online gaming over a 56K modem, you'll probably agree that the main issue you had was *lag*—the time between pressing the trigger and actually shooting someone on screen. As broadband connections became widespread, lag ceased to be the main killjoy of online gaming—but the issue itself is still present. When testing a multiplayer FPS, pay attention to any *connectivity* issues. Lag must be kept to a minimum, and players mustn't be dropped constantly (the infamous "dropped connection").

You will also have to spend time *balancing* the weapons and the map. This is a time-intensive activity, but it pays off in spades once the game goes to market. The secret of blockbusters such as *Halo* is in the balancing of gameplay; a balanced game is a fair one, and this perception will make players came back to it over and over again.

Reprinted with permission from Microsoft Corporation

When testing a multiplayer FPS such as *Halo 3*, pay close attention to any connectivity issues.

Racing

Racing games depend heavily on *physics*. With consoles sporting powerful multi-core processors and very capable GPUs, it's a given that vehicle dynamics will be pushed to the limit. There is, however, a problem with this; since racing is a fast-paced, precise undertaking—both in the real world and inside a game—bugs that affect car dynamics will seriously undermine the gameplay.

It's also important to pay close attention to player *progression*. In games such as *Forza Motorsport* and *Gran Turismo*, players can spend months going through the single-player portion. If something happens to a save game and progress is lost, they might abandon ship. Losing a garage of 30 cars or so is something we don't wish on our worst enemies.

Reprinted with permission from Microsoft Corporation

Bugs that affect car dynamics will seriously undermine the gameplay in racing games such as *Forza Motorsport 2*.

A final area that requires attention is *performance*. Racing games are fast. Players don't pick Lamborghini Murciélagos because they look nice—but because of their extreme performance. If you have a 600 horsepower vehicle on the racetrack in a game running at 20 frames per second, you've got a problem. Thirty frames per second is the bare minimum for racing games. Ideally, the game should be running at *60* fps. The only way to make sure the frame rate is adequate is to constantly pay attention to it. If you don't notice a problem until late in the production phase, developers might not be able to fix it in time for launch.

Fighting

For many, *fighting* games have become a passion since Capcom's *Street Fighter 2: The World Warriors* first showed up at the neighborhood arcade. Others played Sega's *Virtua Fighter* once it came out in 1993 and adopted 3D fighters for life. Ultimately, fighting games get our attention because pummeling friends on screen and owning an entire arcade population is fun. Fighting games are all about *quick responses*. While not necessary in other genres (e.g., turn-based strategy games), immediate *feedback* is required in fighting games. If you throw a punch, it needs to be seen on screen immediately. When you're testing a fighting game, always pay attention to *reaction time*. (If your game is online-enabled, this becomes a lot more serious because online games can suffer from lag.)

In a fighting game such as *Virtua Fighter 5*, always focus on reaction time and balance.

The second main issue in fighting games is *balance*. When the game is unbalanced, one character will be stronger than the other to a point where it affects matches. All early fighting games suffered from it; one of the reasons new "editions" were launched from time to time was to balance the original, flawed gameplay. This was the case with *Street Fighter 2: Champion Edition* and many others. Now that consoles are wired to the internet 24/7, it's a lot easier to drop bug fixes. Even so, poor balance will hurt a title's initial sales due to bad reviews—so you will want to stay on top of it. The best way to spot balance issues is to always pick different characters and make notes of their strengths and weaknesses. Anything that's not "by design" is clearly a bug.

Adventure

Adventure games live and die by their puzzles. Great graphics and a haunting soundtrack can't fix a single broken puzzle because adventures are *linear*: one broken puzzle can prevent the player from advancing in the game. That's why testers need to conduct numerous playthroughs to be absolutely sure that *progress* is never interrupted. Particularly weak areas in adventure games are *player control* and *camera control*. When the genre moved to 3D with *Alone in the Dark*, navigating the environment suddenly became a challenge. Controlling characters with a keyboard is already difficult enough, but these early 3D efforts also had to deal with "cinematic" cameras that clumsily got in the player's way.

If you happen to land a testing job on an adventure game project, focus on player and camera control; this needs to be transparent so that there's no interference whatsoever with gameplay. Some say that adventure games never recovered from the transition to 3D. In fact, we can blame bad QA for it; if developers paid more attention to the issue of control, perhaps games such as *Fade to Black* (the sequel to *Flashback*) wouldn't be such disappointments—and the genre would be in better shape today.

Sony Computer Entertainment America

Testers need to do numerous playthroughs of adventure games such as *Heavy Rain* to be absolutely sure that progress is never interrupted.

Action-Adventure

Action-adventure games are sometimes placed alongside third-person shooters because both share the third-person point of view. However, you can easily differentiate between the two by comparing *Gears of War* and *Tomb Raider*. While *Gears of War* focuses heavily on the shooting aspect, *Tomb Raider* relies on exploration and puzzle-solving. So while a problem with aiming can "kill" a *third-person shooter (TPS),* an action-adventure game can get by if control and puzzles make up for it.

Sony Computer Entertainment America

When you test an action-adventure game, pay close attention to every single puzzle. Like pure adventures, puzzles can stop progress; this is known as *progression break.* Given that movement is much more varied (e.g., climbing ladders, jumping between platforms, and performing acrobatic movements), precision is key. Faulty controls in action-adventures guarantee a bad score.

When you test an action-adventure game such as *God of War II,* play through every single puzzle multiple times.

Role-Playing

Role-playing games (RPGs) are extremely complex; from early Commodore Amiga titles to graphically intense PC games, these massive games are always a challenge to test. If you land an RPG project, prepare yourself for a maddening workload; you may call it the "insane" difficulty level of game testing. Every single item needs to be tested alone and then tested again in tandem with everything else. Playthroughs might take 80-120 hours instead of the usual 10-20 hours. Alternative paths must work as well as the "main" path. All weapons need to be tested against all enemies—or *non-player characters (NPCs)*. In short, RPGs can be tricky—so you really should enlist a large and capable team. (You might also consider the *automated* testing technique, discussed in Chapter 6.)

© 2008 Bethesda Softworks LLC, a ZeniMax Media company

Role-playing games such as *Fallout 3* are always a challenge to test.

The Trouble with RPGs

Open-ended RPGs tend to be the most buggy. Their large scope, combined with the fact that many quests tie into each other, can usually cause a pretty big headache for QA. Add to the mix that each character can usually be customized—as far as stats, skills and abilities—and there can be some pretty insidious bugs hidden throughout the game.

Brandon Adler (QA Lead, Obsidian Entertainment)

Simulation

Simulation games attempt to "slice and dice" reality into workable, manageable chunks. In some racing games, *vehicle* dynamics are faithfully reproduced—but not so with *weather* dynamics. *The Sims* attempts to simulate human relationships but (wisely) avoids controversial life issues. When testing simulations, the most important factor is *real-world relevance*. Whether it's a car or a plane, every element must behave as expected. A car is not supposed to "float" over the road, for example. Neither can a plane be immune to stalling. You must keep watch over the model; visual and audio bugs are important, but the core of a simulation is its *realism*.

Reprinted with permission from Microsoft Corporation

When testing simulations such as *Flight Simulator X*, the most important factor is real-world relevance.

Strategy

At their core, *strategy* games are about *resource management*. They base their gameplay on the premise that resources are always limited. With that in mind, it becomes clear that when testing strategy games, you should focus on *gameplay balance*. In the *Civilization* franchise, for example, nations have different strong suits; this is an organic way to differentiate them from each other. However, if a civilization that's strong in agriculture is underperforming, the game is unbalanced. *Artificial intelligence (AI)* should also be a focus when testing strategy games; faulty AI can greatly diminish the fun factor of the game.

Firaxis Games, Inc.

When testing strategy games such as *Sid Meier's Civilization IV: Colonization*, you should focus on balance issues and artificial intelligence.

Puzzle

Puzzle games are relatively easier to test than other more sprawling genres. Even a more sophisticated puzzle game such as *Lumines* shouldn't be too involved. In puzzle games, your focus should be on everything related to programming. Pay attention to *collision detection*, *scoring*, *control precision*, and *gameplay dynamics*. Even if an element isn't a "proper" bug (e.g., an unimpressive power-up), it should still be reported as a suggestion. Control precision is particularly important. There's nothing worse than misplacing a strategically important piece due to faulty controls.

Reprinted with permission from Microsoft Corporation

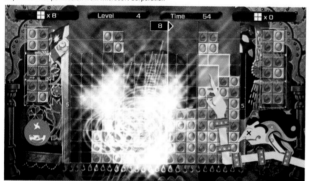

In puzzle games such as *Lumines Live!*, your focus should be on everything related to programming—especially control precision.

> **E**verything just clicks with *Portal*—so much, that most players don't realize until quite late that it's not so much a game as a puzzle.
>
> *Dr. Richard Allan Bartle (Visiting Professor in Computer Game Design, University of Essex)*

Casino

Casino games have lost popularity with the console crowd but still draw an audience on casual gaming web sites. (Xbox Live has also attracted casual gamers through traditional casino games such as poker.) Like puzzle games, casino games are also relatively easy to test. In casino games, the rules are often centuries old, so no game can deviate. For example, even if a game calls itself "Blackjack Special," it can't base all play on the number 22 instead of the traditional 21.

Programming Cheats in Casino Game Testing

I've done audio for many casino video games in my career, and I found out early on that I have got to be *the* unluckiest person on the planet. Imagine my chagrin trying to test the symbol "win" sounds in a game—an effort in futility. After several projects into a contract, I was discussing some other issues with the programmer when it hit me that this is the guy who could make my life infinitely easier by programming cheats into the game so I could "win." It turns out that I stumbled on a fix that the animator, testers, and producer also benefited from and gave "hero" status to the programmer all at the same time. Of course, the programmer now has the burden of remembering to remove the cheats before the game is delivered.

Aaron Marks (Composer & Sound Designer, On Your Mark Music Productions)

If you're testing any casino games, make sure you first *understand the rules* so that you catch all the basic issues. Furthermore, most casino games have some kind of online connectivity—so you also must pay attention to *networking performance*.

When testing a casino game such as *Texas Hold 'Em*, make sure you know the rules so that you can catch all the basic problems.

Survival-Horror

Survival-horror (SH) games are derived from the very first 3D adventure games. *Alone in the Dark*, usually classified as an action-adventure game, is also responsible for sparking the SH genre. More recent franchises include *Resident Evil* and *Silent Hill*. Unlike most other game genres, SH distinguishes itself based on story rather than gameplay elements; in this way, it resembles a movie genre rather than a traditional game genre. Most SH games share gameplay elements with action-adventure games.

When dealing with SH games, it's essential to pay attention to *controls*. Earlier examples of the genre had fixed cameras and that made controlling one's character nearly impossible. Also, take a close look at any *puzzles*; although not a main component of the SH genre, a single broken puzzle will ruin your game.

When dealing with survival-horror games such as *Alone in the Dark: Inferno*, pay attention to its controls and puzzles.

Massively Multiplayer Online

Massively multiplayer online games (MMOGs or MMOs) have entered the mainstream in the last 10 years. *World of Warcraft* and its 11 million subscribers popularized MMO gaming throughout the world. If you get to work on a MMO, congratulations: This is truly the Mount Everest of testing. (You can get a taste of this by participating in open beta testing conducted by almost all MMO developers.) Not even RPGs are this difficult to test. MMO testing is still the "Wild West"—where the law doesn't apply, and every mistake has the potential to be your last. You will have to work with a large team to have any hope of catching the most important bugs. A gigantic beta testing effort will also be necessary, with both closed and open beta programs.

Courtesy of Blizzard Entertainment, Inc.

A massively multiplayer online game such as *World of Warcraft* is the "Mount Everest" of testing.

There is no specific "tip" for MMOs; your best bet is to let every tester focus on certain elements of the game, such as *items* or *quests*, while others ensure that *progression* is okay. You will need a strike team of *networking* specialists to test online connectivity, lag, and other networking bugs that affect every MMO in existence. Automated testing (discussed in Chapter 6) will most certainly make some of this easier—but until computers are smart enough to observe bugs on their own, it's your responsibility to find them yourself.

MMO Testing Challenges

In MMOs, the testing challenges relate to balancing and tuning in the actual multiplayer environment. Players also play differently in a Live game than they do when testing (due to their character persistence being permanently affected while in Live). . . . Both *City of Heroes* and *World of Warcraft* were particularly polished when they came out, and relative to other games in the MMO arena they seemed nearly bug free.

Gordon Walton (Vice President & Studio Co-Director, BioWare Austin)

Dr. Richard Allan Bartle on MMOG Players as Bug Hunters :::::

Richard Bartle co-wrote the first virtual world, *MUD (multi-user dungeon)*, in 1978 and has thus been at the forefront of the online game industry from its inception. A former lecturer in artificial intelligence and current Visiting Professor in Computer Game Design at the University of Essex (U.K.), he is an influential writer on all aspects of virtual world design, development, and management. As an independent consultant, he has worked with most of the major online game companies in the United Kingdom and the United States for more than 20 years. His 2003 book, *Designing Virtual Worlds*, has established itself as a foundation text for researchers and developers of virtual worlds.

Dr. Richard Allan Bartle
(Visiting Professor,
Computer Game Design,
Essex University)

For MMORPGs, it would be an advance to resort to a technique that used to be popular in the old textual worlds but has since fallen out of favor: rewarding players for finding bugs. The way MMOs work, it's like you have something big and complicated like a car, and you want to make it waterproof. The testers can go through and check every seal on every joint to make sure it's water tight—but as soon as you let the players loose, it's like it's immersed in water. If there's a leak, the players will find it. They'll find leaks in places you didn't even check. They outnumber you tens of thousands to one. So, they *will* find the bugs. The question is: Will they tell you about them? Actually, the answer doesn't matter; it's the perception that does. Say you're a regular player and you come across a bug: Do you report it? Well at the moment, your reasons for doing so are all stick and no carrot: If you don't, and someone else does, you could be banned for exploiting it. This is the case even if you genuinely want to report the bug because you're a responsible player (as most are). It sends completely the wrong message to players if they feel they have to report bugs or face the "wrath of the developer." It's much better if you say you'll reward them for being the first to report a bug. Of course, most players never find a bug. Nevertheless, their opinion of you will be colored by your policy in this area. In other words, playtesting can be a customer service tool to enhance the relationship between developer and player. Compared with what we have at the moment, that's certainly an advance!

Bug Reports

Most people think that testing games is all about having fun. You'll probably agree that we've already debunked *that* misconception! What few people suspect is that game testing requires a great deal of writing—and bad writers make for horrible game testers. *Bug reports* are text documents that describe to developers how a bug can be exactly reproduced. The more detailed a bug report is, the easier it is for the developer to fix it. Let's take a look at the elements of a bug report.

Title

Bug *titles* need to be absolutely clear and to the point—like newspaper headlines. A good rule of thumb is to follow the five "W"s from journalism: who, what, when, where, and why.

"Bad" Bug Titles:

A. Fell though the ground

B. Shotgun sucks

C. Can't load level

Problems:

A doesn't say *where* this happened.

B is an *opinion* (and an incomplete one at that).

C doesn't specify *which* level.

Revised Titles:

A. Fell through the ground when crossing Hangar toward the exit

B. Allied shotgun is underpowered when compared to Axis shotgun

C. Can't load Poisson map in Capture the Flag mode

What did we do differently? We supplied detail in the title. Now developers can grasp what the bug is really about without having to open the report. You absolutely need to supply details such as where you were, what was happening, and the name of the map/mode.

> Testers must communicate clearly and efficiently in both spoken and written word. You need to be able to describe very accurately the problems you are finding and the steps to reproduce them.
>
> *Brian Reynolds*
> *(Founder & Creative Director, Big Huge Games)*

Description

While the title supplies some of the raw data, the bug *description* fleshes it out. The description provides more context and detail on the bug.

"Bad" Descriptions:

    A. I was walking through the level when suddenly my char fell through a humongous hole in the ground. He kept falling for ages until he died.

    B. I can't stand the shotgun. I shoot from really close and the other guy doesn't die.

    C. Every time I try to load the Poisson level, something happens and the screen goes dark.

Problems:

    A lacks detail, making use of a silly abbreviation ("char" instead of "character") and unnecessary adjectives.

    B continues to be heavy with opinion; the one bit of extra detail is the fact that he shot the other player "from really close."

    C adds the level name but stops there; it's simply not enough information.

Revised Descriptions:

    A. Crossing the Hangar, about to finish the Enemy Fields level, I suddenly fell though a map hole. Facing the exit, the hole is about two feet to the left of the alien jet engine. I kept falling until my character finally died and I was taken back to the Load screen.

    B. The Allied shotgun seems to be underpowered in comparison to the Axis shotgun. If I stand four feet from an enemy soldier and fire, it takes me two or three hits to kill him. If he shoots me from the same distance, he can kill me with a single shot. Other testers have been reporting the same issue in the past week or so.

    C. The Poisson level failed to load 3 out of 10 times. This seems to happen a lot in Capture the Flag mode. We had a team of 16 in the lobby, all set, when two other machines got stuck on a black screen. (We readied at roughly the same time.)

The new descriptions contain much more detail. In **A**, the developer can now locate the map hole. In **B**, the tester explains *how* he or she ensured that the shotgun damage value was actually a bug. In **C**, a probability is given, the game mode is specified, and the tester also mentions other testers who had a similar problem. The tester even says that everybody readied at roughly the same time—a fact that might point to a specific location in the code.

A good description is *everything*. You need to provide percentages, game modes, exact locations, number of testers playing simultaneously, and everything else that might be relevant. This is the only way the developer will be able to understand exactly what you're talking about.

Steps

Steps work as instructions—explaining to the developer exactly what to do in order to *replicate* the bug.

"Bad" Steps:

A. 1. Walk toward exit.

    2. Die.

B. 1. Load game.

    2. Equip shotgun.

    3. Shoot anyone.

    4. Nothing happens.

C. 1. Boot game.

    2. Select multiplayer.

    3. Attempt to load Poisson.

Problems:

A is too simplistic. In fact, it sounds like a joke.

B attempts to describe the problem but fails to explain the exact order of events. Much happens between Steps 3 and 4!

C doesn't add any new information. The developer is left in the dark.

Revised Steps:

A. 1. Load Enemy Fields level.

    2. Advance through level following the usual path.

    3. Close to the end of the level, you'll see an alien jet engine.

    4. Position your character about two feet to the left of the jet engine.

    5. You'll fall through a map hole.

B. 1. Load any multiplayer level.

    2. Have another tester join in.

    3. Equip the shotgun.

    4. Have the other tester equip the shotgun as well.

    5. Have the other tester shoot you in the chest. You should die with 1 hit.

    6. Once you respawn, shoot the other tester from the same distance. It will take 2 or 3 hits to kill the other tester's character.

C. 1. Boot game.

2. Start a multiplayer match in Poisson.

3. Change the game mode to Capture the Flag.

4. While in the lobby, have a second tester join your game *at the same time.*

5. You should get a black screen 3 out of 10 times.

Steps allow developers to perfectly reproduce bugs at their own stations. Keep in mind that while production testers have developers with offices in the same building, QA testers might be working on a game that was actually developed across multiple time zones. Without detailed steps, developers will not be able to work on a fix. Above all, steps need to be precise and clear. Give as much detail as possible—sparing nothing. One missing detail is all you need to make your bug *non-reproducible*; if this happens, it will come back to haunt you with "can't reproduce" in the notes section.

Version

The three elements (title, description, and steps) we've discussed so far are the main components of a bug report. However, there are other sections that can still make or break your report. The *version* associated with your report is one such essential component. Games go though several versions before being regarded as "done." These versions are updated copies of the game. One version might have new network code. Another might have a reworked graphics engine. Once you're about to start writing a bug report, you will need to input the associated version. Let's examine a possible scenario that could occur if you include the wrong version of the game:

1. Once the developers get their hands on it, they choose *the wrong disc.*

2. They boot the game.

3. Now they start going over the steps in your bug. But they apply these steps to a different version of the game.

4. They can't reproduce your bug. They try over and over again—wasting time.

5. The bug comes back to you.

6. Your lead finds out you input the wrong version. Ouch!

As you can see from the above scenario, it's essential that you include the correct version of the game for each bug you report. Although only one version of the game is usually tested by the team, multiple versions of the game are occasionally tested at the same time—making version tracking much more important.

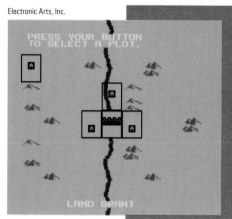

Electronic Arts, Inc.

> What I like about board games is that they bring people together. Computer games tend to isolate people, and even multiplayer video games tend to pit people against each other. There are a few people out there that recognized the computer could offer a backdrop for people to bond. *M.U.L.E.* (developed by a friend, the late Dani Bunten) is one of those games; it was balanced, educational, fun, humorous, addicting (my favorite word for a great game), and it had heart. How much more polish can you ask for?
>
> *Baron R.K. Von Wolfsheild (Chief Software Architect, Qtask, Inc.)*

Repeatability

Repeatability refers to how often a bug occurs. A "five out of five" type of bug is much more serious than a "one out of five" one. Every bug report must contain this information. Most bug tracking software reserves a field to include bug repeatability. The usual scales are 5 and 10; the intention is to give developers a snapshot of the bug's repeatability. Even if it's a rough estimate, this information is still useful. If there isn't a field available for it, be sure to add repeatability to the description.

The All-Important Repeatability Factor

I want [a tester] who has submitted bugs while playing games and who can answer the question: "What is the most important thing you put down when writing a bug?" (The answer to this can determine what kind of tester you would make; the best answer is "repro steps": How do you get it to happen repeatedly?)

Floyd Billings (Assistant Lead QA, Sony Online Entertainment)

Ancillary Documentation

When submitting a bug, having only your word might not "cut it." Even a perfect description might not properly detail the entire bug; this is when *ancillary documentation* such as a diagnostic log, screenshot, and even a video capture comes into play.

Diagnostic Log

If you're testing a PC game, you must always add the Directx diagnostic log: *dxdiag*. This is a snapshot of the computer you're using—and it contains important information about the driver's versions, RAM size, GPU make, video RAM size, and so forth. If you *don't* attach the *dxdiag* file, you might actually get in trouble!

How to access the *dxdiag* log:

1. Go to the "execute" field in the Windows Start menu. (Use the "Search" field in Vista.)

2. Type "dxdiag"and then hit enter.

3. You'll see an application with tabs for System, Display, Sound, and Input.

4. Choose "Save All Information."

5. Save the log file to your desktop.

6. Attach it to your bug!

Having a *dxdiag* log can be a game changer. Many bugs are caused by incorrect versions of the GPU drivers. The *dxdiag* file will give developers all they need to address a complicated PC bug.

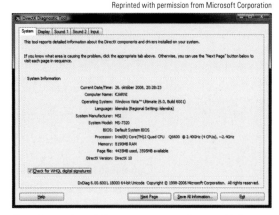

If you're testing a PC game, you must always add the DirectX diagnostic log: *dxdiag*.

If you're testing a console game, you mostly likely will not have a Directx log. In this case, you might have to provide developers with a *memory dump*; not all consoles can provide this, but here are the steps if yours can. (You would only need to access a memory dump in a console testing situation if you encountered a crash bug.)

1. Enable "developer" mode.

2. Search through the developer (dev) menus for the memory dump function.

3. Select the memory dump function and execute it.

4. The console will probably copy a .txt file to a host PC connected to it.

5. Attach this file to your bug.

Whether you're working on a console or PC, a log can save the team if you have an unruly bug on your hands. Careful observation and detailed notes can only go so far; the technical minutiae provided by the log will act as "forensics" of the bug's mischief—greatly enhancing your chances of catching it in time.

Bug Reporting Guidelines

B e specific in your reports. Don't skimp on the details. Many seem vast to us as testers/players. Imagine what it's like looking at all of that code that drives the game! That's what the engineers have to sort through to find the bug in your report. Describing how you got to the bug in great detail is the key to writing a good report. This means you have to be cognizant and precise about what you're doing while you're testing. You're not just playing; you're looking for something that's not working, which means you've got to recreate the process you used to get where you discovered the bug. Stay alert and be specific!

Todd M. Fay (Owner, DemoNinja.com)

Screenshots

There's nothing like a good *screenshot* to convince developers you actually have a bug. Taking screenshots with PCs is easy:

1. Use "Print Screen" key; a screenshot will appear in your clipboard.
2. Paste the screenshot into Paint or Adobe Photoshop.
3. Attach the file to your bug.

Consoles might be a little trickier; you'll need to go into the dev menu again and choose "save screenshot" or "screen capture."

Advanced Screenshot Tips

■   *Always take more than one screenshot.* It's important to cover different angles. Make sure you compress your images in JPEG. BMP files are too big and may clog the network.

■   *Use the highest resolution possible:* Developers have big LCDs; let them make use of all that real estate!

■   *Take extreme close-ups, medium shots and far away views:* All distances are useful.

■   *Mark the affected area with a "red marker":* Use the tools you have in each software package to better explain your bug.

■   *Identify the bug with text (optional):* Providing an identifier such as as "z-fighting" or "missing texture" can't hurt, as long the text doesn't cover the bug itself.

■   *If you have taken several screenshots, zip them up into one file:* Everyone will thank you for this!

Video Capture

Video capture can be even more illuminating than a screenshot. Although video also takes more time to produce, and resolution will probably be low, it also has one big advantage over screenshots: *movement.* You can actually cover all the steps in your bug report (and replace several screenshots) with a single, well-made video. You will surprise many developers if they see video attached to your bug. Video captures separate the amateurs from the pros!

Courtesy of Beepa   Reprinted with permission from Microsoft Corporation

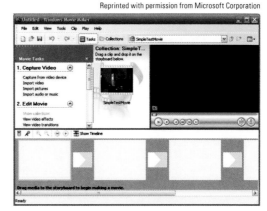

You can actually cover all the steps in your bug report with one well-made video, using tools such as FRAPS (left) and Movie Maker (right).

Advanced Video Capture Tips

When testing on a PC:

- Download FRAPS; it's free and easy to use.

- FRAPS has a 30-second limit if you skip registration. Work within it or pay up!

- Rehearse your video before recording. You don't want to be stuck facing the wall.

- Record a good run. Now start Windows Movie Maker on your computer.

- The video you originally recorded is uncompressed. Several megabytes won't cut it with your bug tracker and you will waste everybody's time. Windows Movie Maker can help you compress it in a tidy WMV file.

- Better yet: Use Windows Movie Maker to slow down the footage. This will make it even easier for developers.

When testing on a console system, you'll have one of two choices:

1. Not do any kind of video capture; or

2. Record the gameplay on a VHS VCR and digitize it.

Option 2 is not very fun, but it just might be your last resort. While cumbersome, it's not actually that hard and we're sure your lead will tell all about it in the very first week of testing. Just imagine that in the not-too-distant past, *everyone* had a VCR in the living room!

Using video in your bug reports will make it impossible for developers to doubt your version of the facts. It will also make their lives much easier! Think YouTube meets DevTrack with a little taste of G4.

Start Your Engines! bare bones bug hunting   chapter 5

Verification

Once your bug report is done, it goes back to the developer for a fix. A week later, it will come back to you. If you did your job well, the lead will give you a high stack of paper and call them "verifies." These are your bugs, now supposedly fixed. Your job now will be to make sure they were indeed fixed. We call this process *verification*. Here are the primary steps:

1. Go over your own steps multiple times.

2. Explore the bug again, with different steps this time. (Establish an alternative set of steps, but don't spend too much time on this process.)

3. If the bug has been fixed, write "verified" in the bug report and *sign your name to it.*

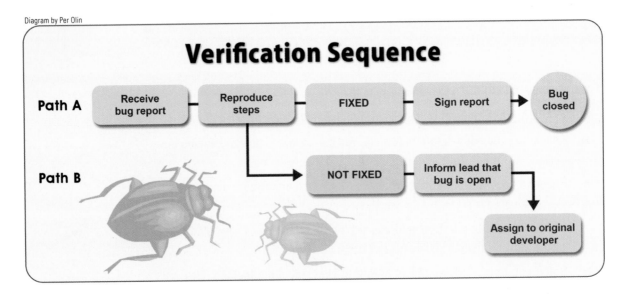

Diagram by Per Olin

The reason developers have testers sign verifies is due to *accountability*. If a tester says that a bug is fixed and it really isn't, this can snowball into a huge issue later in development. If a tester verifies several bugs as "fixed" and they're still there, chances are that tester will get fired. Publishers and developers don't tolerate lazy testers. One mistake can cost them millions once the game is out in the market.

In this chapter, we discussed the basics of testing. You now understand that each genre has its "pet bugs," and that bug reports can make or break your career. In the next chapter, we'll dive into advanced bug hunting techniques, such as ad hoc testing and coordinated teamwork. You will need to understand these techniques to tackle the most complicated bugs in existence.

:::CHAPTER REVIEW:::

1. How does a game's genre affect the type of bugs that might appear in the game? Play 3 games for at least 2 hours each and see if you can find at least one bug in each game. Are the bugs you found associated with the genre?

2. Write a bug report for the 3 bugs you found in Exercise 1. Following the bug reporting guidelines discussed in the chapter, provide the title, description, steps, and repeatability of each bug.

3. Verify each of your bugs using the three steps discussed in this chapter. Discuss the alternate steps you took to verify each bug. (These steps must differ from the original steps you used when you found each bug.)

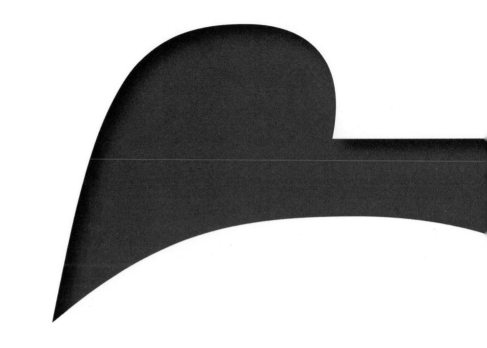

CHAPTER

6

Race to the Finish Line

elite bug hunting

Key Chapter Questions

- What's the difference between *normal* and *tough* bugs?

- When is it best to test *solo*, within a large *team*, or as part of a *task force*?

- What are some *advanced skills* that you need to excel in game testing?

- What are the various testing *techniques* such as ad-hoc and progression—and how can they be applied in testing situations?

- How can you achieve *greatness* as a tester?

Playing games is easy, but playing well is hard. Testing games is easy, but testing like a pro is hard. When you become a great tester, no bug is too complicated, no steps are too numerous, and no bug report is NAB'd. Increased skill levels and use of techniques such as ad-hoc and progression will make you a great tester, but you need to add sheer determination and a bullet-proof work ethic to stand among the best. This chapter focuses on the life of the elite tester, and it will change the way you see the job. Get ready to take a ride on the wild side!

Creepy Crawlies

Bugs that you can see and reproduce at will are considered "easy." They're so easy to spot, in fact, that most games ship without them. Even a mediocre testing team will find them without breaking a sweat. "Medium difficulty" bugs are not always visible and might give you some trouble when trying to reproduce them. They are the 8 in 10 bugs: there for the most part, but not there at times due to some fluke that you can't really pinpoint. Still, most testers can handle them. Eight bugs out of 10 are not that difficult to troubleshoot, and the bug report will be mostly correct. Really tough bugs, though, will not be visible at first. They appear way before you noticed anything wrong. They exist behind the screen and affect separate consoles for no apparent reason. They are notoriously difficult to reproduce; you might spend 4-5 hours trying to determine the steps, only to fail miserably sometime after midnight on a Saturday. Your lead will throw the whole team at it. When that fails, the lead might split everyone into duos or trios—smaller units that *should* be able to determine the steps. Even then, chances are high that you will fail—and the bug will still be there, waiting.

Diagram by Per Olin

Normal vs. Tough Bugs

Normal	Tough
Can be seen	Invisible or very difficult to see
Fairly easy to reproduce	Difficult to reproduce
Occur immediately	Take a while to occur
Observable (cause can be determined)	Not observable (result of hard freezes)

Fight the Nightmare

Remember when you were young? Remember those terrible nightmares that woke you up night after night—almost like a horror movie? Most suffer in silence, but some fight back. Fighting a nightmare is taking control over it, making use of important, often forgotten skills. Dealing with a difficult bug is very similar.

Here's how an inexperienced tester might deal with a tough bug:

1. When the bug hits for the first time, you're stumped. You didn't see it coming.

2. You try to reproduce the bug. You fail. You give up and go back to your checklist.

3. The bug hits again. You're now forced to report your findings to your lead.

4. The lead asks "Do you have the steps?" You answer "No."

5. You try again. You don't make notes and don't invite others to join the fray. Alone and confused, you spend five hours trying for the elusive steps. Nothing.

6. By the end of the day (or night), you go to the lead with an unfinished checklist. You receive no praise.

In contrast, here's how an experienced tester would react:

1. You're playing the game carefully, with your notebook by your side. Suddenly, the bug hits. It's a freeze.

2. You've been playing the game for about 45 minutes: multiplayer match, 11 other testers. Fierce fighting all around. (You write it down.) You take a screenshot with the dev menu, including all debug data.

3. You immediately talk to your lead. "Hey, got a freeze here. I got a screenshot and I'm also saving the dump on the desktop." The lead asks "Do you have steps?" You reply, "No, way too early. We're gonna need everybody to reproduce this. We had a 12-player match going on. Is it okay to work on that other stuff later?" The lead can't say anything other than "Okay."

4. With a team of 12, you reproduce the exact steps. Nobody freezes for the first four times, but then two testers freeze on the fifth.

5. You go to the two testers, notebook in hand. You take notes on their actions. You compare them to your own.

6. You start a new game. Everybody has their instructions. They fail several times, but they're also compiling information essential for accurate steps.

7. After five hours, they have working steps. They don't work every single time— it's a 5 out of 10—but they're good enough.

8. You compile all the information from everyone involved, sit at the computer, and write the report. You attach the memory dump to the report, along with a screen capture taken at the moment of the freeze.

Remember: The difference between a gamer and a tester is like the difference between an amateur actor and legends such as Jack Nicholson or Meryl Streep. Amateurs can act, but only the professional actor will take a movie to a new level by creating an engaging, soul-stirring character. It's not merely enough to know what to do; you need to know *yourself* and be open to the endless possibilities in a game. When you reach this level, no bug is too hard to crack.

chapter 6

The Lone Wolf

Most of your life as a tester will involve working alone. Other than multiplayer testing, it will be "you and the checklist" for days on end. Even production testers work primarily alone. There are various reasons for this:

- Higher productivity (through division of labor)
- Increased focus
- Ease of management (from the lead's perspective)

You're much more likely to be "in the zone"—working at your own pace and rhythm—if you work on your own. You will also take better and more detailed notes, and you'll tackle your checklist more quickly. Entering bugs is also easier if you have all the information already at hand instead of having to rely on others. Here are the situations in which it will be necessary to "go it alone."

On a single-player focused game such as *The Club*, you will be doing most of the testing on your own.

Checklists

All checklists are tedious, and they can put testers in a bad mood. Extended checklists in particular can be a nightmare! Try testing all of the elevators in *Quake 4* over and over again—teleporting between locations. Your output depends on concentration, and this is tough to do when you have 11 other people screaming at you.

Visual & Audio Bugs

Some visual and audio bugs demand more attention to detail than usual. In a multiplayer match, you could easily miss these bugs while trying to avoid getting beaten by your fellow testers. Bugs like these should be taken on by a single tester.

Verification Overload

If you have dozens of *verifications* (bugs that need to be verified as fixed) on your desk, you'll need to work alone. Your objective is to attempt to reproduce the steps to these bugs and *then* sign your name. If you get distracted, you run the risk of making a serious mistake.

It's important to know when to stick to your guns and go solo. Fighting by yourself is an easy way to get killed, but it's the only way to tackle some of the challenges in testing—such as detailed checklists, visual and audio bugs, and a pile of verifications.

Hunting in Packs

If the game allows for a large number of players (multiplayer or co-op), expect to work in a group in order to tackle most of the bugs. Here are a few reasons to "hunt in packs":

- Necessary for networking bugs (which demand a large group of testers)
- Higher odds of reproducing exact steps (easier to accomplish with more minds involved)
- Increased "esprit de corps" (morale and team spirit will rise)

Sometimes you absolutely need the team to back you up. There's a wealth of information flowing in a testing lab; having teammates contribute and cooperate with you makes it easier to grasp the many bits of information and process them. Your teammates' eyes and ears will be yours; eventually, this information will be distilled into the precise steps that have eluded you.

Multiplayer games such as *Brothers in Arms: Hell's Highway* require a team effort to test.

Complicated Network Bugs

There's no way to avoid it: Most games are multiplayer now. Some titles might not have proper "multiplayer mode," but they'll at least offer co-op play and shared high score tables. The days of exclusive single-player modes are quickly waning. One day you might be testing a massively multiplayer online puzzle game (MMOPG) such as *Puzzle Pirates*, or a racing game with eight simultaneous drivers and an audience of millions watching the race at home. You will need to find out why positions are not updated or why certain items don't "drop" as they're supposed to. The only way to do this in a multiplayer title is within a team environment.

Balance Issues

When balancing a multiplayer title, you will need to have the team play on all sides and make use of all weapons and other relevant props and accessories. The team will also help you make correct assertions and verify balance issues by playing the game over and over again. In first-person shooters (FPSs), it's common to have unbalanced weapons until late in the development process. You will never be able to figure this out by yourself.

Massive Tasks

Prior to going gold, some tests will be executed *one last time*. One of these might be the loading of maps. In *Call of Duty 3*, a bug that prevented maps from loading was discovered late in the game, and the whole team had to spend from 10:00pm on a Friday to 7:00am on Saturday to locate it. While all members of the team were not necessarily testing during the same sessions, they were all on the same task. This is similar to using a cluster of PS3s to figure out the cure for cancer; the sheer number of individual elements doing exact the same thing turns the team into one very powerful entity. It takes a lot of leadership to extract this kind of performance from testers, but the end results can be outstanding.

You will have a lot of fun hunting for bugs with your teammates. The feeling of inclusiveness is intoxicating; you now belong to a pack of wolves that fights together. While you should never let go of your solo skills, working well within a team might be even more valuable. There's a shortage of leaders out there. Imagine what it would be like to *lead the pack*!

Reviewing the Basics

Before we move on to advanced testing techniques, let's more deeply analyze the basics—many of which were introduced in Chapter 5. First of all, the most important thing to know before testing a game is *what should happen*; we call this *expected behavior*. This is the reason why testers start a new project by merely playing the game and asking questions about what they see; it's important to get acquainted with the game first. This process might take a day or two. There's simply no other way to develop your observation skills other than to *know what to expect*. Let's take a look at other basic techniques.

Take Notes

Keep a notebook at your desk at all times. Write down everything out of the ordinary—bugs large and small. Add as much detail as humanly possible—in an organized fashion.

Don't Rush

Take your time, and don't rush the level. The only person rushing is the tester who is responsible for doing playthroughs. If you're not that person, you should be focusing on details and *not* speed.

Follow Procedure

Let's say your team is following a detailed procedure regarding save games. This may seem silly to you, but there's usually a good reason for it. If you ignore the prescribed procedure, you'll jeopardize the entire team and throw a monkey wrench into all of your bug entries.

Check the Version

You don't want to do all of your testing on an old version of the game. Always read the version numbers of the discs the lead distributes and ask your fellow testers about theirs. Testing the wrong version is a sure-fire way to waste time, money, and your reputation.

Pay Attention

There is something to be said about having too much fun. If you're laughing and making jokes while the lead explains the steps that *everyone* must follow, you might not follow instructions and make a huge mistake. If you get pigeonholed because of this, say goodbye to your career.

Focus on the Game

With Internet-enabled phones and PDAs, and a room full of testers, it's just too easy to lose focus. When you pay more attention to tester "drama" than what just happened onscreen, you're doing a disservice to the team. You're being paid to test, not to chat.

If you follow these basic directives, you will become a good tester. You'll be able to *see* bugs for what they are—and describe and report them. You will also rise among other testers.

Growing Up

Advanced skills will allow you to go one step further and crack bugs that most let go. In order to apply these techniques, you need to develop a basic understanding of programming/scripting, strong analytical/critical thinking skills, advanced knowledge of photo/video editing software, and college-level writing skills.

Programming/Scripting

Even just knowing the basics of programming/scripting allows you to look at bugs from the developer's point of view. You cease to be a victim of effects and begin targeting the underlying causes. Most games are heavily scripted; knowing how scripts "break" and how this affects the game can make a huge difference in your effectiveness.

The Untouchable Tester

Luis used to work with a tester who had the elusive *previous programming experience*; in a team of 14, this tester was the only one who could quickly identify and replicate scripting and artificial intelligence bugs. No one on the team could touch him!

Scripting Skills

Learning scripting skills can be particularly useful; I would highly recommend scripting to all QA testers who want to stay in the industry for any length of time.

Brandon Adler (QA Lead, Obsidian Entertainment)

Analytical/Critical Thinking

Analytical/critical thinking involves the ability to break down a *whole* into its constituent *parts* in order to study these parts and their relations. The *whole* is the game. The *parts* are the different areas affected by bugs. In order to become a professional tester, you need to be able to integrate disparate systems into a single, coherent event. Detail is nothing without form; your analytical thinking skills will be essential to construct the bug report inside your head first, which will lead to a better bug report.

Writing Skills

When writing bug reports, some testers default to a "high school" style that doesn't fit the job. Some can't spell. Some can't write a coherent report. To become a good tester, you need to know how to write! Advanced writing skills make a huge difference. You need to expand your vocabulary and write sentences that connect and follow a thread. There's no other good way to write a bug report. Most publishers and developers now pay attention to writing skill; sometimes they give it more weight than being a gamer!

Becoming the best not only involves "competing" with other testers but stretching yourself. Recognize your weak areas and work hard on them. Push yourself every day, and challenge your weaker side to become the best it can possibly be. If you play MMOs, you know that leveling up is not a matter of playing the same inefficient strategy four hours a day; it's all about finding the *quickest, most efficient way to beat the toughest opponents*. If you can do this in *World of Warcraft*, you can do it while testing games!

Diving in Head First

Game projects usually begin with a large pool of testers. However, by the time the project ends, only a few manage to survive the chopping block; if you don't *ace* the basics and work hard on the advanced skills we've discussed in this chapter, you will meet this fate. You need to know all of these skills, and you need to get good at them. Think *Survivor* meets *The Running Man* meets *The Lawnmower Man*: you don't want a millionaire Jobe to run you over with Big Red while your collar explodes. Testing might seem like a reality show sometimes; make sure you're still standing at the end.

Playthroughs

Playing a game quickly without cheating is a very desirable skill. There was one tester on the *Quake 4* project who could go though the entire game in roughly three hours; the other players took 10 hours! These "sprinters" conduct *playthroughs*, which are necessary to make sure the game can be completed and allow developers to focus on everything else. In the first days of the project, the lead will watch everyone play and even have some kind of competition to discover the "speed stars" of the team. Once established, these testers become responsible for doing quick playthroughs every time a new build is done—scouting the territory before other testers are fully engaged. When the project is close to completion, those testers who can perform under pressure and complete the game quickly will be kept on for other projects.

Playthroughs Are Not Speedruns!

On the surface, playthroughs may seem identical to *speedruns*; they're both about reaching the end really fast, right? Actually, no. Playthroughs cannot include any sorts of codes or cheating because they're part of the testing process. Cheating and game testing never go together; a cheat can easily break the game. Speedruns, on the other hand, are usually *tool-assisted*. Emulators allow you to save and load a game at will; speedrunners can save time by avoiding certain death and/or scores of enemies. Speedrunners can also cheat by using *exploits*—flaws in the game that, while not bugs, still allow the player to gain an unfair advantage.

Playthrough Guidelines

Here are a few guidelines you should follow during the playthrough process:

- No cheating whatsover. Cheats unbalance the game and might also introduce instability.

- Complete all basic objectives.

- Play in all difficulty levels. Most testers forget about anything other than "normal."

- Use headphones (to avoid distractions).

- Mark your start and end times. Subtract any breaks.

- If you encounter a crash or progression break, stop everything. Talk to your lead and start working on a *thorough* bug report.

Used by permission from id Software, Inc.

Repeat playthroughs are necessary to make sure the game can be completed (*Quake II*, shown).

Playthroughs can be incredibly fun—or infuriating. That's why very few testers actually get to be sprinters. If you've got what it takes, a lead will notice you and put you through "trials." If the lead is convinced that you're the one, get ready to play the game from beginning to end dozens of times—from the "Peek-a-Boo!" intro level to "Chuck Norris Cried while Playing This Game."

Task Force

Sometimes a bug is so complicated that it can't be taken on by either one ace tester or the entire team. In this case, a middle ground is needed; enter the *task force*, which shares the same objective of hunting a particular bug, but pursues different strategies. With a task force, the lead can have each of the subteams follow slightly different steps in an attempt to nail down all the details. The possibility of varying steps within a team saves an enormous amount of time in the end. Task forces are also great for uncovering leadership talent among testers who don't usually get to lead. In the future, those same testers can be called to action again and perhaps even be prepared to lead their own teams in different projects.

BigStockPhoto

Sometimes, a bug is so intricate that it needs a task force—like a SWAT team!

If you are part of a task force:

- Don't be a smart aleck. Speak when you have to, and be silent when you don't.
- Follow instructions to the smallest detail.
- Work with your teammates. Don't "go rogue" on them. Put any Jack Bauer fantasies aside!
- Report your findings to the task force lead.
- Take detailed notes.

If you are the lead of a task force:

- Work alongside the other leads. You all have your roles.
- Be respectful with each member of your team. They are *not* inferior to you.
- Keep the end goal in sight at all times.

You can easily compare task forces to the way the human body works. Each organ remains alive in its own way—but brain, heart, and lungs serve different purposes. They work well together because *they share a mission-critical objective*; they thrive because each is *the best at what it does*.

Race to the Finish Line: elite bug hunting

chapter 6

Coordinated Effort

Sometimes a bug demands a *coordinated effort* from everyone in the team. This is the case with networking bugs that are often the result of sloppy network code. When scale is needed, a task force won't do; you need an army! Team efforts are usually helmed by the lead. If your lead is not especially hands-on, he or she might pick a trusted tester for the job instead, who will then have command over the entire team and will tell each tester which map and classes to use.

Coordinated Effort Guidelines

Here are a few guidelines you should follow if you are leading a coordinated effort:

- Set your priorities straight. Keep the main objective in mind at all times.

- Avoid a bossy or professorial tone. Your job is to organize and guide the team, nothing more.

- Start from known steps and build a steady case. Avoid taking shortcuts.

- Compliment the team for a job well-done, and remind them of the objective if they lose focus.

- Make sure everyone is taking notes.

- Respect breaks. Testers lose effectiveness if they don't take a break every three hours or so.

- Keep an open mind. Even the craziest hypothesis might turn out to be true.

- Lead by example. If you want cooperative testers, be cooperative yourself.

Above all, keep in mind that some bugs are simply too difficult to crack in the first attempt. Give all the information you have to the developers and let them have a go at it. They might come up with new test cases for the entire team to iterate on.

Becoming an Expert

It's hard to do everything well. In fact, no one can quite claim this honor. When you're testing games for a living, you feel the pressure to excel at everything—visual bugs, scripting, artificial intelligence (AI), balance . . . you name it. Your lead will constantly push you to "know what you're doing" and "think for yourself." Newsflash: It just doesn't work. It's better to be an expert at one topic than to not be an expert at all. (Don't be a "jack of all trades and master of none," to quote an age-old adage.)

Choose Your Field

Becoming an expert means making use of your natural talents and focusing on your aptitude. Here are some suggestions:

- If you love programming, put energy into it to become an expert in scripting/programming for games.

- If you're into film, use your "eyes" to dominate visual bugs.

- Musicians can become amazing audio testers. This has happened right before our eyes: One tester who was in a band was quickly hired to join the sound department!

- If your obsession is game design, strive to become the new "Balance Czar." Your talent will be very much in demand!

- If your gaming skills are out of this world, think about being the official play-through "sprinter."

Becoming the best in one field is a sure-fire way to break free from the pack. As a professional tester, the last thing you want is to "blend in" with a thousand other testers. By learning advanced techniques and becoming proficient in them, you minimize the chance of being laid off. More than that, becoming a great tester is a solid step toward an actual career in game development. Some of the greatest designers of all time started in the testing lab; all it takes to "escape" is the drive to succeed and the discipline to hone your skills.

Testing Techniques

As if the previous techniques weren't enough, here's some food for thought: Testing can be numbers—or music. Ad-hoc testing is an art, but automated testing is firmly within a programmer's realm. Progression testing is going through the game in a linear fashion; regression testing has nothing to do with past lives. Let's now take a look at more techniques from the (fascinating) world of game testing.

Ad-Hoc

BigStockPhoto

Ad-hoc testing is free-form testing. When you ad-hoc, you leave the checklist behind, relax, and play without thinking—almost as if you were at home sitting in the couch. The one difference, though, is that when you ad-hoc, you are still looking for bugs and exploring the game; you might not be sweating over a checklist, but you have eyes and ears focused on what's happening onscreen. Ad-hoc testing can allow you to find bugs that you'd never find otherwise. It's almost like a "magic power" guides your every move; all you have to do is "listen"!

When you ad-hoc, "not-testing" is the best testing there is.

Ad-Hoc Steps

- Load the game. Put all of your focus on the screen. If you have headphones, use them.

- Forget about finding bugs. You're in a different world now.

- You're not a tester. You were never a tester. In fact, you were never *born*.

- There is such a thing as a "stream of gameplay." Dive into it.

Ad-hoc testing is almost like a flow of consciousness. By relaxing and isolating yourself from the other testers, you enter a different level of awareness. You will find your biggest bugs in ad-hoc testing, so make sure you're comfortable with the process.

Floyd Billings on Advanced & Ad-Hoc Testing :::::

Floyd spent seven years working for Dell Computers as a sales rep before entering the game industry. He had been a longtime MMO gamer—so when the opportunity to work for Sony Online Entertainment presented itself, he jumped at the chance to see how games are made.

Anyone can see and do the positive test cases. It takes thought to come up with an edge negative test case that gets results. This is not to say to ignore the others; after all, our job is to find and report bugs. The more you identify, the better the game ultimately will be! But being able to think outside the box like a lot of our players will attempt to do is *worth* the effort you put into it.

Floyd Billings
(Assistant Lead QA, Sony Online Entertainment)

Focused ad-hoc testing is valid, and it's of great value to the game you may be working on. After all, this is when you find a bug that was caused by the implementation of a system that should not effect what you are seeing—but it somehow does. This has happened numerous times with us—so if you are done with your assigned testing, you should be testing a specific system using the ad-hoc technique.

The Value of Ad-Hoc Testing

Ad-hoc testing is very important for the types of games that Obsidian makes. I have noticed that using test plans and checklists tends to catch the obvious bugs on the game's surface, but the most despicable bugs seem to be found during ad-hoc sessions.

Brandon Adler (QA Lead, Obsidian Entertainment)

Ad-hoc testing is valuable for usability and gameplay validation, but it is not a substitute for methodical quality assurance practices.

Gordon Walton (Studio Co-Director, BioWare Austin)

Ad-hoc testing is where QA for games really stands apart from all other aspects of quality assurance. In my book, an experienced QA tester playing ad-hoc can devastate any producer, and ruin any programmer's day. But it's all for the collective good, right?

Jerome Strach (QA Manager, Sony Computer Entertainment America)

Automated

Game testing is better done by humans, but certain games can be so complex that testers need the help of a computer to go over all the possible permutations. If we take *Forza Motorsport* as an example, it becomes obvious that some bugs will only be found with a thorough, super-human effort: hence *automated* testing. Can you imagine making sure every single upgrade in *Forza* has the desired effect? This is tough enough; now imagine ensuring that each upgrade doesn't conflict with all the other upgrades. The sheer scope of the task makes computers a necessity. Chris Dickens (*Software Test Engineering @ Microsoft* – blogs.msdn.com/chappell/articles/106056.aspx) explains:

> "I'm a smart guy and I know a lot about software development, so it's clearly not the best use of my time to click on the same button looking for the same dialog box every single day. Part of smart testing is delegating those kinds of tasks away so I can spend my time on harder problems. And computers are a great place to delegate repetitive work. That's really what automated testing is about. We try to get computers to do our job for us. One of the ways I describe my goal as a tester is to put myself out of a job—meaning that I automate my entire job. This is, of course, unachievable, so I don't actually worry about losing my job. But it's a good vision. My short-term goal is always to automate the parts of my job I find most annoying with the selfish idea of not having to do annoying stuff any more."

Reprinted with permission from Microsoft Corporation

Can you imagine making sure every single upgrade in *Forza Motorsport* has the desired effect?

In *Forza Motorsport*, a tester with programming knowledge could wrote software that goes over all the permutations in the game and looks for error messages of any kind. If those errors exist, it warns the tester. This way, a huge amount of time is saved during the testing itself—releasing time for polishing or other important tasks.

Functionality

Functionality testing is considered the primary testing variety and involves making sure the game functions properly and also *looks* like it's supposed to (i.e., no visual bugs). If the game crashes, it's not functioning; that's a "fail." If the game fails to load, you guessed it—that's a fail. If you have "expected behavior" on one hand and "actual results" on the other and they *fail* to match—just go ahead and write it up!

Courtesy of Blizzard Entertainment, Inc.

Functionality testing ensures that levels load completely and correctly (*World of Warcraft*, shown).

Functionality Requirements

The following requirements should be followed in all functionality testing situations:

- If you select a character, you're able to play with that character.

- You start the game, and "load game" actually loads your saved game.

- You are able to finish the game (i.e., *playthrough completion*).

- In a role-playing game, a new item works as intended (e.g., stronger sword adds more damage).

- In a racing game, a new engine upgrade is clearly felt once you take the driver's seat.

- Nothing you can do can actually crash the game.

- All art assets such as walls or picture frames look spot on.

In short, functionality testing involves being absolutely sure that all features in the game return the expected results—whatever they may be. Bear in mind that you're not worried if the game is fun or not; that really doesn't matter at this point, since the focus is to make sure the basics are covered.

Progression

Progression testing involves playing the game linearly—merely trying to get to the end. It's not about speed at all; you're looking for progression *breaks*. You can play the game leisurely, explore, try new things, save, and load at will. Your objective is to make sure the gameplay is never interrupted. You might think we're talking about crashes and freezes; yes, these can interrupt gameplay, but they're not progression breaks. If the game is still running, but you simply *can't open that door* (the one that leads to the next area), *that's* a progression break. About 99% of the time, progression breaks are caused by scripting issues. The other 1% are caused by especially nasty stuck spots.

BigStockPhoto

Progression breaks will interrupt gameplay even if the game itself is still running.

Regression

Once developers fix a bug, it's fixed forever . . . in a perfect world. In reality, bug fixes can easily generate other bugs. To curb the potential damage from an important bug sneaking past you, it's essential to conduct *regression* testing. Not part of the daily routine, regression testing will only be done a few times a week. In regression testing, you're essentially looking for old bugs in current code. Let's say a nasty crash was fixed in Version 0.5. You're working with Version 0.9 now, and the crash was supposed to have been fixed. Your lead might request that you look for that bug in Version 0.9—just in case. While seemingly simple on the surface, regression testing is very important.

Courtesy of NAMCO BANDAI Games America Inc.

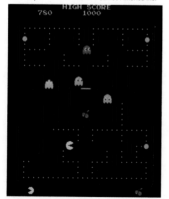

Courtesy of NAMCO BANDAI Games America Inc.

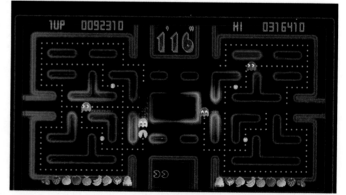

Old code (*Pac-Man*, left) can help you understand new code (*Pac-Man Championship Edition*, right).

Achieving Greatness

The great tester: This elusive creature is said to exist deep inside the best development studios on earth. A great tester is like "The Stig" on BBC's *Top Gear*; he doesn't work for money, doesn't care whether he's "liked" or not, and doesn't stop until he hits the performance limits of every car he drives. He cares for one thing and one thing only: to be the very best.

Courtesy of nahtanoj on flickr (Wikipedia)

You might call this attitude a strong *work ethic*. Great testers avoid the gossip and conspiracy of a testing room; they test, learn, and explore in silence—and when the time comes, they write crystal clear bug reports. Think about the difference between "What I Did on My Summer Vacation" and a doctoral thesis; this is what stands between a tester and a great tester.

But how do you get there? We should assume that *everyone* wants to reach this level. Unfortunately, this is not the case. Many testers are happy being "okay" (i.e., not fired). They might still want to work in game development, but years of testing have made them jaded and reckless. Like many, they see no hope of ever getting out of the test room. Most likely, this attitude will ensure that they *never* leave that room! In your quest for greatness, you'll need several skills and characteristics.

A great tester is like The Stig on BBC's *Top Gear*.

Flexibility & Dexterity

A standout tester has got to have the following two characteristics:

- *Flexibility*: Programmers are creatures of habit; have the programmers show you the game (or product). In other words, have them show you a given feature, play a level, etc. Now, don't do *anything* the same way they did it. If they used the mouse, use the keyboard. If there are two ways to get somewhere, take the "other" path.

- *Dexterity*: A company called Epyx used to spend more time on testing than most game companies of the time (and perhaps even today). They even hired a programmer to write tests to learn how fast humans could actually control a joystick. You want at least one or two people on your test team who have extremely high reaction times. This will reveal the more subtle rendering and interaction issues.

Baron R.K. Von Wolfsheild (Chief Software Architect, Qtask, Inc.)

Determination

You can never give up working on a bug. If a solution is impossible for now, take a break but keep the bug in your "short list." Keep it in your head for months if necessary. One day, you'll find out the bug is gone. Then you can forget it.

Energy

You must be able to work for hours on end. Eight-hour days will soon become 12- and 15-hour days. You need to learn how to "modulate" your energy so that you always have some available. If you fail, you will crash and become useless as a consequence.

Friends

Get to know your superiors—making "friends in high places." Go beyond your immediate lead and producer; meet artists, tool programmers, the receptionist . . . everyone. One sincere friendship with a key coworker might make the difference between unemployment and promotion.

Aspirations

You need to expect a lot from your game. Perfection is impossible, but *high quality* is not. You need to seek the very best product possible under the time you have to test it. Anything less and you soon start to treat smaller bugs as "annoyances" and not something that needs to be fixed.

Being the Best Possible Tester

Attention to detail and good writing skills are the most important characteristics for an entry level tester to have. Anyone can find a crash bug, but the best testers I have known have been the ones that can recognize inconsistent behaviors in the way the game behaves from Level 1 to Level 10 and then communicate that information effectively to a developer. While overall gaming skill is valuable, being able to beat every game on the hardest difficulty doesn't necessarily translate to being the best possible tester.

David Price (Test Lead, THQ, Inc.)

Technical Knowledge

The technology in testing is not overly complicated. There are computers or consoles waiting for bug input—not to mention devkits, HDTVs, and servers. In order to grow, you absolutely need to take the equipment head on and make it work to your benefit. You need to know how to dump the memory contents of the game, connect a console to the HDMI port, and burn the most recent version of the game. You *will* receive some training for most of these tasks, but you should have a basic knowledge of them anyway.

Investigative Skills

Complicated bugs are like the plots in a hard-boiled novel. They twist and turn, throwing a hundred red herrings at you in any given day. They are stubborn and unpredictable. Investigative skills will go a long way toward clearing the noise from testing. Method and organization will put everything into perspective and give you solid next steps. Even if you fail, your notes will have enough information on them to support a new and improved attempt.

Outstanding Work Ethic

Be at work on time, avoid pointless arguments, always tell the truth, follow protocol, focus on the bug(s) at hand, and inform your lead ahead of time if you have scheduling issues. You will go a long way by keeping your job in check and respecting common sense.

People Skills

Understanding machines is great, but you also need to be good with human beings; it's your "people skills" that will separate you from the socially awkward. You'll need these skills to relate to fellow testers, get hired, or fire someone working under you. Lack of people skills is one of the biggest challenges in an industry that's technical and binary by definition.

Curiosity

A great tester has an unending curiosity about the world—reading when off work and researching everything under the sun online. Learning is a passion—not a chore. A thirst for knowledge creates smarter, more resourceful testers; it expands them into future developers, serving as reminders of how much they still have to learn.

Confidence

Sometimes, your lead will make a mistake—perhaps due to being too busy or worried sick about a higher-level issue (studios also have office politics). Anyway, you can't let your lead's mistake sink the entire team. You must have the confidence to stand up for your opinion in a respectful way, pointing out *why* that bug is important and *how* it affects the game. If your lead still decides to shut you down, then you need to keep a precise record of what happened. When the time comes, you will return to the topic. Confidence can mean the difference between a serious bug caught in development and one in the wild, once the game is in the players' hands.

:::

In this chapter, we explored advanced skills and testing techniques. You learned about single and team testing—along with the characteristics you'll need to truly "achieve greatness" in the testing arena! In the next chapter, we'll discuss what you can do right now to prepare yourself for a career in the game industry—getting the education you need to shine, searching for a job as a game tester, and creating the next "ridiculously-expensive-mod-that-happens-to-be-a-hyper-profitable-franchise-in-disguise."

:::CHAPTER REVIEW:::

1. Consider the advanced skills discussed in this chapter: programming/scripting, analytical/critical thinking, and writing. Which of these skills have you already developed, and how? If you haven't yet developed any of these skills, choose one that is the most attainable and focus on it—by training yourself, taking classes, working on outside projects, and practicing. Discuss how you will tackle these skills in preparation for a testing position.

2. Conduct a playthrough for an original game or one that is currently on the market. How many "hours of gameplay" are specified for the game? (Check reviews on GiantBomb.com for official specs.) How long did it take you to play through the game? Do you think you might be fit to be a "sprinter" on a testing team?

3. Describe the various testing techniques discussed in this chapter. Select 3 games that are currently on the market. For each game, choose at least one testing technique that might be most appropriate for that game. Provide rationales for your decisions.

Part III:
End Game

Ready, Set, Go!

entering the world of game testing

Key Chapter Questions

- What are different ways that prospective testers can *research* and *apply* for available testing positions?

- How can a prospective tester *get noticed* by game development studios and publishers?

- What are some *educational opportunities* for those interested in pursuing careers in game testing or the game industry in general?

- What are some requirements for an effective *cover letter* and *resumé*?

- How can a candidate for a testing position prepare for an *interview* at a game developer or publisher?

Getting a job in game testing is far from difficult—but getting a *good* job is! Before jumping head first into job hunting, you need to assess your options. Will you immediately apply for a job as a game tester? Will you be a step ahead of the competition by working on projects such as mods before you begin hunting? Or will you take some time to learn and hone new skills by taking game development courses or even enter a degree program in game development? This chapter will also discuss what you need to do during the job application process—and how to conduct yourself during the interview. At that final point, you will need to plan your strategy before facing the interviewer—your personal "mini-boss" of sorts!

Get Yourself Noticed!

For further reading on this topic, please see *Game Industry Career Guide* (Moore/Novak)—part of the *Game Development Essentials* series.

In order to start working as a game tester, you first need to get noticed. This does not translate into coming up with a rushed resumé full of gaming references. Instead, use the proper channels. If you're technically inclined, you might want to consider creating a mod. Participation in game forums, on the other hand, is the choice of those who are adept at expressing themselves through writing. An always helpful addition to *any* job hunt is attending industry conferences such as the Game Developers Conference in San Francisco and E3 (Electronic Entertainment Expo) in Los Angeles. We'll also describe other, less conventional ways of getting hired as a tester. While none of these methods are guaranteed, the novelty factor alone might be enough to get you through the door.

Modding

Modding involves using a game's assets—such as textures and geometry—to create *mods*, or modifications of the original game. "Partial conversions" are superficial changes (e.g., new character skins, altered weapons values), while "total conversions" involve creating an entirely new game using the engine originally shipped with the game. Modding came into the spotlight with the first *Doom*, when id Software allowed players to make their own maps and exchange them over *bulletin board systems* (BBSs), early methods of exchanging files and chatting online—and later, the web. Once *Quake* was released, id went one step further and shipped the official level editor with the game—giving a boost to the modding scene. Valve and Epic followed suit a few years later, with both Valve and Unreal engines becoming extremely popular among PC users. Modding is a great way to get your foot in the door. The team that created *Counter-Strike* was originally hired by Valve after developing the extremely successful mod with Valve's *Half-Life* engine. Many of the level designers in major franchises such as *Quake* and *Call of Duty* come from modding as well.

Courtesy of Mod DB

Participating in a site such as MODdb.com can help you get your foot in the door through modding.

Pick a popular game, make sure the publisher supports modding, and start working on a single original level or multiplayer map. This will become your demo and the key to getting hired. If you lack scripting skills, why not *join* a modding group as an artist, designer, or other team member? Working as part of a team will not only be much easier, but it will also better prepare you for the studio environment.

Beta Testing

Beta testing is sometimes regarded as a long shot, but it just might work for you. The idea is to enroll in the open beta program of a game you love and be exceptional at it. You're supposed to prove yourself to the developers through thoughtful suggestions, detailed bug reports, and pristine behavior in the game's forums. A developer might very well spot you among thousands of users and offer you a job. It sounds too good to be true, but we know from personal experience that it can work.

Courtesy of Cartoon Network

It might be possible to get noticed by the dev team if you participate wisely in open beta testing for titles such as Cartoon Network's *FusionFall*.

Balancing Opinion & "Malleability"

I look for testers who are gamers first. I like testers who have opinions about the game. As a designer, this provides me with great feedback. However, I try to stay away from gamers that feel as though they know everything there is to know and whose views are not "malleable."

John Comes (Creative Director, Uber Entertainment)

Forums

Participating in *forums* can yield similar results to beta testing—but forums are not quite as effective. It's easy to be an outspoken fan nowadays. When everyone is online, you lose the advantage of actually being there—and you need to do more than that. Giving good suggestions is a plus, as well as helping the developers run the forum. If you really want your participation in forums to be worth your while, enroll in the moderation team. This is the best—and possibly only—way to call attention to yourself.

Courtesy of Evil Avatar

If you really want to make your participation in forums such as Evil Avatar to be worth your while, enroll in the moderation team.

The Squeaky Wheel Can Get the Grease

A successful senior producer currently working at an AAA game development studio got his start in the industry when he made a series of outspoken forum posts for one of his favorite games. The developers moderating the forum hand-picked him for a position—and the rest is history. Being a squeaky wheel has its rewards—especially when you've got something meaningful to say!

Sharpen Your Skills

Take part in the game industry now. Attend GDC conferences and try to be active in indie projects. Having skills related to game development will always help, so if you're not studying a game development related degree then try picking up some skills on the side. A great learning activity while playing games is to practice finding as many bugs as you can with released video games. The longer you practice sharpening your skills of finding bugs (especially small ones!) the better a QA tester you'll become.

Nathan Madsen (Composer & Sound Designer, Madsen Studios / NetDevil)

Conferences

Conferences are essential to attend when looking for a job. In the end, getting hired is often about *who* you know—and how much they know about you. Attending a conference such as GDC will give you the chance to mingle with the greatest developers on earth. You will learn how they think and speak. You will chat with them during a booth crawl, root side-by-side for your favorite "battle-bot" during a publisher's after party, and maybe play a match of *Wii Sports* at a snooker bar. Anything goes, really. However, in addition to all the schmoozing, you'll need to meet recruiters and apply for jobs during the Game Career Seminar at GDC. Apply for as many jobs as you can—showing the flexibility to relocate if necessary. If you approach the conference experience this way, not only will companies have an official job application from you but they will actually *know* the face behind the resumé.

Courtesy of Game Developers Conference

The annual Game Developers Conference may have more developers recruiting new talent than any other game-related event.

Getting out and about is essential for *any* kind of job hunting. But this doesn't mean you have to wear out the rubber on your shoes to meet like-minded individuals. Why not do it virtually? Using the Internet to break into the game industry is not only easier, but far more sensible than knocking on developers' doors. Get your name out there, learn, and make yourself available to help others just like you. You'll get positive results in no time.

Making the Most of Networking

Persistence is key. There are a lot of people out there that want to become game testers. Being able to hang in there while you're looking for openings is key. Also, knowing someone helps. Networking is so important in this industry. The more people who know you and like you, the more likely you are to get the nod. I know it's not pretty, but it often comes down to who you know. Don't get bent out of shape over it, though; it's human nature. Better yet, work with it: Get out to trade shows and meet industry veterans, listen to what they have to say and befriend them. Once you make some contacts, pick someone you respect and develop a mentoring relationship with him—where he can take you under his wing and show you the ropes. Don't overlook newcomers to the industry though; friends I made eight years ago at my first GDC have gone on to great places and we continue to help each other out.

Todd M. Fay (Owner, DemoNinja.com)

Josh Bear on Hiring Testers

Josh Bear
(Chief Creative Officer
& Co-Owner,
Twisted Pixel Games)

Josh Bear is chief creative officer and co-owner of Twisted Pixel Games—an independent game company that specializes in high-quality downloadable games for Xbox Live Arcade, PlayStation Network, PC, and WiiWare. Twisted Pixel's latest game, *The Maw*, won the 2008 Penny Arcade PAX 10 Audience Choice Award. Before helping form Twisted Pixel Games, Bear worked for High Voltage Software where he worked on several games for the PlayStation 2, Xbox, Gamecube, and Wii. Bear is a graduate of the Ringling School of Art and Design, with a Bachelor's Degree in Illustration.

When the time comes to hire testers, I want someone who is really into games and loves to play them, but not a "know-it-all" who thinks he knows everything about game design and what makes games fun. If you haven't worked in the industry or you haven't designed a game before, you'll quickly learn that most development studios aren't devoid of good ideas. It all comes down to time and money—and above all, creating great games is a team effort. So the tester who would work with us would need to understand how that process works, and become an important part of the team.

The Hunt Begins

Let's take a look at some time-tested ways to get in the game industry as an entry-level tester. None of these are especially difficult, but they offer a longer path towards becoming a game developer. During your job hunt, you should focus on finding the available opportunities through game company web sites, job boards (e.g., Craigslist), and professional and social networks (e.g., LinkedIn). You also want to consider your own relationships you have cultivated in recent years, along with connections you've made through school.

Game Company Web Sites

Publishers usually have a "jobs" section on their company web sites. When resumés are submitted to a job through an online form, they all go to a tidy database, where searching for the right "match" is a lot easier. Although this can be an effective way to apply for mid- to high-level positions, testers and other entry-level positions don't fare nearly as well. QA managers often prefer quick-and-dirty online classified sites such as Craigslist instead.

It's always a good idea to register with several major game company databases. The initial process of enrolling, adding your resume, and filling out what can sometimes seem like a web-based job application can be lengthy, but the whole thing can be put on auto-pilot after this—with custom emails sent to you once a new position opens. All you initially must do is to choose the top three publishers/developers you're interested in working with, get your name in there, and pray (or *play*) for the Gaming Gods to pick your name out of a hat!

Electronic Arts, Inc.

Publishers such as Electronic Arts usually have "jobs" sections on their company web sites.

"It Doesn't Mean They Aren't Hiring"

The best advice I can give to someone looking to break into the industry is to stay focused and don't assume that one company saying "no" is the final word on your career. Send your resume to every video game company you can find, even if they don't have the specific job you want. Just because they don't list any positions on their "career" page, it does not mean that they aren't hiring.

David Price (Test Lead, THQ, Inc.)

Job Boards

While publishers have adopted Craigslist as an easy way to reach prospective game testers, there are other job boards/forums that warrant your attention. They include, in no particular order: CreativeHeads.net, GameJobs.com, GameDev.net, IGDA forums, and Gamasutra.com. All of these sites include job listings for game testers—and some of them, such as GameDev.net, have very active forums where "breaking into the game industry" threads are a common sight.

Courtesy of CreativeHeads.net

CreativeHeads.net contains job postings for tester positions.

Even general purpose job sites such as Monster.com and Careerbuilder.com often list openings in QA or production testing. To get a job this way, you need to keep an updated version of your resumé on file and have the service send you all testing-related jobs daily, if possible. Then all you have to do is hit the "submit" button if you find something that works for you. General purpose job sites are not as efficient as Craigslist (which better suits the needs of some QA managers), but they are more efficient than the tedious process required to register at game company online databases. No matter what, you should always have an updated resumé stored and ready to grab the attention of prospective employers!

Relationships are "Gold"!

If you have contacts inside a development studio or publisher, you can use those relationships to help get your foot in the door. Your contacts will give a heads up if they're aware that certain positions are about to open up, and they might help you place your resumé on Human Resources' desk. Other than that, you need to make sure the relationship is managed appropriately so that they don't put their job at risk for you. You'll also have to be extra careful if you *do* get the job, since your presence will be forever linked to your person "inside."

Professional & Social Networks

Professional and social networks are quickly becoming significant factors in the job hunt. From the "civilian" MySpace and Facebook to "professional grade" Plaxo and LinkedIn, these networks will help you connect with important people and apply for jobs in a somewhat more intimate setting than the cold company web site. LinkedIn in particular can play a big role in your job hunt, since it includes a wealth of game industry insiders. If you don't have a LinkedIn profile right now, you can create one immediately. Make sure all of your education is included, as well as professional history—and then join all the professional "game" groups. If you see a position, go for it.

One warning, though: Testing-specific positions are not all that common on these networks—and it might be easy to burn yourself by attempting to connect with people you don't know directly. As you reach out to people, be sure to go through the proper mediation/introduction process that has been put in place by the network.

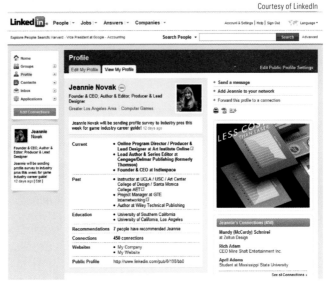

Courtesy of LinkedIn

The LinkedIn community is purely professional, and many game industry insiders are members.

The Importance of Networking

Make LinkedIn your best friend, and get all your associates to keep in touch—if only occasionally. I am a firm believer that it isn't only what you know; who you know goes a very long way as well. Remember that many people started in the industry by having to pay their dues. Long gone are the days where gamers and developers were rare and companies wanting a taste of the annual profits would hire just anyone and give 'em a shot. There's a *ton* of competition now, and lots of talent. So the biggest trick is getting your foot in the door: QA testing is often viewed as the best step. Unless you're simply a very talented programmer or artist/modeler, you're going to have to put in the time. Once your foot's in the door, this is half the battle. Simply network and meet people as time allows—and without becoming a pain in the neck, keep your ear to the ground and listen for winds of change. Don't be afraid to take chances and jump at opportunities that might develop into something bigger. It's a slow process sometimes, but the most important step on the longest of journeys is that first one.

Jerome Strach (QA Manager, Sony Computer Entertainment America)

Twitter

Twitter—a micro-blogging tool in which users exchange 140-character "tweets"—has been increasingly used to cut off intermediaries by connecting people directly. In job hunting, this means you can reach out to developers or publishers in a much more personal way. It's a good idea to have an active profile on Twitter that's industry focused—but remember that there is such a thing as "TMI (too much information)"!

Do Your Research!

You most likely want to become a tester for one of two reasons: 1) You *want* to test games; or 2) You want to do something *else*, and you regard testing as a soul-destroying task that you're willing to endure to show how much you *REALLY, REALLY* want to do that "something else." Different developers have different attitudes. Some only want testers who see testing as their future, and some only want testers as a filter to find out if they have a future elsewhere. My advice in either case would be to know what the studio you're applying to expects. In other words, do your research!

Dr. Richard Allan Bartle (Visiting Professor in Computer Game Design, University of Essex)

Hunting is all about *not* giving up. Eight out of 10 times, you will face rejection. Your email messages, phone calls, and tweets will be ignored. You need to prepare yourself psychologically for failure. But doing so doesn't mean giving up; it should make you even more determined to land a job. Each "no" has to push you forward, like the welcome challenge of a well-designed game. Keep a positive attitude, polish your resumé, and let your drive to succeed do the rest.

Anatomy of a Job Posting

Let's analyze a typical ad for a game testing position:

Sports Game Testers Wanted!

XXXX, the publisher of XXXX, XXXX, XXXX is looking for outstanding game testers to help make the best sports games in the business even better. We are staffing both our night shift and day shift with Quality Assurance Game Testers for long-term temporary positions. Have you ever played a game and wondered how they are made? Do you have a love of sports and have wondered if there was a job out there that you could feel passionate about? This may be your opportunity. Previous testing experience is welcome, but not required. Come be part of a great team, working on some great games.

Responsibilities
- Identify software defects, run test checklists, verify fixes
- Enter bugs into Bug Tracking System
- Be able to follow directions

To qualify for this exciting position you must:
- be at least 18 years old and able to verify eligibility to work in the U.S.
- be able to work standard working hours: 7AM-4AM OR 5PM-2AM, Monday through Friday.
- be ready to work overtime hours when needed, including weekends.
- be able to work independently with minimal supervision.
- be able to write clearly in English and have good verbal communication skills.
- be able to learn quickly and effectively.

This job posting is for XXXX only. Local candidates only, please. Part time positions are not available. Please apply by emailing or faxing your resumé and cover letter.

What can we learn from this?

1. The company would like someone with experience, but it's "okay" if you have none.
2. Enjoying sports games is a good thing for this particular project.
3. You will work overtime if necessary. (It always is.)
4. Part-time positions are *not* available. (This is common.)
5. You need to send a cover letter along with your resumé.

To apply, write a brief cover letter explaining why you're such a good tester and send it with your resume. (Guidelines for effective cover letters and resumés will be discussed later in this chapter.) If the recruiters like what they see, they will follow up with an email message or phone call. Even better, add supporting evidence of your writing skills and observations. Writing samples are a great way to show them you can actually write a decent bug report, for example. Remember that you have everything to gain by adding proof of your talent with a job application—and nothing to lose if they ignore it.

Make Your Job Application Stand Out!

In addition to submitting the expected cover letter and resumé, consider providing a writing sample. Contrary to what you might expect, a "critique" or even "negative" review of a game developed or published by the company you're pursuing can get you in the door. Luis attached a caustic (but constructive and well-written) critique of *Doom 3* to his cover letter and resumé when applying for a testing position at Activision—the game's publisher. He was hired on the spot. It turns out that Activision was looking for that kind of impartial view of the game, not the *ooohs* and *aaahs* of *Doom* fanboys.

Education

Game testing has become a "shadow skill"—such as understanding what animals think, changing a tire during a storm, and even being able to complete *Mass Effect* 10 times in a row. Many in the industry still see testing as something that "cannot be taught," depending primarily on personal experience and innate talents; you already know from previous chapters that this couldn't be further from the truth! If you want to work as a game tester and also be educated, there's really only one way: a college degree, certificate, or coursework focusing on game development.

Education Has Its Perks: School "Connections"

Sadly, game testing in its "purest" form is not part of the curriculum of most schools; however, we're confident that this is beginning to change—which is one of the reasons this book has been written! (See Chapter 9 for a discussion of educational opportunities.) However, game art, design, programming, and even production are increasingly being offered as degree programs or tracks at a wide variety of educational institutions. If you currently attend school in one of these disciplines, perhaps your school has a partnership or close association with a game publisher or developer. Even if the school doesn't have an "official" partnership with a game company, consider geographical proximity—such as the Art Institute of California and Activision's Santa Monica headquarters, situated just a few *feet* from each other!

Courses

Non-degree coursework such as classes offered at community colleges, game academies, university extensions, and even software training from companies such as Autodesk can help you acquire some of the knowledge necessary for a career in games. Luis actually started out like this—taking a class called "Careers in the Game Industry" at UCLA Extension. He didn't come out of it knowing how to create a game, but the class gave him an understanding of the industry as a whole, as well as numerous writing samples—cited previously as one of the reasons he was hired by Activision. Taking non-degree game classes can be an inexpensive, more work-friendly way for you to get an education in games. Remember to make sure you pick a well-regarded institution; some schools are only interested in making a quick buck on gamers. The right school can be the difference between playful unemployment or *gainful* employment at the developer of your dreams, so research both online and onground courses.

Courtesy of Game Institute

Game Institute offers game courses online.

Degree Programs

Knowing about game development will always be a huge plus for a tester. A basic knowledge of programming, design and art can go a long way toward making you a great tester and setting you apart from scores of testers with no real experience in game development. Several schools have advanced courses, and the good news is that most of them can be attended online. Established names are DeVry University, Westwood College of Technology, ITT Technical Institute, Full Sail, Carnegie Mellon University, DigiPen, the Art Institutes, the University of South Florida, and the University of Southern California. (See the Resources section in the back of the book for a complete list.) These courses will also help you determine your "higher calling" in game development. Although testing is fun and an essential part of game development, you won't necessarily want to stay in the QA department forever. You will need to choose an area of expertise if you want to move up in the studio. A degree specializing in game art, design, programming, or production will make this obvious by exposing you to all aspects of game development—and will also enable you to build an effective portfolio.

While game-specific college degrees are few and far between, graduate degrees in fields such as computer science and graphic design can provide you with many of the skills needed when applying for a position in the game industry. These degrees also provide a solid foundation for the game-specific knowledge you'll invariably acquire once you join the industry.

Courtesy of the Art Institute of Pittsburgh - Online Division

An undergraduate degree in Game Art & Design from the Art Institute of Pittsburgh - Online Division (formerly the Art Institute Online) can provide you with training and skills needed for a career as a game artist or designer.

Interactive Media Division, USC School of Cinematic Arts

USC (University of Southern California) is home to the Electronic Arts Game Innovation Lab and Interactive Entertainment program—which offers a Master's degree in Interactive Media.

Unrelated Disciplines

Although having a game-related degree can give you a leg up on the competition, a degree in a seemingly unrelated discipline can give you the breadth necessary to be an asset to any team you join! In fact, many in the industry went to college to specialize in other interests—even if game development was their true passion. The advantage of pursuing education in a different field is that you can apply it to games with very interesting results.

Luis received his BA from a film school in Brazil—learning how write scripts, direct productions, and edit his work; in the process, he developed a critical sense that happens to be perfect for evaluating video games. College taught him to write, observe, and analyze—and those skills were essential once Luis started working as a tester. Luis' lead in *Quake 4* was an English Literature major who was an outstanding employee—knowing how to express himself clearly and helping the entire team write better bugs.

Jeannie received her BA at UCLA and an MA at USC—in Mass Communication and Communication Management, respectively. At the time, there were *no* game development degrees—so she created her own projects and theses focusing on games (e.g., using MMOGs as online distance learning applications). She found that her degrees in communication were so interdisciplinary that she's been able to apply what she learned in various aspects of her career—game design, production, usability, business consulting . . . and even education management!

A college degree in Game Development, Design, Programming, or Production (or even an unrelated discipline) will certainly put you ahead of the pack. As you may remember from our discussion of demographics in Chapter 2, there *has* been a shift in the educational level of most testers: The majority of them now have Bachelor's degrees under their belts. Your best bet might very well be to invest in an education!

Farhad Javidi on Game Testing Expectations & Preparations :::::

Farhad Javidi
(Director,
Simulation, Modeling
& Visualization Center,
Central Piedmont
Community College)

Farhad Javidi currently serves as Director of the Simulation, Modeling & Visualization Center at Central Piedmont Community College (CPCC)—North Carolina's largest community college and the fourth largest college in the nation. He developed the first state-approved associate degree program in Simulation & Game Development in the nation. He is a recipient of the 2007 National Institute for Staff and Organizational Development Excellence Award and was CPCC's Instructor of the Year in 2006. In 2005, he was named Outstanding Faculty Advisor by the National Academic Advising Association and an Unsung Hero by the Charlotte, NC Chamber of Commerce. Javidi also serves as chair of CPCC's Senate Technology Committee. He has served as an adjunct faculty member in the computer science department at the University of North Carolina–Charlotte and has taught various courses in the computer science department at the University of South Florida. From 1997 to 2002, Farhad served as director of information technology for Epley Associates Inc.—one of the largest communications firms in the southeastern United States. In 1998, he co-founded Digiton Corporation, a North Carolina consulting firm.

"Video game tester" is not a dream job and it's certainly not "getting paid to play." It is hard work—and it can be tedious. You will be asked to evaluate incomplete games with many bugs. You'll do whatever your employer asks of you, no questions asked. You may have to play games that don't appeal to you. You may be asked to do everything possible to lose the game. You'll have to follow a set of instructions. Rarely will you have the opportunity for free play. Game testers are asked to work long hours, including weekends, and must meet specified deadlines. Game testing is not playing games. Your job may be opening and closing a door or climbing a wall for 12 hours a day, seven days a week. Sometimes your task is to break the game. Sometimes your task is complex; for example, you may be asked to isolate a platform-specific bug that only occurs when multiple variables are set a certain way. You'll have to take detailed notes as you evaluate games and record bugs in the database; communicate with developers and other testers; come up with ways to improve games and create reports. All communications must be clear and thorough. To get yourself ready for a game-testing job:

- Play as many video games as you can. Buy them, rent them, borrow them, download demos . . . whatever it takes.

- Familiarize yourself with all game genres.

- Read game magazines and online game news and reviews.

- Exercise your observation, evaluation and writing skills by setting up a blog. Write your own game reviews, previews, hints, cheats, tips, strategy guides, walkthroughs, and tutorials.

- Create a resumé that demonstrates your game knowledge and contains a link to your blog.

- Don't look for a game testing job in the newspaper; they aren't usually advertised. Contact the company directly to see if they need you. If possible, head to corporate headquarters.

"Anyone Can Find a Crash Bug . . ."

Attention to detail and good writing skills are the most important characteristics for an entry level tester to have. Anyone can find a crash bug, but the best testers I have known have been the ones that can recognize inconsistent behaviors in the way the game behaves from level 1 to level 10 and then communicate that information effectively to a developer. While overall gaming skill is valuable, being able to beat every game on the hardest difficulty doesn't necessarily translate to being the best possible tester.

David Price (Test Lead, THQ, Inc.)

Packaging Yourself

In many ways, game testing is just like any other career. If you want to get a job, you need to submit a cover letter and a resumé. Most candidates don't go past this stage due to sloppy resumés and missing cover letters. In this section, we'll look into ways to perfect your resumé and guarantee you an interview for a game testing position.

The Cover Letter that Wasn't

Most candidates for testing positions don't bother to write cover letters when applying for jobs, perhaps because they see testing as outside the system when it comes to the application process. Testing is just like any other job—and cover letters are expected. If you do not provide a cover letter, one or more of the following will happen:

- You will appear *lazy* to recruiters and will only be contacted if "emergency" testers are needed.
- You will miss an ideal chance to introduce yourself to your future superiors and discuss your reasons for pursuing a career in the game industry.
- You will be eliminated automatically from the "short list"—since most testing jobs *require* a cover letter.

A cover letter is essential; you can't escape it. Don't bother applying for a testing position if you hate to write cover letters; if you hate writing at all, you're in the wrong business. (Remember our discussion of bug reports in previous chapters!) The cover letter will introduce you to the publisher or developer and tell them why you deserve to be considered for a position. Chances are, whoever's responsible for the selection process has more important things to do—so if your cover letter is muddled or plain, the initial "filter" will skip your resumé altogether. You need to grab them by the horns, like every good game does in its first 10 minutes.

For email submissions, paste your cover letter in the message body. If you're using an online form instead, ensure that you have uploaded your cover letter to the system so that the prospective employer will have a cover letter to go along with your resumé. Here are a few guidelines:

- Start with a brief description of yourself. Make sure it presents you in the best possible light.
- Now describe how your skills match the current job opening. Address the top 3-4 needs.
- Next, include a short paragraph that integrates your personal goals with the company's needs. For example "With my passion for games and attention to detail, I will make sure the project I'm working on is as bug-free as possible."
- Close with a polite phrase such as "Thank you for your consideration."

chapter 7

Crafting a Winning Resumé:
It's Easier than it Seems!

Think of your resumé as a one-page professional portrait of yourself. (There's no need for more unless you have a wealth of relevant experience.) A resumé must sell who you are as a perfect fit for the testing job, leading to a live interview. A resumé for a testing position is very different from a resumé for a mall clothing store. Game development has specific needs, like a fair knowledge of technology and passion for games. More than the format itself, you must infuse your resumé with "professional gamer" DNA and add desired skills such as troubleshooting and writing. Here are a few guidelines:

- Go through your work history and compile a document containing all of your achievements. Add as much detail as possible, using active verbs such as developed, implemented, improved, created, and maximized.

- Think about a goal. What do you really want to do in the game industry? What are your major aspirations? Write a short objective that defines who you are ("eager college graduate," "experienced modder") and what moves you ("seeking to advance the stage of MMOs," "looking for a creative, engaging studio to learn the trade of game development").

- Edit your work history until it becomes a collection of strong bullet points.

- Start a separate document with all of your skills. Categorize them in different groups: technical, writing, and verbal skills. Edit them in bullets as well.

- Find a template by searching online. If you use Microsoft Word 2007, Microsoft's website has some great templates (office.microsoft.com/en-us/templates/CT101043371033.aspx). Sample Resumés (www.freeresumesamples.org) has a nice selection of templates as well. Incorporate your goal, skills, and work history using short, tidy sentences. Avoid paragraphs at all costs.

- Check your draft several times for inaccuracies, misspellings, grammatical errors, and inconsistencies. It also helps to print a hard copy and read the resumé from bottom to top starting with the last section. This will help you with typos, a "deal breaker" for most companies.

- Enlist friends or family to read your resumé. Make sure they understand everything. Ask if it's impressive or "punchy" enough.

"The Biggest 'No-No'"

The biggest no-no in my book is sending a resumé or cover letter riddled with spelling and grammar problems. Since our job involves documenting bugs and communicating those issues as clearly as possible, it is really tough to look past something that is difficult to read. Also, If a potential employee couldn't take the time to proofread his own resumé, why would it be any different when writing bugs becomes his job?

Brandon Adler (QA Lead, Obsidian Entertainment)

The Interview

If the prospective employer likes your resumé, someone from the company (usually in the human resources department) will give you a call or reply to your email—and may schedule an interview. Keep in mind that interviewing for a testing position at a game company is considerably different than many other interview experiences. Game companies will usually administer a test of sorts during the interview—sometimes asking fairly technical questions such as:

- What company makes the GPU on the Xbox 360 and PS3?
- What are three differences between the online services for the Xbox 360 and PS3?
- How do you install a video card on a PC?
- What are three differences between Vista and Windows XP?
- What are three bugs that you have seen while playing a game?
- What are your favorite games in the following genres (e.g., racing, RPG, strategy, FPS)?
- What are the last five games you've played?

Your performance on the test will determine whether or not you'll be hired, and it will also affect which type of project is given to you; high scores can guarantee a PC project, while lower scores might send you straight to portables such as the Nintendo DS. As you learned in Chapter 2, the testing environment for portables is less than ideal.

---

7 Interview Rules

1) Interviews are all about impressions, and you won't have much time.

2) Listen as much if not more than the time you spend talking.

3) Keep all answers relevant to the questions being asked of you.

4) Use a firm handshake and strong eye contact.

5) Re-read #4.

6) Always . . . always . . . always ask questions of your potential employer if given the chance to demonstrate interest in the company and position.

7) Convey enthusiasm and desire (without coming across like a nut job).

There's more, but that's a great start—and 7 is a lucky number!

Jerome Strach (QA Manager, Sony Computer Entertainment America)

A sure-fire way to succeed in a testing interview is to dress properly and show off the good sides of your personality. Of course, you need to know what you're talking about as well. Here are some pre-interview preparations:

- Check the company's website. Read everything you can.

- Read reviews of the company's games. Better yet, play most of them.

- Google whoever you'll be meeting (if you have this information ahead of time). You never know if you uncover useful information such as "loves poodles, hates cats, partial to pythons"—or better yet, common interests ("Dr. Who fan, never misses Comic-Con, enjoys LARPing in spare time").

- Dress a level above the position. Since lead testers are not the best dressed, use "Associate Producer" as a target. "Nice casual" dress is appropriate: slacks, shoes and shirt for a man, a dress or blouse and skirt/dress pants for a woman (no T-shirts).

- Use the web to research typical "challenging" (or even uncomfortable) interview questions such as "What are your biggest flaws?" "What are five adjectives that describe you?" and "Why are you the best candidate for this position?" Make sure you have decent answers, and practice with a friend.

- Read the top trades. *Edge Online, Gamasutra, Develop Magazine, GameDaily,* and *GamesIndustry.biz* all talk about what's happening in the industry. (See the Resources section in the back of the book for additional references.)

Diagram by Per Olin

Interview Guidelines

Do	Don't
Keep your voice at an even volume	Mumble or scream
Give succinct answers	Give long-winded answers
Show you're eager to learn	Be cocky
Come prepared with examples of bugs (and describe them in detail, if asked)	Show up empty-handed
Discuss your gaming background, along with favorite genres	Spend a lot of time talking about yourself
Be honest	Lie
Dress professionally	Look like a "typical gamer"

Stand Out from the Crowd

Since the supply of people knocking on the door to become a tester is much higher than the demand, you have to set yourself apart.

- ■ Dress well, but not so well they know you are using the test department as a stepping stone.

- ■ Prove you are good at making lists. Your resumé is your proof. Make sure it is impeccable, with not a single spelling error. You're asking to be tester; if you can't see your own errors, how can you be trusted on the team?

- ■ Since the person who might hire you can hire anyone, this is going to be about your personality; they need to work with you every day (and night). If you can't build rapport you are probably not going to be selected.

- ■ Show enthusiasm for testing (I'm not saying to lie!)—just be clear, you might be asked to jump [<-this->] high, seven thousands time in a row.

- ■ Know Excel. Prove you can use it. Be flexible with your hours. This is one of those businesses where it is "who you know," so if you know *anyone* in the business, ask them to help.

Baron R.K. Von Wolfsheild (Chief Software Architect, Qtask, Inc.)

You need a natural inquisitiveness, an ability to work independently, strong critical thinking skills—and you must be a good communicator with an eye for detail.

Edward Rotberg (Chief Technology Officer, Mine Shaft Entertainment)

Publishers and developers are always looking for QA, and it isn't too tough to get an interview. Experience may not be immensely important, but you need to show people why they should hire you versus generic QA Tester #7. Show them that you mean business and that you take games very seriously.

Brandon Adler (QA Lead, Obsidian Entertainment)

Knowledge of the game industry and an in-depth understanding of games are very important. Technical skills covering computers and networking could put you ahead of others during the job hunt.

Dave Dawson (Environmental Artist, Snowblind Studios)

The ideal interview should actually be *fun*. You need to be relaxed enough to look your best. If you take it in stride, the chances of being hired go through the roof—even if you're not a perfect match or have little or no experience. Once you're past the interview, you will be sent home with the promise of a phone call. (Yes—the old "Don't call us; we'll call you" routine.) If they never call, you know what that means. If they do, congratulations: You are now a game tester and will begin to play games for a living!

"Anyone Can Find a Crash Bug . . ."

Attention to detail and good writing skills are the most important characteristics for an entry level tester to have. Anyone can find a crash bug, but the best testers I have known have been the ones that can recognize inconsistent behaviors in the way the game behaves from level 1 to level 10 and then communicate that information effectively to a developer. While overall gaming skill is valuable, being able to beat every game on the hardest difficulty doesn't necessarily translate to being the best possible tester.

David Price (Test Lead, THQ, Inc.)

::

This chapter was all about getting your foot on the door. However, testing is an entry-level position—and there's much more to game development than playing through broken code. The next chapter will look into how you can keep your job, grow into it, grow out of it, and take the next step in a game development career. One day, you'll find out that making games is much more rewarding than breaking them.

:::CHAPTER REVIEW:::

1. Using at least 3 methods discussed in this chapter, research positions available at developers and publishers associated with your favorite games. Analyze each job listing and determine which ones you should pursue; consider your strengths, skill level, and the location and working conditions associated with each company.

2. Research educational programs and courses associated with at least 3 institutions. Come up with a list of institutions that you feel are best suited for you. Assess your existing educational background and incorporate it in the resumé you create in Exercise 3.

3. Create or update your existing resumé—targeting it for the positions you selected in Exercise 1. Write a sample cover letter that you can use as a template for your job hunt.

CHAPTER

8

Surviving & Escaping the Dungeon

transcending testing

Key Chapter Questions

■ How can testers avoid being put *on call*?

■ What is the *testing ladder*, and how can it be climbed effectively?

■ What are the biggest *mistakes* a tester can make?

■ What are some beneficial *side quests* testers can pursue?

■ What are some *achievements* associated with testing?

Game testing can be a step toward a position in the game industry or a one-day ticket to professional limbo. There are those who remain testers for a couple of years, only to be hired by the developer as a texture artist or sound designer. Others will still be testing games for a living, stuck in the same entry-level job for years. The latter fate can be avoided—if you have what it takes. This chapter will show you how to climb the testing ladder by applying knowledge from real life experiences. You'll learn about "evil" mistakes to avoid, beneficial "side quests," and brilliant achievements of the best testers on earth.

The Forever Job?

Being a game tester has one major disadvantage: It's a relatively easy-to-live-with, fun job. In other industries, entry-level positions are usually unbearable—so employees work hard to move up and leave them behind. Not so with testing. Complacency and lack of opportunities might result in a person doing the same job for an extended period of time without ever complaining about it.

Stuck in Limbo

A distinct lack of ambition coupled with no formal education might help keep a "status quo" that really carries no status. This is the fate of testers stuck on the job—incapable of moving up, and moving on.

Here are a few tell-tale signs that you're "stuck":

- You are never promoted
- The projects change, but the job remains the same
- Your colleagues are promoted instead of you
- You are never given any complex tasks
- You would rate your job performance as "so-so"
- You like working under a lead tester because it makes you feel "safe"

These are all clear indications that you're stuck. Don't settle for this fate. We'll show you the way out!

Getting Unstuck

Everyone hates *stuck spots*. We hate them because a stuck spot prevents our characters from moving forward in the plot, stopping them from getting "somewhere." However, if the stuck spot sent you to an interesting bonus level, full of goodies and unlockables, would you complain about the main plot being "interrupted"? You would not. You'd appreciate that comfortable, *pleasant* interruption. Similar to this type of siren's call, getting unstuck from an entry-level job in testing requires constant effort on your part. You literally need to *fight yourself*!

Here are a few ways to get unstuck:

1. As much as you love testing, understand that a game tester is still an entry-level position.

2. Look around and consider this: Do you really want to be in the same situation for the next five years?

3. Do you have any goals? Working in the same testing position for a living does not necessarily lend itself to "attaining goals."

4. Secure a financial parachute and/or go back to school to leave testing for a while and expand your horizons.

5. Offer to do complex tasks. Become exceptionally good at them.

6. If the job gets too comfortable, you're not working hard enough.

In the next section, we'll turn to another type of nightmare that can often be much worse than being stuck. We'll also discuss techniques that will help you make sure this does not happen to you.

The "On Call" Predicament

Being put *on call* is like getting the short end of the stick. Testers are usually temps, which means that the publisher or developer hires them through a third party. Around May or June, these third-party companies start contacting hundreds of "out of work" testers and newbies, attempting to fill all the positions. Once everyone is hired, they will then manage the testers—leaving the publisher or developer responsible only for specific on-the-job instructions and training. Everything else, including human resources, will be handled by the temp agency. The job itself will last between six and seven months. Once the game is ready to be launched ("gold" in industry jargon), the temp agency will put 90% of those testers "on call." That's precisely *how* all those testers were out of work in the first place!

Sometimes being put on call is unavoidable. You never know what kinds of problems the publisher or developer is facing. Maybe the company is running out of money or was just bought! Perhaps the company decides to dump the entire QA department—and there's nothing you can do about it. Let's take a look at a few qualities that might very well prevent you from being put on call.

Eagerness to Learn

You'd be surprised at the number of testers who begin a new job thinking they already know it all. Brazilians call that "having a King in the belly"—considering yourself special and therefore all-knowing and infallible. On the opposite side of the spectrum, you'll find testers who admit they know little but are always ready to improve. They talk to developers about the best way to do their jobs, spend their free time researching testing and game development, and always follow directions.

Strong Work Ethic

There are many testers who see their jobs as "playing" instead of "working"—and they show their disregard by being constantly late, ignoring directions, and picking fights with other testers. They become liabilities because in their eyes, they're not really working. Testers with strong work ethics—who consistently get to work on time, warn their supervisors if they're running late, and do their jobs as they are told—are highly regarded by their superiors and peers.

Communication Skills

Being a "good" tester is simply not enough. You need to have superior communication skills in order to work better within a team *and* write better bugs. When testers fill their bugs with typos and incorrect information, they're soon flagged by management. They might be able to save their jobs if their testing skills are off the charts—but they won't survive otherwise. Communication skills are also helpful when you need to present an elevator pitch to a high-level executive. You never know when you're about bump into someone important.

Leadership Skills

Leads are overworked by nature. They hold a lot of responsibility in their hands, sometimes unwillingly. Leads will gladly welcome help from testers. If you have leadership skills, use them. Offer help to your lead—organizing task forces and taking on some of the lead's work load. Being a de facto leader (or even a willing leader-in-training) is a surefire way to escape being put on call.

Developing one or more of these abilities (eagerness to learn, strong work ethic, communication skills, and leadership skills) is the best strategy to avoid being put on call. An additional advantage: Your chances of being promoted get a nice boost as well!

Brandon Adler on Moving Up :::::

Brandon Adler
(QA Lead,
Obsidian Entertainment)

Born and raised in Southern California, Brandon attended Cal Poly Pomona's Computer Science program before entering the military in early 2001. After spending four years in the U.S. Air Force, he decided to pursue his true passion—video games. Brandon has worked at Obsidian on *Neverwinter Nights 2* as a quality assurance tester, *NWN2: Mask of the Betrayer* as a production tester, and *NWN2: Storm of Zehir* as the lead tester.

Once you're in, there are plenty of opportunities for good testers to move out of quality assurance—but you have to be persistent. If you want to be a designer, find out what tools are popular in the industry and create a few levels. If you want to be a programmer or scripter, learn the different scripting languages that are being used to create games. If you are good, people will notice—but only if you put yourself out there to be noticed.

QA: The "Killer Career Path"

QA is a killer career path, because it gives you many chances to demonstrate your professionalism: writing documents, staying organized, communicating with team members, adhering to strict schedules, checking off completed milestones, and so on. Put the effort in here, and it will reflect very well on you down the road. Don't worry too much about being "pigeonholed"—this isn't Wall Street! The game industry is wonderfully dynamic, with plenty of start-up companies, and room for new ideas and advancement.

Jamie Lendino (Composer & Sound Designer, Sound For Games Interactive)

The Testing Ladder

Game testing is a career in itself. The sad part is that reaching the top as a tester might mean you won't actually make games for a living. This will not be a problem for some, so let's take a look at this career choice. Although it's not a favored career goal today, we believe it will increase in popularity as it continues to professionalize.

When you get hired as a QA or production tester, you're really choosing testing as a career. This is an entry-level position, which means that you can specialize in other skills and end up doing something completely different. However, this section is about what happens when you *do* decide to take testing seriously for the long term. We'll show you the end of the road—in a good way. Let's take a look at the natural progression of a tester.

QA Tester

QA testers, hired by publishers, often have literally no experience in testing. That's why they get to do the most boring, repetitive work—consisting of going over checklists, making sure there are no offensive (i.e., religious) icons, checking all elevators, doors, walls, and so forth. Often, only one mere day of training (and sometimes no training at all!) and rushed schedules result in QA testers being regarded by many in the industry as the lowest rung on the ladder; by the same token, it can be the easiest way to get your foot in the door.

Production Tester

Most testers are hired first as QA testers and are snapped up by a developer as *production testers* if they demonstrate good performance and professionalism. Even so, sometimes "green" testers are hired straight as production testers—another example of hurried schedules and too much work. That's why being a production tester doesn't necessarily mean you actually got a promotion. Being a production tester is a surefire way to be in daily contact with developers and producers, maximizing your chances of moving up.

Lead Tester or Floor Lead

If testing is your thing, the next step up is *lead tester* at a developer, or *floor lead* on a publisher's QA team. In QA, the first promotion is floor lead, an entry-level leadership position. Floor leads organize the testers for the lead tester, freeing the lead for more senior tasks such as compiling case files and keeping in touch with the producers and developers. In production testing, the floor lead position might not exist—which means a promotion will make the tester into a lead tester. We discussed lead testers early in Chapter 3; they are responsible for the testing reports and low-level management of the testing team. Lead testers are also those who burn each build to several discs in preparation for testing.

> **W**e've always viewed QA as a core part of the team, and hope that good testers can both learn the game development process and grow into larger roles in the company.
>
> *Jason Kay (Chief Operating Officer, RKG Games)*

QA/Testing Manager

Becoming a *QA* or *testing manager* is the end of the line for testers. If a lead tester is very effective at managing a team and is able to work a schedule, chances are that the lead will be retained as a QA/testing manager—a fairly stable developer position with responsibility over the hiring, management, and firing ostarr longf all testing personnel. The QA/testing manager is also responsible for budgeting—working along senior producers when estimating the testing costs for each title.

This is it. Rising through the ranks of game testing will lead you to an office job where playing games ceases to be the main activity, not to mention making them. Still, those who are not technically or artistically inclined might thoroughly enjoy it, especially if they have an appreciation and a knack for management.

Diagram by Per Olin

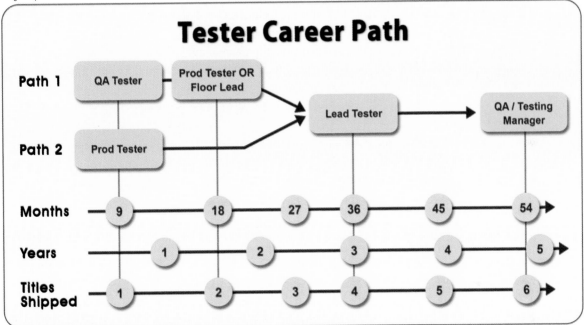

Tester Career Path

Path 1 — QA Tester → Prod Tester OR Floor Lead

Path 2 — Prod Tester

Lead Tester → QA / Testing Manager

Months	9	18	27	36	45	54
Years		1	2	3	4	5
Titles Shipped	1	2	3	4	5	6

QA as a Jumping Off Point

If you have computer graphics, development, or designer skills but do not have the experience to get hired for these roles: Testing is a great jumping off point. After starting in our QA department, many people are now producers, assistant producers, developers, designers, artists—and so on. All of the areas are open to you, *but* I would stress that if you are interest in any of those jobs to make sure you continue to train yourself in them. Go and get those degrees at night—and once you have them, get into an apprenticeship program with your company that will allow them to see what you can do and help you get the knowledge you need in order to move into that field. It is a "win-win" situation for the company, QA, those fields, and for you.

Floyd Billings (Assistant Lead QA, Sony Online Entertainment)

Todd M. Fay
(Owner,
DemoNinja.com)

Todd M. Fay is the owner of DemoNinja.com, a coaching company assisting creative professionals in advancing their crafts and their careers through access to veterans of their respective industries for coaching, critique, and inspiration. Since 2000, Todd has enjoyed a successful career as an entertainment industry consultant (Todd M. Fay Consulting) working with companies such as GameInvestors.com, CMP Media, Creative Labs, G4 Media, Ubisoft Entertainment, 1C Company, Tommy Tallarico Studios, Threewave Software, and Video Games Live. Todd served as the first Director of Development for the popular game industry international trade organization, the Game Audio Network Guild. His writing is published in *Game Developer Magazine*, Gamasutra.com, Music4Games.net and in his book *DirectX 9 Audio Exposed* (Wordware)—the first technical book on audio for games. Todd is also a contributing author of *Introduction to Game Development* (Steve Rabin) and *The Complete Guide to Game Audio* (Aaron Marks). He is the technical editor of *The Game Producer's Handbook* by Dan Irish. Todd has been a featured speaker at Los Angeles Music Productions, International Game Developers Association (IGDA), Art Institute of California, University of Colorado, Game Developers Conference (GDC), and *Xtreme Game Developers Xpo*.

My first day at Blizzard Entertainment was an amazing day for me personally because I'd landed at my favorite developer in the world, on the ground level, anxious to work my way into their audio department from the testing pool. That was September 10, 2001. Obviously the mood of the following day was about as far as you can get from the elation I felt arriving at my first day at work. Tension was high, and everyone was on edge. I remember at some point I was working on the build looking for bugs and this guy was standing behind me watching me over my shoulder. With everything that was going on with the country and my desire to do a good job at the company, I was under so much pressure that I thought I was going to snap under it—and I almost did. Let's just say I was able to keep it together—and it's a good thing I did, because the guy standing behind me was Mike Morhaime, one of the founders of Blizzard. The moral of the story: Testing games for hours and hours can wear on you. Take care of yourself, clear your head, and keep your eye on the prize. Remember: You're there to do a great job and to work your way up to the position with your name on it!

"Kill-Switch" Mistakes

Like everything in life, some mistakes get you in trouble, while others get you killed. If you work as a game tester, you need to understand what kind of mistakes can send you hurtling towards the dungeon's door—never to be seen again. We're calling these mistakes "kill-switches." In telecommunications, a kill-switch is a mechanism that service providers use in order to remote-delete unlawful/buggy applications. Some mistakes will get you fired. Let's learn how to avoid them.

Don't Snoop

Snooping in the publisher/developer's private files is a big no-no. A colleague of ours, working for one of the leading first-person shooter (FPS) developers, was caught looking though the public folders in the email system—only to find out they were not quite public. He was fired on the spot.

Don't Talk About the Game to Anyone

Every game project requires testers to sign a Non-Disclosure Agreement (NDA). If a tester signs it and then proceeds to post a picture of the game online, he will be caught, fired and maybe prosecuted. Leaking protected information to the press or the public can also be punished with sizeable fines, especially if it leads into piracy.

Don't Be Late

Being rarely or occasionally late is very different than being frequently or constantly late. If the project is in full swing, you might not get fired for this. But when things slow down, you'll be the first to go. Being late is nothing that serious at first, but it says a lot about how you do work and what kind of employee you are.

Don't Sleep on the Job

Testers are known for going to bed late and falling asleep on the job. If you work with game consoles, the joystick's vibration might keep you awake, but PC testers can easily fall asleep at their keyboards. Sleeping on the job is taken very seriously by managers. While awake, you might be doing your job right—but when asleep, you're not doing it at all. You snooze, you lose (your job)!

> QA is a great way to get into the game industry, and it can lead to any job within it. I myself started in QA, and I'm now a producer. We have testers who have moved on to be designers, programmers, and producers on my team.
>
> *Starr Long (Executive Producer, The Walt DisneyCompany)*

Don't Disrespect the Workspace

Eating on the job is okay; everybody does it. However, leaving your half-eaten Egg McMuffin on the desk for others to smell is not. Gamers feel comfortable among their peers, but some rivers are not meant to be crossed—or spat in. Keep the workspace professional!

Don't Compete Like a Gamer

They're not paying you to be the best. They don't care about your Xbox Live gamer score either. So put a pin in your hardcore competitive instincts. Resist the impulse to teabag the executive producer. (When this happened at a major publisher, it wasn't a pretty sight.) You have a job to do; get going!

Don't Gossip

Gossiping is bad habit anywhere, but it's worse in a small room full of testers. It's far too easy to get into stupid arguments or non gender-specific "cattiness" with friends, enemies, or frenemies. You never know when something like this will escalate and take a life of its own. By avoiding gossip, you'll improve your image among other testers. They'll invariably see you as a fair person as well, which is a good stepping stone for a future leadership position.

Don't Take Pictures

In addition to not *talking* about the game to anyone, you also should *not* be taking any pictures (with the exception of screenshots for bug reports, of course). Your pictures *will* be tracked, and you *will* be fired. For the 8, 12, or 18 hours you're working, pretend your cell phone doesn't exist (unless you have to make an emergency call or want to use it for its primary purpose during a break). Taking pictures is a big "no-no."

Don't Bring Your Personal Life

We have seen fellow testers break up with their significant others several times a week via cell phone—within audible range, from a nearby chair. Airing your relationship grievances to everyone in close range will erode any respect the team has for you. It will also make your problems worse; blame it on "karma."

Don't Lose Focus

With web-enabled phones and iPods, it's very easy to put your attention on anything but the job at hand. If you do that, your performance will suffer and you'll open yourself to potentially serious mistakes. All it takes is one misstep, one bug unreported, to break the game. If that happens, they *will* track this and fire you. Use your *breaks* for games, web searches, and music; the company is not paying you to Google "What's faster, a PlayStation 3 or an Xbox 360?"

Michael E. Moore on the Reality & Opportunity of Testing :::::

Michael is a 24-year veteran of the game industry. For the first 10 years, he designed, developed, and produced board games (mass market, role-playing, and military simulations). He then moved into computer games as a designer and producer—working for such publishers as Infocom, Activision, and 3DO. In addition, he helped start up several game development companies. Over the years, he designed and produced such games as *Circuit's Edge*, *Shanghai II: Dragon's Eye* and *BattleTech II: The Crescent Hawks' Revenge* (Activision), *SpellCraft* (ASCII Entertainment), and *The Shadow of Yserbius/Fates of Twinion* and *Alien Legacy* (Sierra). Michael joined the Game Software Design & Production department at DigiPen Institute of Technology in January 2004—where he has taught game design and project management to both undergraduate and graduate students and served as department chair. Michael continues to teach part-time at DigiPen and is lead author of the *Game Industry Career Guide* (part of the *Game Development Essentials* series).

Photo courtesy of DigiPen Institute of Technology

Michael E. Moore (Professor, DigiPen Institute of Technology)

Testing is not glamorous. It is tedious. You usually replay one section of a game over and over and over until all the bugs are worked out. You have to be observant and able to reproduce the bugs you find, and you have to report them clearly in your bug reports. Testing is for the detail-oriented perfectionist. However, it can be a path into game design and producing at companies if you demonstrate a knowledge of games and how they're made. Many companies prefer to hire internally for these positions, and testers are the group they draw from.

Jason Kay on the Skill Set That's Always in Demand :::::

Jason Kay
(Chief Operating
Officer,
RKG Games)

Jason Kay co-founded Flektor with Jason Rubin and Andy Gavin, creators of *Crash Bandicoot* and *Jak & Daxter*. He previously served as a consultant to Home Box Office, Inc., the largest pay television service in the world, where he consulted on a variety of projects in games and new media. Prior to his work at HBO, he was involved in the sale of direct marketer Columbia House, Inc., which is now owned by BMG Direct, Inc. Jason began his career in entertainment as a Producer and Business Development Executive for Activision. Jason holds a Juris Doctor degree from the University of Southern California Law Center, and a BA *magna cum laude* with honors in English from Tulane University.

Testing is a great way to get into the game business—and skilled and insightful people will move up quickly. The most important skill to develop is analytical reasoning. It's easy to say that something doesn't play well or that the level is badly designed. It's much harder to be able to say *why* something doesn't work and suggest fixes; *that* skill set is always in demand and can lead to a larger role as a QA lead or even as part of the development team.

Making the Best of Side Quests

If you're an avid MMO player, you're well-aware of *side quests*. For the uninitiated, side quests are any quests that do not belong in the game's main storyline. So if you decide to spend your time in a side quest, you won't get any new details on the princess' mating habits or the reason why your entire world is gray. Side quests will give you:

a) Money

b) Experience

c) Skills

In a way, this is actually similar to real life. The main storyline is often divided into two paths: your personal life and your work life. Everything you do in those areas advances your story. Everything *else* is a side quest.

Bad Side Quests

Let's take a look at bad side quests in both your personal and work life. Some of it may seem a little weird to see in a book about game testing; bear with us. Hopefully this chapter will show you that everything you do—every choice you make—can have an effect on your performance as a tester. The following three bad side quests have been observed in actual testing situations—and they have all resulted in disaster. Be forewarned.

Office Relationships

Dating in the office is always a bad idea. It will lead to murky waters in the future. It will distract you. It might also be against company policy, even if at first your superiors don't seem to care. One day, they will—and this is the perfect excuse to fire someone.

Addictions

Being addicted to pretty much *anything* is a big problem. Substance abuse is at the top of the list because you lose yourself to an extraneous element, a *thing* (e.g., drugs, alcohol) that has power over you. A tester who is addicted to a substance *cannot* be efficient—with an inability to focus, lack of discipline, trouble following and understanding direction, lower performance, fatigue, and erratic behavior that can be disturbing to your co-workers. Similarly, any other addictions and distractions will lower your chances on the job. You won't be respected as much. You won't be on the ball 100% of the time. Remember, one single mistake can get you fired. You need to work on minimizing the chances of that, not enhancing them.

Hyperactivity

Sometimes, we're just too curious—too restless. We need to search for something *right now*, buy that new smartphone *right now*. This lack of impulse control will eventually get in the way of your job. The best way to defeat is to set short-term goals for yourself. For example, say you want to catch at least four bugs before lunch. You write it down and focus all of your energy on it. Push yourself to the max, and leave nothing behind. Whether or not you succeed in the end, take a short 10-minute rest break. Then select new goals and start the process all over again.

Good Side Quests

Good side quests expand your reach. They allow you to exercise parts of you that might lie dormant otherwise. Good side quests also the have effect of pushing your main storyline forward. No effort is wasted.

Modding

In Chapter 7, we discussed modding as a way to get a job in game testing. The opposite is also true: Modding can be a great side project if you're already a tester. For example, modding will teach you a lot about environmental art, level design, and game design. If you're already inside a developer, acquiring these skills may put you in the fast lane for a promotion. Better yet, your audience is right there—all the senior producers and designers already working on your game. Although you might have a problem with free time—especially as things get frantic near launch—modding is a very positive, effective side quest.

YouTube Channel

YouTube was the path to fame and fortune for hundreds of thousands of users. First, they were nobody—then overnight, they became *somebody*. This is not our objective. Still, if you start a YouTube channel while working as a tester, you'll gain valuable exposure among your peers. More than that, you'll become a visible part of the industry. Effective YouTube videos could focus on your industry observations, game reviews, walkthroughs, and tutorials. The YouTube way is exceedingly positive except for one scenario: divulging NDA-protected information on a YouTube video. That's bad, very bad. In fact, that's the worst thing you can do with YouTube, bar none.

Schmoozing

If it's not on work time, party away. Go to all the conferences (Game Developers Conference [GDC], Electronic Entertainment Expo [E3], and so forth) and associated parties; become a true social animal! You'll want to know *everyone* at the studio, from the receptionist to the CEO, keeping everything you learn close to heart. "Networking"—the serious word for schmoozing—will get you places. From a new job to a promotion, everything is possible if you truly connect with your peers.

Another Job

Sometimes, you're just a tester. But you might as well be a design intern, working *temporarily* as tester. It's all a matter of perspective. Some studios might be understaffed, especially after the financial crisis that began officially in 2008. See this as an opportunity to take on extra work—possibly in areas other than testing. Take on more responsibility, own it and do a great job. This kind of side quest can help you "transplant yourself out of testing"—effectively placing you among the rest of the staff. We've seen the efficacy of this strategy first hand at a leading developer working with major licenses. The person in question went from roughly $20k/year as a tester to $50k/year as a sound designer.

Side quests can help you advance to the next level in your career and virtually provide insurance against being put "on call." There are many more side quests than those listed here—both negative and positive. In short, if side quests take attention away from the main storyline and don't reward you in any way, they're bad side quests. On the opposite side of the spectrum, if side quests enhance your position within the company and you learn something new and useful, they're good side quests. With side quests, it's important to use your time wisely—especially since you'll have so little of it.

Working Up to Position "X"

Many developers get their start in testing and work their way up because they have their eye on a senior position. Companies have only a few options when it comes to staffing for senior positions, and one of those is grooming from in house. So do a great job testing, show your character, and let it be known that you're looking to climb the ladder to Position "X"—whatever that position is for you.

Todd M. Fay (Owner, DemoNinja.com)

Gordon Walton on Getting Noticed & Promoted :::::

Gordon Walton has been building computer games for over 30 years. He is currently VP and Studio Co-Director at BioWare Austin working on *Star Wars: The Old Republic*. Previously, he was Vice President & Executive Producer at Sony Online Entertainment, Maxis, Origin, and Kesmai Corporation. He also led development at Konami of America, Three-Sixty Pacific, and his own studios.

Gordon Walton
(Vice President & Studio Co-Director, BioWare Austin)

Come to solve the problem we are hiring for, not what your potential is. Focus on how you can be a great tester and improve the quality of the games you work on. If you are doing a great job as a tester, you are likely to get noticed and promoted when there is an opening. If you are overtly trying to get out of testing (pushing what a great designer, programmer, etc. you are), you're less likely to get those opportunities!

Testing Achievements

If you work as a game tester, "doing okay" should never be your main aspiration. Throughout this chapter, we've discussed how testers might get too comfortable at their jobs. This section is exactly the opposite—discussing your highest achievements as a tester. Think of these as "Xbox Live" style achievements. We all know that Xbox Live has some lame duck achievements like "Completed Act 1 of [insert game title here] on Easy Mode." Those are not real achievements; they're bookmarks. We'll only discuss *real* achievements here—those you can be proud of!

Illustration by Ian Robert Vasquez

Bulldog Achievement

Bulldogs are relentless, so the *Bulldog achievement* is for testers who never let bad bugs go. Once you learn about a bug, you don't rest until it's documented and fixed. The longer it takes to locate and fix the bug, the higher the achievement. Being a bulldog is a great competitive advantage if everyone else is a poodle or a lab. (Okay, enough with the dog metaphors!)

Eagle Eye Achievement

Illustration by Ian Robert Vasquez

Not many testers have eyes capable of seeing *everything*. It takes a special skill and very special eyes—henceforth the "Eagle Eye" moniker. You earn the *Eagle Eye achievement* when no visual bug escapes your sight, even if it's marked Will Not Fix later in the game. You need to be able to spot more than visual bugs, though; pay attention to light levels, color balance, jumpy animation sequences, collision detection, and even each character's hair and clothing. You might leave work with a headache, but we guarantee it will pay off in the end.

Nosferatu Achievement

"Nosferatus" are the ugly vampires. While Count Dracula merely had to flick his cape to get some action, Nosferatu needed to pay some serious lip service to achieve the same results. The *Nosferatu achievement* is for those who start with a handicap—such as knowing nothing of scripting in a script-heavy game. Getting the job done despite any weaknesses is the mark of a true Nosferatu.

Illustration by Ian Robert Vasquez

Sherlock Achievement

If your deductive skills are off the charts, you deserve the *Sherlock achievement*. Deductive skills are essential for testing. Several types of bugs are well beyond observation, so deductive skills will allow you to dig deeper and get more from each event. Another quality of the Sherlock achievement is the usefulness of a Watson—a tester who learns from you and simultaneously keeps you in check with intelligent questions.

Illustration by Ian Robert Vasquez

Hail Mary Achievement

Like a "Hail Mary" pass, the *Hail Mary achievement* is the mark of someone who saves the game in the very last second. Maybe your last-minute guess prevented a serious network bug from shipping with the game. Maybe your leadership avoided a nasty fist fight in the last 12 hours of the project's life. To earn the Hail Mary achievement, you must make a decision at great risk and succeed.

Illustration by Ian Robert Vasquez

Achievements are won—but never lost—and you're forever changed by them. So pick your achievements well; give enough of yourself to conquer them fully, but don't allow yourself to be consumed by them in a wasteful frenzy. Once you push yourself to the brink, fearlessly challenging your own shortcomings every step of the way, you'll find out that there are really no limits to what you can achieve. It all depends on you.

Baron R.K. Von Wolfsheild on the Persistence Factor :::::

Baron R.K. Von Wolfsheild (Chief Software Architect, Qtask, Inc.)

Reichart ("The Baron") started playing with computers back when "display" meant eight LEDs in a row. He began his career at a very early age—and before being old enough to legally drink alcohol, he was the art director for Coors, Pizza Hut, Godfather's Pizza, and Pepsi television commercials. In the early 1980s, he helped pioneer those really annoying music videos for the then fledgling MTV. ("Sorry.") It was then that Reichart's life sadly began a steep decline. Booze, cheap women, and world fame combined to bring down the once famous "whiz kid." For years, Reichart roamed the streets, pushing around a shopping cart filled with his ideas and inventions (not to mention his really big foil ball and his lint collection). It should be quite obvious how he went from homelessness to heading multi-million dollar software companies, so we won't go into that. But nevertheless, the foil ball served a critical role.

We had a bug like a bubble under a carpet. This one bug was about to hold up shipping a gigantic title for one of the largest entertainment companies, and for a marketing plan that included the game coming out at the same time as the movie. And it meant not getting paid. We made huge lists of what routines we thought could possibility be causing the problem. It seemed that the closer we got to cornering the problem, the worse it would get. All our tempers were flaring at this point. I have a hardware background—so I literally hooked up a scope to the hardware and began to actually track what the machine was doing outside the software. In fact, it got so bad that I began to question the test tools themselves—but they seemed to be okay. (We tested the test tools, too.) Our deadline was coming, and our team was exhausted. The stress was deep. The lead programmer actually lost it and appeared to be throwing in the towel on the whole project—and he just left one night. I had to step back and become hypercritical. I stayed there all night questioning all my assumptions. There was one routine we all assumed had to be perfect; it was part of the system itself, the "printf" command. I trusted nothing now and began to trace the command itself. I did not like the results. I called the lead programmer, and we had a long talk about our anger at the project—not each other—and he came back to the office in the morning. We sat together and worked all day and into the night again. There it was, in the deepness of one of the simplest and core functions, the very command we were using to tell us what was going wrong. The print command was not allocating memory "for itself." Back then, we used every byte of a machine for the game—so we had indeed cornered this little command. The bug was actually in the system itself. We wrote our own print command in a few minutes, gave it a buffer—and the bug disappeared. We told the company that made the machine—and they were stunned this bug hadn't been noticed before. The game shipped on time, and that programmer is still with me after 22 years!

This chapter introduced you to the most common problems with a career in game testing. We talked about the biggest challenges you may face and what happens if you fail. But we also explored alternative paths to avoid being put on call and even get promoted. In the next chapter, we'll look at the future of testing. We'll find out what the future holds for "lifers"—those who will eventually become QA managers—and entry-level applicants looking for full-time positions making games for a living.

:::CHAPTER REVIEW:::

1. In this chapter, we discussed problems such as being put "on call," making "kill-switch" mistakes, and embarking on bad side quests. Choose one issue associated with each area (a total of 3 issues) and discuss how you personally will ensure that you avoid these issues.

2. In this chapter, we also discussed positive scenarios such as good side quests and testing achievements. Choose a good side quest and a testing achievement, and discuss what you will do to successfully accomplish them.

3. Where do you see yourself in the next five years? After becoming a tester, do you plan to work up the game testing ladder, move to another subteam (e.g., art, design, tech, audio), train for management (e.g., assistant producer), or get a job outside of the game industry? Using the concepts discussed in Chapters 7 and 8, create a five-year plan outlining how you will achieve your career goals.

CHAPTER

9

Testing Future Waters

what's next & how to get there

Key Chapter Questions

- How is it possible to keep *current* when the industry changes so fast?

- How will *portability* change the game industry?

- How will the "next" *next-gen systems* change the way games are tested?

- How can a bug actually *enhance gameplay*?

- What is the *future* of game testing and QA?

Everything changes incredibly fast in the game industry. Consoles appear, thrive, wither, and die in a few years—and games go from "must have" to the discount bin in a couple of months. Testing is also changing quickly, whether you see it happening or not. This chapter will give you a panoramic view of the future of testing and ways to make the best of it. We have also included a summary on the life of a game—along with a special section that illustrates ways in which bugs can actually improve a game.

Is It All About the Robots?

A theory popular among game testers is that automated testing (discussed in Chapter 6) will gain ground, inch by inch, until human testers are suddenly obsolete. This is simply not true. Automated testing does indeed look like the future—and you'll be thankful for it—but human testers will always be part of the equation. Computers can't measure "fun"—and they can't get bored either. Human testers might leave the repetitive stuff behind, but some tasks will always demand a human mind.

BigStockPhoto

Robots were at first seen as crude technological novelties. However, advances in artificial intelligence may one day make them sentient beings!

Looking ahead to the next 10-20 years in testing, we can say at the onset that the biggest difference between the testers of today and tomorrow will be their level of professionalism. The days of "leisure testing"—where lack of tech skills, tardiness, and inappropriate dress were the norm—will be *over*. In its place, there will be slightly older, more educated testers in business casual dress with diplomas and degrees under their arms. They'll be a cross between programmers and producers—career interns who know what they want and how to get it.

Here's what the future looks like:

- Better communication tools (everyone carries a smartphone)
- Superior schools with quality game testing and QA courses
- Professional standards adopted by the game industry
- Mobile gaming becomes mainstream, rivaling console games
- Next-gen games demand a large number of testers, which equals more jobs
- Testing is a respected profession

In the next sections, we'll examine these qualitative changes in testing that are brought forth by technology, superior education, and the proliferation of mobile platforms—taking you to a future that's closer than you might think!

David Price on the Place of Automated Testing in the Future :::::

Born at the start of the '80s, video games have always been a part of David's life. After completing his Bachelor's Degree in Computer Science from Furman University, he decided to pursue a career that combined his talents and interests. David moved back to Southern California to start his search—and within two months of graduating, he had started work as a tester with THQ in the QA department. Hard work and a positive attitude helped him stand out from the rest of the crowd—eventually leading to his position as Test Lead. David now manages teams of up to 50 testers—giving daily assignments and tracking progress on major AAA titles for all platforms.

David Price
(Test Lead, THQ, Inc.)

I think that the future of testing video games will always rely on the ingenuity of human beings, and automated testing programs will never be able to fully reproduce the methodology and creativity of a human tester. That being said, I feel that automated testing programs will be essential to verifying the functionality and appearance of content—while human testers will be the best at providing meaningful feedback on how the game plays and what can be changed to make the game better. Simply put, a computer can tell a program when something isn't right—but it can't tell the programmer how to make it better.

Automation Can't Juggle

Game testing is not something that can be automated. Period. This is not to say that some *aspects* of testing cannot be automated (e.g., stress testing, load testing, installation procedures)—but automate a machine to play ad-hoc while monitoring subtitle text, listening for music anomalies, sound-effect data corruption, and stereo panning glitches, detecting undesired ergonomic behavior with input devices, and detecting un-sync'd vibration or rumble, all while trash-talking your opponent? Maybe in another decade, but not now. The technology is constantly changing, the genres are vastly different, trends in gameplay are subtle and must be finessed—and until AI comes a lot further, I think human testing will remain the most desired method of QA testing.

Jerome Strach (QA Manager, Sony Computer Entertainment America)

Message in a Bottle: Beyond the Age of Information

Can you imagine what testing was like in the 1980s? Bug tracking software was non-existent, electronic spreadsheets ran in Apple II computers, and email (or "electronic mail") was exclusive to the government and academia! Of course, finance departments were starting to experiment with spreadsheets, and email was slowly gaining acceptance—but none of those tools would be used in testing for years to come. The result is that communication wasn't the easiest thing in the world: you had the information, but not the pipes to take it everywhere. Now let's fast forward to the new millennium: We are used to the Internet, email, and DevTrack. We have the capacity to send a direct message to one of the producers (when appropriate, of course). We can "tweet" and microblog about about testing using Twitter (respecting any NDAs, of course). What hasn't changed? When you're sitting in a console testing lab away from a computer, you can't really do any of this—and most testing rooms have one, maybe two PCs.

Courtesy of Twitter

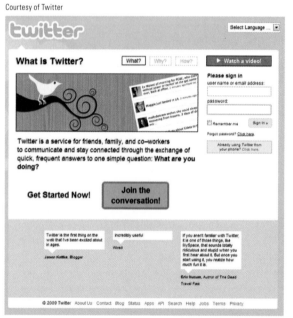

In the near future, developers will increasingly use tools such as Twitter to exchange messages in real time.

In the years ahead, all cell phones will be smartphones. Email will be the bare minimum; more likely, developers will be able to use a professional variant of Twitter to exchange real-time messages with others in the studio. This form of communication will greatly enhance cooperation during the process. By being able to reach decision-makers directly, you'll be able to better deal with cliques and other social "bottlenecks" that would otherwise adversely affect your performance (e.g., stopping you from reporting a bug). There is also a high probability that all testers will be able to access the bug tracking database from their smartphones—saving a tremendous amount of time in the process.

The Science of Fun: Game Education in the 21st Century

If you were around the industry in the 1980s, you'd know that there weren't any game development schools. If you wanted an academic background, you had to resort to a technical degree (e.g., Computer Programming) and apply it to game development. There were no game art, design, production, or audio specializations either. You learned on the job—making mistakes. It was tough, but this white-knuckle approach to development gave us some of the greatest game developers ever, including David Crane (*Pitfall!*), Will Wright (*Sim* franchise)—and Shigeru Miyamoto, who created a very famous Italian plumber named Mario.

Starting in the 1990s, game development courses started to pop up here and there, first with a class of video game programming students accepted at DigiPen in 1994. Several other schools followed suit—including the Art Institute, DeVry University, Westwood College of Technology, ITT Technical Institute, Full Sail, Carnegie Mellon University, the University of South Florida, and the University of Southern California. (See Chapter 7 for more information on game development education.) The new millennium brought with it game development courses and degrees—greatly enhancing the industry. Nonetheless, some developers still reject recent grads, citing their lack of experience and basic skills as the reason. We need to address this problem is to ensure that game development students get involved in internships, game projects, modding, and competitions long before graduation!

Berkman Center for Internet & Society at Harvard Law School

Many schools, including Harvard's School of Business, have utilized multi-user virtual environments such as *Second Life* to enhance learning.

In the future, game development will be a career just like law, medicine, and film. Parents will rejoice when their teenage sons and daughters get accepted by Ivy League schools with Master's degrees (or even PhDs) in game art, design, programming, and production. Game development studios will gladly seek out graduates—offering them jobs before they even leave school. On-ground campuses will still be common, but online learning will be much more prevalent—with many schools attempting immersive learning environments (ILE) for the first time. Similar to *Second Life* and *Multiverse*, these environments may be used as courses disguised as games (a form of "covert" or "stealth" learning). ILEs will also provide students with opportunities to co-author these course-game hybrids, sharing their creations with their peers over incredibly fast, gigabit wireless networks. In the end, game development courses will reach a level of sophistication that might be difficult to imagine right now—providing graduates with skills rivaling today's industry veterans.

The New Professionals: Game Testing Grows a Beard

The computer and game industries both had similar beginnings. At first, games and computers were made in universities equipped with gigantic mainframes. With the invention of the transistor, computers became lighter, simpler, and cheaper—allowing many more people to use them. Hence the very first game designers were born. Since this growth happened in empty garages all across the country, neither industry really had "adult" supervision. This trend continued from the mid 1970s until the late 1980s. In the wake of Atari's self-destruction and Nintendo's rise, the game industry suddenly became wiser—more adult and more responsible. Nintendo has a big hand in this shift—its professionalism serving as the model for other game companies. Today, game development is regarded as a serious profession—but some of that rowdy 1970s behavior still persists. Being late and even skipping work can happen frequently—sometimes to level up through a new *World of Warcraft* expansion. We accept that progress was made, but the game industry is still in its infancy.

Electronic Arts, Inc.

One day, game testing will be as professional as these Sims in *The Sims 2: Open for Business.*

While the film industry is not such a great role model, we dare say that game development will look more professional than the film industry in the future. Game development still has its roots in software development—even though its products will most likely surpass film, television, and music as *the* primary form of consumer entertainment. The high technology focus does attract a more professional workforce and dress code—but we see developers treating their jobs as though they work at major bank (i.e., seriously). Management will be increasingly more professional, led by people who love to manage others; the old trend of artists, designers, and programmers who work up the management ladder and become producers will be a thing of the past. Jobs will be fairly stable, with less of the shuffling we currently see in the market. In a future where the vast majority of the world's adult population will most likely be playing games, the industry will be regarded as one of the pillars of the global economy—helping humans learn, train for dangerous jobs, interact, and connect across nations . . . a far cry from the derisive way the game industry is currently treated by some in the media.

Evan Call & David Dawson on the Professionalization of Testing ∶∶∶∶∶

With over 20 years work with or within the broadcast and digital media space, Evan has a broad understanding of the application of media business models and technologies as they pertain to the distribution of information and entertainment. Most of his background includes the coverage and broadcast of sporting events, including the Olympic Games. For several years, his focus has been on providing technology solutions for the digital media, video games, and social networking industries.

As games become more sophisticated and reach or even exceed movie production budgets, the role of QA and testing will become even more important. With ever-increasing video game sales numbers, testing will evolve to become more rigorous and professionalized.

Evan Call
(Business Development Manager, iBeta Quality Assurance)

David Dawson has an Associate's degree in Advertising & Design and a Bachelor's degree in Game Art & Design from the Art Institute of Pittsburgh-Online Division. David started working in the computer graphics industry in 1990; specializing in interactive media design, he created interactive training for corporations on both CD-ROM and the Internet. David has taught classes in art, design, and computer software. He enjoys playing MMORPGs and RTS games.

Testing has already has become professionalized in the game industry. Any game released to market that is buggy or just plain doesn't work is a bad mark for a game company. Gamers are not forgiving when it comes to wasting their money on a game that contains bugs or, worse yet, is non-functional. We have full-time people whose sole job is testing and debugging the game. I can't imagine us *not* having people in those positions.

David Dawson
(Environmental Artist, Snowblind Studios)

Gaming On the Go: The Growth of Mobile Game Development

The first mobile games, powered (or underpowered) by salt-of-the-earth cell phones, had no business running games. You might remember attempting to play these games using shoddy keyboards, with graphics that would make a Game Boy cringe. This is how it all began in the 1990s, when telecoms realized there was money to be made in mobile gaming. The iPhone changed all of this. With an advanced PowerVR GPU, plenty of storage, and fast 3G access, iPhone users all over the world are discovering that mobile games can indeed be very impressive. With installed user bases in the hundreds of millions and widespread connectivity, nothing can stop the advancement of mobile games now. The iPhone is the most cited example, but everything we see on the web points to similar developments with T-Mobile's G1, the Google-powered smartphone. The G1 is also capable of 3D graphics—with a rumored performance of 3-4 *million* polygons per second.

Imagine what an iPhone will be like two generations from now. Bear in mind, this is enough time for its 3D performance and storage to outpace an Xbox 360. When every phone is a smartphone and standards are shared among all platforms, widespread mobile gaming becomes a reality. This will translate in an explosion in the number of mobile game developers, a huge jump in revenue, and all-around acceptance of gaming as a cell phone activity. You will see increasingly more job opportunities, with hundreds of thousands of open positions available for testers. Global gaming networks such as Xbox Live *for mobile users* will also add to these numbers. Part of this change has already taken place, but the scale will increase dramatically in a very short time.

Courtesy of Apple Inc.

When every phone is a smartphone such as the iPhone 3G and standards are shared among all platforms, widespread mobile gaming will become a reality.

Hardware Complexity Will Fuel Growth

Game development is incredibly complex. Today's consoles are mind-blowing in their capabilities, and mobile devices involve dozens, even hundreds of hardware SKUs that require polishing and re-polishing. Pardon the double-negative, but I *can't* imagine testing *not* being an area for growth!

Jamie Lendino (Composer & Sound Designer, Sound For Games Interactive)

The Next Gen Cometh: When Giants Roam the Earth

When video games transitioned from the PlayStation 2 and Xbox to the PlayStation 3 and Xbox 360, several things did not change: Graphics were still king, online gameplay was a proven way to enhance a game's value proposition, and traditional genres such as the first-person shooter (FPS) and racing game had guaranteed places in gamers' hearts. One thing did change, though: development costs. The next generation of consoles—with its six-fold jump in resolution (480p-1080p)—exponentially raised the money necessary to actually make a game. And you thought the PS3 was expensive! There was a time in the '70s when making games cost practically nothing. In the '90s, $100,000 would have been a very big budget. Currently, we're looking at millions of dollars per game—more than $25 million, in fact, if you add marketing. Games have grown in size and complexity to the point where new players are sometimes relegated to casual games that only take a few minutes to learn and play.

The future brings good and bad news. First, the bad: The next generation of consoles will repeat the cycle and make game development yet more expensive. An initial budget of $150 million is just around the corner; we expect this in the next five years. Now, for the good: As games get more complex and expensive, QA will become paramount. There will be a demand for a very large number of testers, and quality standards will be fiercely enforced by both publishers and consumers. Game testing jobs will thrive for this reason alone. Even better, mobile gaming will also demand testers. Mobile games are gaining in complexity, so expect to see growth there as well. Publishers, as always, will have to fork out the money—but testers will have plenty of work!

Reprinted with permission from Microsoft Corporation

Gears of War 2 goes well beyond the first *Gears of War*—pushing the limits of current generation configurations.

"Testing for Greatness"

If technology advances well enough, the need to test will change form—since programs will become sandboxed, isolated in a way that protects the program and the environment. Programmers will become self-healing, and testing might move more toward QA—which is to say there would be less testing for failure, and more testing for greatness.

Baron R.K. Von Wolfsheild (Chief Software Architect, Qtask, Inc.)

The Rise of the Tester

Being a tester in the 1980s meant that nobody paid you. After all, you were paid for being a developer in your current game; testing was just a favor you did for your employer. Then, as 8-bit computers gave way to 16-bit powerhouses such as the Atari ST and the Sega Genesis, testing suddenly became "a job." Two or three testers would work on the average 16-bit title, make some money, and call it a day. But they got no respect; testers were regarded by the industry as "a bunch of high-school kids playing games for a living." We might be well into the new millennium, but testers still "get no respect." For the most part, they're still ignored, mistreated, or sometimes even maligned as foul-smelling geeks who aren't fit to do anything else. They can be fired unceremoniously and re-hired—being promised "easy money" and the opportunity to have some fun. The good news, though, is that our survey (discussed in Chapter 2) shows that the status of testers is already changing for the better!

iStockphoto

Elite professional testers will specialize in certain game areas and will be chosen to join other teams.

We see a future where testers are hired and treated just like today's programmers. Testers will specialize in certain areas of the game, become very good at their jobs, and then get chosen by knowledgeable leads to join other teams (e.g., art, audio, design, tech). They'll assemble teams such as superior task forces—playing on each other's strengths and with a clear sense of hierarchy. In this environment, testers will always dress appropriately, keep quiet when necessary, and tackle the most difficult bugs with a clear head. The new testers will be respected—and feared, in a way, because they'll know their way around code. Testers will be like hired guns, always ready to strike. This change in attitude will transform the industry from the bottom up.

Testing Paradigm Shifts

Game testing will not become more professionalized until it is considered a valid career choice in the industry. Quality assurance is something you could spend your life doing in other types of software development, but I don't know if I see it happening for games. It is considered a stepping stone to other jobs in games—and until that changes, not much else will.

Brandon Adler (QA Lead, Obsidian Entertainment)

Until the pay rate is increased, you will not be able to pull in the level of testers you would need for that to become a reality. At the current level, you get some really good people—but they do not stick with it because they can move to another area within the company or to a different career and earn quite a bit more.

Floyd Billings (Assistant QA Lead, Sony Online Entertainment)

The Future of . . . Bugs?

In his blog post in *Crispy Gamer*, "If These Bugs Are Wrong, I Don't Want to Be Right," John Teti compiles a list of 10 famous bugs that turned out to be beloved features in games. These "programming mistakes" were eventually found to add to the gameplay, and not the opposite. Among his examples, "Guile's Handcuffs" allowed savvy *Street Fighter II* arcade players to freeze the opponent in a stunned pose. (See this YouTube video for more info: www.youtube.com/watch?v=VSBjqSV40Uw.) In *Super Mario Bros.* on the Famicom Disk System, it was possible to reach Minus World (-1!) by jumping backwards into a solid wall in World 1-2. This was an entire level born out of a computer *glitch*. (See this YouTube video for more info: www.youtube.com/watch?v=_BNr1Az7MJM.)

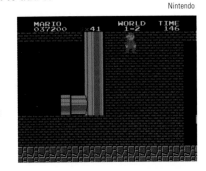

Nintendo

Rapid Iteration & the Engineering of Bugs

In the past, creating video games didn't allow for much trial and error. Even small changes to the code required lengthy recompiling, making tinkering and tuning with the game undesirable as a deadline approached. With modern game engines, developers can have a much higher degree of freedom since the engine avoids most of the recompiling seen in the old days. Levels, particle effects, and enemy placements can be changed on the go, taking the concept of "polishing" to a whole new level.

Nintendo

It's not inconceivable for bugs to pop up during polishing. Minus World had to be left in *Super Mario Bros.* (Developers didn't have the time to "fix it" before launch.) If a modern engine is in use, an especially interesting bug not only can be left in, but may be finalized—and polished. This is a complete change in the way games are made; it's almost as if developers, empowered by rapid iteration, can now allow chaos to play a part in the design phase. They can change gameplay 100% between versions, play it for a couple of hours, and then change it again. Testers can discover new uses for what seem to be bugs—and possibly take the game in a hyper-creative, never-before-seen direction.

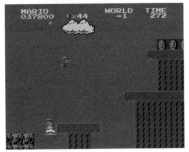

Nintendo

It's almost as if bugs are evolving. They graduate from merely slips of the mind to creative seeds laid down by Game Muses living high above the clouds—or in a PlayStation 1 memory card. If better games can come out of it, who's to say that bugs are really inferior to "planned" features?

Minus World in *Super Mario Bros.* (Famicom Disk System) gave players a glimpse into the unexpected. Minus World path from World 1-2 (top), level screen (middle), and game screen (bottom).

Shepherd Duties

It's your job as a game tester to detail your finds while keeping the big picture in mind. When developers and publishers pay you to test video games for a living, they're not looking for "trained monkeys"; they need sensitive, smart human beings to think *beyond the code* and spot any valuable opportunities. You need to make sure everything is written down so that prospective producers can see the value of even the smallest bug. Do a good job at this, and you won't be a tester for long.

Courtesy of Atari, Inc.

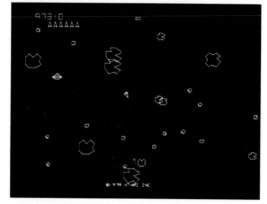

A bug allowed you to become invincible if you hid your ship behind the score in an early arcade version of Atari's *Asteroids*.

In John Teti's post mentioned earlier in this section, *Asteroids* is cited as having another "positive" bug: By standing behind the score, players could suddenly become invincible. If a tester spotted this bug during testing and *didn't* report it, the tester could have been fired. As a bug, this would be categorized as high-priority because it can fundamentally change gameplay. Now imagine that a tester *did* catch it and report it in time (not that any testing teams were in place during this era, as discussed in Chapter 1). Two results would come out of this:

1. Playtesting sessions would uncover all the different effects of the bug
2. Those effects could become the basis for new gameplay

For example, developers could implement new code that gives the player limited time to clear the level when using the invincibility "cheat." If time runs out, the ship would simply explode. As you can see, this could be a very welcome change in the way *Asteroids* is played. It could have made the game even more popular—and certainly more accessible.

Becoming a game tester is much more than just finding bugs; it's important to develop critical sense as well. In this section, we showed you how bugs can actually play a constructive role in the way a game plays on certain occasions. In time, you'll gain a deeper understanding of how the separate pieces of gameplay and planned features or bugs can affect the total sum of the finished game. Until then, watch out for any "special" bugs; you never know when one of them might actually *improve* things.

Cradles, Graves & Lions

When we decided to write this book, we wanted to educate and inform anyone interested in becoming part of the game industry through game testing and QA. Unfortunately, there's a lot of misinformation out there—from clichés to incomplete conceptions of what game testing is all about. This book has attempted to correct these assumptions with some good old-fashioned information based on first-hand experience. Let's step back and look at the big picture—reminding ourselves of what game testing is all about, from the early days of almost unplayable code to the final hours before submission. Hopefully, you will recall this journey with us and get ready to take your first step into the world of game testing.

Conception & Birth

A game is born as a prototype—its first incarnation. Its concept needs to be proven with a simple demo, securing the publisher's support. This is the only way to get funding and then give the studio the green light to start hiring. No testers will ever be hired to look at prototypes. Testers already working on other projects might be called in, though, to provide their opinions. Traditionally, when a game is in the prototype phase:

- There are no testers involved
- The game is presented to the publisher by the developer
- Only sample gameplay exists (which does not represent the final game)

In the early stages of game development, testers are *not* included. Sometimes, a producer will show a prototype to a tester—but this is a focus test of sorts, not actual testing. The producer needs an opinion, and testers are full of them!

Childhood

As the prototype is approved, the studio starts hiring developers. Soon enough, the initial team is put in place and production begins. The team will work toward alpha—the game's first milestone. If a game were a human being, it would be a child right now—slowly learning to walk and talk.

Let's take a look at the definition of the alpha phase again (from Chapter 3):

> Alpha demands feature-completion, which includes a full play-through (playing a game from beginning to end). Contrary to what some may think, alpha is more about locking in the features than having a bug-free game.

No testers will be hired for early alpha. By this time, there's no game per se—just a collection of different systems that don't add up. There is nothing to test. However, as systems mature and programmers start "plugging in"—each one of them to the main engine—the game finally begins to take shape. Once all main features and temp assets are put in place, the game will be in late alpha. Enter the production testers. Here are the requirements for the "alpha" milestone:

- Feature-complete
- Temp assets
- Testers hired at around late alpha

But testing a game in late alpha is very different from doing the same in late beta. Let's take a look at the typical activities done in late alpha in the accompanying diagram.

Diagram by Per Olin

Testing Activities (Alpha)

- Check main features
- Make sure a full playthrough is possible
- Balance gameplay (an essential part of alpha testing)
- Hunt down critical bugs; crashes and freezes need to be dealt with early in the testing process

Even in late alpha, sometimes there won't be a game to test. It's easy to break a game when attempting to fix a serious bug, so don't be surprised if that new build you waited two hours to play gives you a black screen. In this case, the lead might make everyone default back to the old build. You have to be ready to deal with crazy distorted player models, missing artwork, no sound, no connectivity, and other crippling issues during alpha. It's your job to help them get through these issues and arrive at a stable, feature-complete title by the end of the alpha stage.

The Teenage Years

Let's go ahead and add the tweens to this category as well. We are talking about beta. By the time the studio hits alpha, the publisher sends the developer another check so they can hire additional developers and testers. The game is growing by leaps and bounds now, with all major systems in place and final assets being readied for gold. Beta is a tricky period because developers sometimes indulge in what we call *feature creep*—insisting on adding new features or mechanics late in development. Most of the time, this proves to be a fatal mistake, resulting in delays and a ballooning budget. Navigating the beta period properly is essential if you want the game to rise above 80% in review scores.

Let's look at our previous definition of beta again (from Chapter 3):

> Beta is roughly a time when all assets are in place and the game is essentially done. A game doesn't fully hit beta until all high priority bugs are all addressed; therefore, the days before beta can be terrifying—especially if you take into consideration that a good chunk of the funding is conditional on hitting beta on time.

Production will be deeply entrenched by the time early beta hits, but QA testers are just beginning. This is the time when both jobs start to differentiate—since production testers focus on bigger bugs and gameplay issues, while QA addresses minor bugs and submission guidelines. Here are the requirements and parameters for the "beta" milestone:

- Feature-complete
- Final assets in place
- Plenty of low-priority bugs
- Polish starts during late beta *if* developers have enough time

Beta is the developer's final chance to fix any major bugs. It's also an opportunity to polish the game before it hits gold. While some games get plenty of time for polish (e.g., id Software's titles and the *Halo* series), others are not so lucky. This period will usually be the difference between 75% and 95% review scores, since games become truly great after polishing.

Diagram by Per Olin

Testing Activities (Beta)

- Search for low bugs; sound and visual bugs need to be addressed in early beta
- Focus on multiplayer gameplay
- Find and fix all high networking bugs
- Test community features in Xbox Live and the PlayStation Network
- Find and fix any progression breaks
- Check for loading bugs
- Verify all items/weapons/accessories
- Make sure the game hits its performance targets (30 or 60 frames per second)

The full list for typical beta activities is considerably larger than those listed in the accompanying diagram. The one thing to keep in mind, though, is that beta includes dealing with serious bugs *and* addressing small ones; go ahead and add a pint of polish to the mixture. It's a very diverse period during which several things can go wrong. We can safely say that beta will be the most demanding phase of testing—more than gold, in fact.

Adulthood

Ah, adulthood—the sweet taste of freedom. Games go through the same challenges as all of us. As beta comes and goes, there's only one objective: gold. By the time the game you're working on hits gold, the team will be exhausted and nobody will be sleeping more than a few hours per day. Gold is the end of the line.

Let's look at our previous definition of gold again (from Chapter 3):

> When a game hits gold, it's ready for the marketplace. Bear in mind, we didn't say "done." Today, with consoles perennially connected to the Internet, games are regularly released in "almost-ready" states and then fixed though downloadable updates.

As we've mentioned, there is actual development work after a game hits gold. A small percentage of the testing crew will stay behind—working on patches and other last-minute issues. Even with this new reality, your job as a tester will mostly be over during gold. All showstopper bugs must be dealt with. Here are the requirements for the "gold" milestone:

- The game is now polished and ready to ship
- All assets are final
- All features have been implemented
- No showstopper (critical) bugs exist
- All levels load properly
- Only a small percentage of low priority bugs remain

By the time the game hits gold, there's a good chance you'll either be: (a) placed on a different project; (b) promoted; or (c) put on call. If you happen to stick around with the "patch squad," keep in mind that one of these outcomes will either be delayed or nullified.

Still Undecided?

If you're still on the fence, just do it! Even the worst day testing games is better than the best day in any other job I have had. Who knows, you may end up really loving it!

Brandon Adler (Quality Assurance Lead, Obsidian Entertainment)

Imagine a game as that tiny lion cub at the top of Pride Rock. It will one day rule the market, but in the beginning it's just a funny-looking cat. The game is one of many in a long list of projects you'll work with. Feed the lion cub, and help it grow stronger and more powerful—but don't let it eat you in the end. It's just a project . . . not your entire life.

We hope this book has expanded your view of testing games for a living. You now have the knowledge to make your dreams a reality—to become a novice tester and then move on to bigger and better things. We can see a day when testers are respected and, frankly, sought after by studios and publishers. That day depends on you. It's your job to leave your mark in the industry by breaking in, moving up, and changing it from the inside. You've seen this movie before—so go ahead and take the first step. *Press start!*

Nintendo

:::CHAPTER REVIEW:::

1. How will the growth of communication technology, hardware (such as next-gen systems and mobile devices), and game industry education affect the growth of game testing and QA?

2. Have you ever stumbled upon a bug that you feel actually enhances gameplay? Describe the bug in detail, and discuss how it benefits the game.

3. Do you feel that game testing and QA will become more professionalized in the next 5-10 years? Why or why not?

Resources

There's a wealth of information on game development and related topics discussed in this book. Here is just a sample list of books, news sites, organizations, and events you should definitely explore!

Communities & Directories

APM Music   www.apmmusic.com

Apple Developer Connection   developer.apple.com

ArtBarf.com   www.artbarf.com

Betawatcher.com   www.betawatcher.com

Beyond3D   www.beyond3d.com

CG Society   www.cgtalk.com

CG Textures   www.cgtextures.com

Destructoid   www.destructoid.com

DevMaster.net   www.devmaster.net

DevShed Forum   forums.devshed.com/game-development-141

EntertainmentCareers.net   www.entertainmentcareers.net

Gamasutra   www.gamasutra.com

Game Audio Forum   www.gameaudioforum.com

Game Audio Pro Tech Group   groups.yahoo.com/group/gameaudiopro

GameDev.net   www.gamedev.net

Game Development Search Engine   www.gdse.com

GameFAQs   www.gamefaqs.com

Game Music.com   www.gamemusic.com

Game Music Revolution (GMR)   www.gmronline.com

Games Tester   www.gamestester.com

GarageGames   www.garagegames.com

Giant Bomb   www.giantbomb.com

iDevGames Forum   www.idevgames.com/forum

Indiegamer Forum   forums.indiegamer.com

International Dialects of English Archive (IDEA)   web.ku.edu/idea/

Machinima.com   www.machinima.com

Mayang's Free Texture Library   www.mayang.com/textures

MobyGames   www.mobygames.com

Northern Sounds   www.northernsounds.com

Overclocked Remix   www.overclocked.org

Professional Sound Designers Forum   psd.freeforums.org

PS3   www.ps3.net

Sound Design Forum   groups.yahoo.com/group/sound_design

3D Buzz   www.3dbuzz.com

3D Total   www.3dtotal.com

VGMix   www.vgmix.com

Video Game Music Database (VGMdb)   www.vgmdb.net

Voicebank.net   www.voicebank.net

Wii-Play   www.wii-play.com

Xbox.com   www.xbox.com

XBOX 360 Homebrew   www.xbox360homebrew.com

News, Reviews & Research

Blues News   www.bluesnews.com

Computer & Video Games   www.computerandvideogames.com

Computer Games Magazine   www.cgonline.com

Develop Magazine   www.developmag.com

Digital Playroom   www.dplay.com

Edge Online   www.edge-online.com

Eurogamer   www.eurogamer.net

Game Career Guide   www.gamecareerguide.com

GameDaily   www.gamedaily.com

Game Developer Magazine   www.gdmag.com

Gamers Hell   www.gamershell.com

Game Industry News   www.gameindustry.com

Game-Machines.com   www.game-machines.com

GamePolitics   www.gamepolitics.com

GameRankings   www.gamerankings.com

GamesIndustry.biz   www.gamesindustry.biz

GameSlice Weekly   www.gameslice.com

GameSpot   www.gamespot.com

GameSpy   www.gamespy.com

Games Radar (PC Gamer)   www.gamesradar.com/pc

Guide to Sound Effects   www.epicsound.com/sfx/

Internet Gaming Network (IGN)   www.ign.com

Joystiq   www.joystiq.com

Kotaku   www.kotaku.com

Mayang's Free Texture Library   www.mayang.com/textures

MCV   www.mcvuk.com

Metacritic   www.metacritic.com

Microsoft/Monster Career Center   office.microsoft.com/en-us/help/FX103504051033.aspx

MMOGChart.com   www.mmogchart.com

Music4Games.net   www.music4games.net

1UP   www.1up.com

Penny Arcade   www.penny-arcade.com

Planet Unreal   planetunreal.gamespy.com

PolyCount   www.polycount.com

Recording History: The History of Recording Technology   www.recording-history.org

Resumé Samples   www.freeresumesamples.org

Showfax   www.showfax.com

Slashdot   games.slashdot.org

Star Tech Journal   www.startechjournal.com

Tongue Twisters   www.geocities.com/Athens/8136/tonguetwisters.html

UnderGroundOnline (UGO)   www.ugo.com

Unreal Technology   www.unrealtechnology.com

Unreal Wiki   wiki.beyondunreal.com

Voiceover Demos   www.compostproductions.com/demos.html

Xbox Developer Programs   www.xbox.com/en-US/dev/contentproviders.htm

Wired Game | Life   blog.wired.com/games

WorkingGames   www.workingames.co.uk

Organizations

Academy of Interactive Arts & Sciences (AIAS)   www.interactive.org

Academy of Machinima Arts & Sciences   www.machinima.org

Association of Computing Machinery (ACM)   www.acm.org

Audio Engineering Society (AES)   www.aes.org

Business Software Alliance (BSA)   www.bsa.org

Digital Games Research Association (DiGRA)   www.digra.org

Entertainment Software Association (ESA)   www.theesa.com

Entertainment Software Ratings Board (ESRB)   www.esrb.org

Game Audio Network Guild (GANG)   www.audiogang.org

Game Audio Technical Committee   www.aes.org/technical/ag

Interactive Audio Special Interest Group (IASIG)   www.iasig.org

International Computer Games Association (ICGA)   www.cs.unimaas.nl/icga

International Game Developers Association (IGDA)   www.igda.org

Events

Consumer Electronics Show (CES)
January   Las Vegas, NV
www.cesweb.org

Game Developers Conference (GDC)
March   San Francisco, CA
www.gdconf.com

D.I.C.E. Summit (AIAS)
March   Las Vegas, NV
www.dicesummit.org

SIGGRAPH (ACM)
Summer   (location varies)
www.siggraph.org

E3 Expo
June   Los Angeles, CA
www.e3expo.com

Tokyo Game Show (TGS)
Fall   Japan
tgs.cesa.or.jp/english/

Austin Game Developers Conference
September   Austin, TX
www.gameconference.com

IndieGamesCon (IGC)
October   Eugene, OR
www.indiegamescon.com

Project Bar-B-Q
October   Lake Buchanan, TX
www.projectbarbq.com

Colleges & Universities

Here is a list of schools that have strong game degree or certificate programs:

Academy of Art University   www.academyart.edu

American Intercontinental University   www.aiuniv.edu

Arizona State University   www.asu.edu

Art Center College of Design   www.artcenter.edu

Art Institute of Pittsburgh - Online Division   www.aionline.edu

The Art Institutes   www.artinstitutes.edu

Carnegie Mellon University/Entertainment Technology Center   www.cmu.edu

DeVry University   www.devry.edu

DigiPen Institute of Technology   www.digipen.edu

Ex'pression College for Digital Arts   www.expression.edu

Full Sail Real World Education   www.fullsail.edu

Guildhall at SMU   guildhall.smu.edu

Indiana University - MIME Program   www.mime.indiana.edu

International Academy of Design & Technology   www.iadtschools.com

Iowa State University   www.iastate.edu

ITT Technical Institute   www.itt-tech.edu

Massachusetts Institute of Technology (MIT)   media.mit.edu

Rasmussen College   www.rasmussen.edu

Rensselaer Polytechnic Institute   www.rpi.edu

Ringling College of Art & Design   www.ringling.edu

SAE Institute   www.sae.edu

Santa Monica College Academy of Entertainment & Technology   academy.smc.edu

Savannah College of Art & Design   www.scad.edu

Tomball College   www.tomballcollege.com

University of California, Los Angeles (UCLA) Extension   www.uclaextension.edu

University of Central Florida - Florida Interactive Entertainment Academy   fiea.ucf.edu

University of Southern California (USC) - Information Technology Program   itp.usc.edu

University of Southern California (USC) School of Cinematic Arts   interactive.usc.edu

Vancouver Film School   www.vfs.com

Westwood College   www.westwood.edu

Adams, E. (2003). *Break into the game industry.* McGraw-Hill Osborne Media.

Adams, E. & Rollings, A. (2006). *Fundamentals of game design.* Prentice Hall.

Ahearn, L. & Crooks II, C.E. (2002). *Awesome game creation: No programming required. (2nd ed).* Charles River Media.

Ahlquist, J.B., Jr. & Novak, J. (2007). *Game development essentials: Game artificial intelligence.* Cengage Delmar.

Aldrich, C. (2003). *Simulations and the future of learning.* Pfeiffer.

Aldrich, C. (2005). *Learning by doing.* Jossey-Bass.

Allison, S.E. et al. (March 2006). "The development of the self in the era of the Internet & role-playing fantasy games. *The American Journal of Psychiatry.*

Atkin, M. & Abercrombie, J. (2005). "Using a goal/action architecture to integrate modularity and long-term memory into AI behaviors." *Game Developers Conference.*

Axelrod, R. (1985). *The evolution of cooperation.* Basic Books.

Bartle, R.A. (1996). "Hearts, clubs, diamonds, spades: Players who suit MUDs." *MUSE Multi-User Entertainment Ltd* (www.mud.co.uk/richard/hcds.htm).

Bates, B. (2002). *Game design: The art & business of creating games.* Premier Press.

Beck, J.C. & Wade, M. (2004). *Got game: How the gamer generation is reshaping business forever.* Harvard Business School Press.

Bethke, E. (2003). *Game development and production.* Wordware.

Birn, J. (2006). *Digital lighting and rendering (2nd ed.).* New Riders Press.

Boer, J. (2002). *Game audio programming.* Charles River Media.

Brandon, A. (2004). *Audio for games: Planning, process, and production.* New Riders.

Brin, D. (1998). *The transparent society.* Addison-Wesley.

Broderick, D. (2001). *The spike: How our lives are being transformed by rapidly advancing technologies.* Forge.

Brooks, D. (2001). *Bobos in paradise: The new upper class and how they got there.* Simon & Schuster.

Busby, A., Parrish, Z. & Van Eenwyk, J. (2004). *Mastering Unreal technology: The art of level design.* Sams.

Byrne, E. (2004). *Game level design.* Charles River Media.

Campbell, J. (1972). *The hero with a thousand faces.* Princeton University Press.

Campbell, J. & Moyers, B. (1991). *The power of myth.* Anchor.

Castells, M. (2001). *The Internet galaxy: Reflections on the Internet, business, and society.* Oxford University Press.

Castillo, T. & Novak, J. (2008). *Game development essentials: Game level design.* Cengage Delmar.

Castronova, E. (2005). *Synthetic worlds: The business and culture of online games.* University of Chicago Press.

Chase, R.B., Aquilano, N.J. & Jacobs, R. (2001). *Operations management for competitive advantage (9th ed)*. McGraw-Hill/Irwin

Cheeseman, H.R. (2004). *Business law (5th ed)*. Pearson Education, Inc.

Chiarella, T. (1998). *Writing dialogue*. Story Press.

Childs, G.W. (2006). *Creating music and sound for games*. Course Technology PTR.

Christen, P. (November 2006). "Serious expectations" *Game Developer Magazine*.

Clayton, A.C. (2003). *Introduction to level design for PC games*. Charles River Media.

Co, P. (2006). *Level design for games: Creating compelling game experiences*. New Riders Games.

Cooper, A., & Reimann, R. (2003). *About face 2.0: The essentials of interaction design*. Wiley.

Cornman, L.B. et al. (December 1998). A fuzzy logic method for improved moment estimation from Doppler spectra. *Journal of Atmospheric & Oceanic Technology*.

Cox, E. & Goetz, M. (March 1991). Fuzzy logic clarified. *Computerworld*.

Crawford, C. (2003). *Chris Crawford on game design*. New Riders.

Crowley, M. (2004). "'A' is for average." *Reader's Digest*.

Csikszentmihalyi, M. (1991). *Flow: The psychology of optimal experience*. Perennial.

Decker, M. (2000). "Bug Reports That Make Sense." *StickyMinds.com* (www.stickyminds.com/sitewide.asp?Function=edetail&ObjectType=ART&ObjectId=2079).

DeMaria, R. & Wilson, J.L. (2003). *High score!: The illustrated history of electronic games*. McGraw-Hill.

Demers, O. (2001). *Digital texturing and painting*. New Riders Press.

Dickens, C. (April 1, 2004). "Automated Testing Basics." *Software Test Engineering @ Microsoft* (blogs.msdn.com/chappell/articles/106056.aspx).

Digital Media Wire. *Project Millennials Sourcebook (2nd Ed.)*. (2008). Pass Along / Digital Media Wire.

Duffy, J. (April 2009). "8th Annual Game Developer Salary Survey." *Game Developer Magazine*.

Duffy, J. (August 2007). "The Bean Counters." *Game Developer Magazine*.

Dunniway, T. & Novak, J. (2008). *Game development essentials: Gameplay mechanics*. Cengage Delmar.

Egri, L. (1946). *The art of dramatic writing: Its basis in the creative interpretation of human motives*. Simon and Schuster.

Erikson, E.H. (1994). *Identity and the life cycle*. W.W. Norton & Company.

Erikson, E.H. (1995). *Childhood and society*. Vintage.

Escober, C. & Galindo, J. (2004). Fuzzy control in agriculture: Simulation software. *Industrial Simulation Conference 2004*.

Evans, A. (2001). *This virtual life: Escapism and simulation in our media world*. Fusion Press.

Fay, T. (2003). *DirectX 9 audio exposed: Interactive audio development*, Wordware Publishing.

Feare, T. (July 2000). "Simulation: Tactical tool for system builders." *Modern Materials Handling*.

Friedl, M. (2002). *Online game interactivity theory*. Charles River Media.

Fristrom, J. (July 14, 2003). "Production Testing & Bug Tracking." *Gamasutra* (www.gamasutra.com/view/feature/2829/production_testing_and_bug_tracking.php).

Fruin, N. & Harrigan, P. (Eds.) (2004). *First person: New media as story, performance and game.* MIT Press.

Fullerton, T., Swain, C. & Hoffman, S. (2004). *Game design workshop: Designing, prototyping & playtesting games.* CMP Books.

Galitz, W.O. (2002). *The essential guide to user interface design: An introduction to GUI design principles and techniques.* (2nd ed.). Wiley.

Gamma, E., Helm, R., Johnson, R. & Vlissides, J. (1995). *Design patterns: Elements of reusable object-oriented software.* Addison-Wesley.

Gardner, J. (1991). *The art of fiction: Notes on craft for young writers.* Vintage Books.

Gee, J.P. (2003). *What video games have to teach us about learning and literacy.* Palgrave Macmillan.

Gershenfeld, A., Loparco, M. & Barajas, C. (2003). *Game plan: The insiders guide to breaking in and succeeding in the computer and video game business.* Griffin Trade Paperback.

Giarratano, J.C. & Riley, G.D. (1998). *Expert systems: Principles & programming (4th ed).* Course Technology.

Gibson, D., Aldrich, C. & Prensky, M. (Eds.) (2006). *Games and simulations in online learning.* IGI Global.

Gladwell, M. (2000). *The tipping point: How little things can make a big difference.* New York, NY: Little Brown & Company.

Gladwell, M. (2007). *Blink: The power of thinking without thinking.* Back Bay Books.

Gleick, J. (1987). *Chaos: Making a new science.* Viking.

Gleick, J. (1999). *Faster: The acceleration of just about everything.* Vintage Books.

Gleick, J. (2003). *What just happened: A chronicle from the information frontier.* Vintage.

Godin, S. (2003). *Purple cow: Transform your business by being remarkable.* Portfolio.

Godin, S. (2005). *The big moo: Stop trying to be perfect and start being remarkable.* Portfolio.

Goldratt, E.M. & Cox, J. (2004). *The goal: A process of ongoing improvement (3rd ed).* North River Press.

Gordon, T. (2000). *P.E.T.: Parent effectiveness training.* Three Rivers Press.

Hall, R. & Novak, J. (2008). *Game development essentials: Online game development.* Cengage Delmar.

Hamilton, E. (1940). *Mythology: Timeless tales of gods and heroes.* Mentor.

Hart, S.N. (1996-2000). "A Brief History of Home Video Games." *geekcomix* (www.geekcomix.com/vgh/main.shtml).

Heim, M. (1993). *The metaphysics of virtual reality.* Oxford University Press.

Hight, J. & Novak, J. (2007). *Game development essentials: Game project management.* Cengage Delmar.

Hornyak, T.N. (2006). *Loving the machine: The art and science of Japanese robots.* Kodansha International.

Hsu, F. (2004). *Behind Deep Blue: Building the computer that defeated the world chess champion.* Princeton University Press.

Hunt, C.W. (October 1998). "Uncertainty factor drives new approach to building simulations." *Signal.*

Jensen, E. (2006). *Enriching the brain: How to maximize every learner's potential.* John Wiley & Sons.

Isla, D. (2005). "Handling complexity in the *Halo 2* AI." Game Developers Conference.

Johnson, S. (1997). *Interface culture: How new technology transforms the way we create & communicate.* Basic Books.

Johnson, S. (2006). *Everything bad is good for you.* Riverhead.

Jung, C.G. (1969). *Man and his symbols.* Dell Publishing.

Kent, S.L. (2001). *The ultimate history of video games.* Prima.

King, S. (2000). *On writing.* Scribner.

Knoke, W. (1997). *Bold new world: The essential road map to the twenty-first century.* Kodansha International.

Koster, R. (2005). *Theory of fun for game design.* Paraglyph Press.

Krawczyk, M. & Novak, J. (2006). *Game development essentials: Game story & character development.* Cengage Delmar.

Kurzweil, R. (2000). *The age of spiritual machines: When computers exceed human intelligence.* Penguin.

Laramee, F.D. (Ed.) (2002). *Game design perspectives.* Charles River Media.

Laramee, F.D. (Ed.) (2005). *Secrets of the game business. (3rd ed).* Charles River Media.

Levy, P. (2001). *Cyberculture.* University of Minnesota Press.

Lewis, M. (2001). *Next: The future just happened.* W.W.Norton & Company.

Mackay, C. (1841). *Extraordinary popular delusions & the madness of crowds.* Three Rivers Press.

Marks, A. (2008). *The complete guide to game audio.* Elsevier/Focal Press.

Marks, A. & Novak, J. (2008). *Game development essentials: Game audio development.* Cengage Delmar.

McConnell, S. (1996). *Rapid development.* Microsoft Press.

McCorduck, P. (2004). *Machines who think: A personal inquiry into the history and prospects of artificial intelligence (2nd ed).* AK Peters.

McKenna, T. (December 2003). "This means war." *Journal of Electronic Defense.*

Meigs, T. (2003). *Ultimate game design: Building game worlds.* McGraw-Hill Osborne Media.

Mencher, M. (2002). *Get in the game: Careers in the game industry.* New Riders.

Meyers, S. (2005). *Effective C++: 55 specific ways to improve your programs and designs (3rd ed).* Addison-Wesley.

Michael, D. (2003). *The indie game development survival guide.* Charles River Media.

Montfort, N. (2003). *Twisty little passages: An approach to interactive fiction.* MIT Press.

Moravec, H. (2000). *Robot.* Oxford University Press.

Morris, D. (September/October 2004). Virtual weather. *Weatherwise.*

Morris, D. & Hartas, L. (2003). *Game art: The graphic art of computer games.* Watson-Guptill Publications.

Muehl, W. & Novak, J. (2007). *Game development essentials: Game simulation development.* Cengage Delmar.

Mulligan, J. & Patrovsky, B. (2003). *Developing online games: An insider's guide.* New Riders.

Mummolo, J. (July 2006). "Helping children play." *Newsweek.*

Murray, J. (2001). *Hamlet on the holodeck: The future of narrative in cyberspace.* MIT Press.

Negroponte, N. (1996). *Being digital.* Vintage Books.

Nielsen, J. (1999). *Designing web usability: The practice of simplicity.* New Riders.

Nomadyun. (February 23, 2006). "Game Testing Methodology." *CN IT Blog* (www.cnitblog.com/nomadyun/archive/2006/02/23/6869.html).

Novak. J. (2007). *Game development essentials: An introduction. (2nd ed.).* Cengage Delmar.

Novak, J. & Levy, L. (2007). *Play the game: The parent's guide to video games.* Cengage Course Technology PTR.

Novak, J. (2003). "MMOGs as online distance learning applications." University of Southern California.

O'Donnell, M. & Marks, A. (2002). "The use and effectiveness of audio in *Halo:* Game music evolved." *Music4Games* (www.music4games.net/Features_Display.aspx?id=24).

Omernick, M. (2004). *Creating the art of the game.* New Riders Games.

Oram, A. (Ed.) (2001). *Peer-to-peer.* O'Reilly & Associates.

Patow, C.A. (December 2005). "Medical simulation makes medical education better & safer." *Health Management Technology.*

Peck, M. (January 2005). "Air Force's latest video game targets potential recruits." *National Defense.*

Pepastaek, J. "The PlayStation Gamemaker: Disassembling Net Yaroze" *Gamespot* (www.gamespot.com/features/vgs/psx/yaroze).

Pham, A. (October 20, 2008). "Mom, I Want to Major in Video Games." *Los Angeles Times* (www.latimes.com/business/la-fi-gamesschools20-2008oct20,1,1900670.story).

PHP Quality Assurance Team. "Handling Bug Reports?" *PHP-QAT* (qa.php.net/handling-bugs.php).

Piaget, J. (2000). *The psychology of the child.* Basic Books.

Piaget, J. (2007). *The child's conception of the world.* Jason Aronson.

Pohflepp, S. (January 2007). "Before and after Darwin." *We Make Money Not Art* (www.we-make-money-not -art.com/archives/009261.php).

Poole, S. (2004). *Trigger happy: Videogames and the entertainment revolution.* Arcade Publishing.

Prensky, M. (2006). *Don't bother me, Mom: I'm learning!* Paragon House.

Ramirez, J. (July 2006). "The new ad game." *Newsweek.*

Rheingold, H. (1991). *Virtual reality.* Touchstone.

Rheingold, H. (2000). *Tools for thought: The history and future of mind-expanding technology.* MIT Press.

Robbins, S.P. (2001). *Organizational behavior (9th ed).* Prentice-Hall, Inc.

Rogers, E.M. (1995). *Diffusion of innovations.* Free Press.

Rollings, A. & Morris, D. (2003). *Game architecture & design: A new edition.* New Riders.

Rollings, A. & Adams, E. (2003). *Andrew Rollings & Ernest Adams on game design.* New Riders.

Rouse, R. (2001) *Game design: Theory & practice (2nd ed).* Wordware Publishing.

Salen, K. & Zimmerman, E. (2003). *Rules of play.* MIT Press.

Sanchanta, M. (2006 January). "Japanese game aids U.S. war on obesity: Gym class in West Virginia to use an interactive dance console." *Financial Times.*

Sanger, G.A. [a.k.a. "The Fat Man"]. (2003). *The Fat Man on game audio.* New Riders.

Saltzman, M. (July 23, 1999). "Secrets of the Sages: Level Design." *Gamasutra* (www.gamasutra.com/view/feature/3360/secrets_of_the_sages_level_design.php?page=3).

Saunders, K. & Novak, J. (2007). *Game development essentials: Game interface design.* Cengage Delmar.

Schildt, H. (2006). *Java: A beginner's guide (4th ed).* McGraw-Hill Osborne Media.

Schomaker, W. (September 2001). "Cosmic models match reality." *Astronomy.*

Sellers, J. (2001). *Arcade fever.* Running Press.

Shaffer, D.W. (2006). *How computer games help children learn.* Palgrave Macmillan.

Standage, T. (1999). *The Victorian Internet.* New York: Berkley Publishing Group.

Strauss, W. & Howe, N. (1992). *Generations.* Perennial.

Strauss, W. & Howe, N. (1993). *13th gen: Abort, retry, ignore, fail?* Vintage Books.

Strauss, W. & Howe, N. (1998). *The fourth turning.* Broadway Books.

Strauss, W. & Howe, N. (2000). *Millennials rising: The next great generation.* Vintage Books.

Strauss, W., Howe, N. & Markiewicz, P. (2006). *Millennials & the pop culture.* LifeCourse Associates.

Stroustrup, B. (2000). *The C++ programming language (3rd ed).* Addison-Wesley.

Szinger, J. (1993-2006). "On Composing Interactive Music." *Zing Man Productions* (www.zingman.com/spew/CompIntMusic.html).

Trotter, A. (November 2005). "Despite allure, using digital games for learning seen as no easy task." *Education Week.*

Tufte, E.R. (1983). *The visual display of quantitative information.* Graphics Press.

Tufte, E.R. (1990). *Envisioning information.* Graphics Press.

Tufte, E.R. (1997). *Visual explanations.* Graphics Press.

Tufte, E.R. (2006). *Beautiful evidence.* Graphics Press.

Turkle, S. (1997). *Life on the screen: Identity in the age of the Internet.* Touchstone.

Van Duyne, D.K. et al. (2003). *The design of sites.* Addison-Wesley.

Vogler, C. (1998). *The writer's journey: Mythic structure for writers. (2nd ed).* Michael Wiese Productions.

Weems, MD. (October 5, 2008). "10 Steps to Becoming a Video Game Tester." *Bright Hub* (www.brighthub.com/video-games/pc/articles/9819.aspx).

Welch, J. & Welch, S. (2005). *Winning.* HarperCollins Publishers.

Weizenbaum, J. (1984). *Computer power and human reason.* Penguin Books.

Wilcox, J. (2007). *Voiceovers: Techniques & Tactics for Success.* Allworth Press.

Williams, J.D. (1954). *The compleat strategyst: Being a primer on the theory of the games of strategy.* McGraw-Hill.

Wolf, J.P. & Perron, B. (Eds.). (2003). *Video game theory reader.* Routledge.

Wong, G. (November 2006). "Educators explore 'Second Life' online." *CNN.com* (www.cnn.com/2006/TECH/11/13/second.life.university/index.html).

Wysocki, R.K. (2006). *Effective project management (4th ed).* John Wiley & Sons.

Index

Extended Copyright & Trademark Notices

Alone in the Dark®: Inferno © 2008 courtesy of Atari Interactive, Inc. All rights reserved. Used with permission.

Ikaruga © 2003 courtesy of Atari Europe SASU. © 2001-2003 Treasure. All rights reserved. Used with permission.

Fallout 3 © 2008 Bethesda Softworks LLC, a ZeniMax Media company. Fallout is a registered trademark of ZeniMax Media Inc. All Rights Reserved.

Warcraft ® and World of Warcraft ® images provided courtesy of Blizzard Entertainment, Inc.

Xbox®, Xbox 360®, Forza Motorsport®, Halo®, Zoo Tycoon® 2: Marine Mania® are trademarks or registered trademarks of Microsoft Corporation. Gears of War® (Epic Games, Inc.} Lumines™ (Q Entertainment Inc.), and Conker™ (Rare) are trademarks or registered trademarks of their respective owners. Art/images/game demo reprinted with permission from Microsoft Corporation.

PAC-MAN® ©1980, GALAGA® ©1981, SOULCALIBUR® ©1998 1999, PAC-MAN® CHAMPIONSHIP EDITION ©1980-2008 NAMCO BANDAI Games Inc. Courtesy of NAMCO BANDAI Games America Inc.

Bug Notes

Bug Notes

Bug Notes

Bug Notes

Bug Notes

Bug Notes

Bug Notes

Bug Notes

Bug Notes

Bug Notes

Bug Notes

Bug Notes

Bug Notes

Bug Notes

Bug Notes

Bug Notes

IMPORTANT! READ CAREFULLY: This End User License Agreement ("Agreement") sets forth the conditions by which Cengage Learning will make electronic access to the Cengage Learning-owned licensed content and associated media, software, documentation, printed materials, and electronic documentation contained in this package and/or made available to you via this product (the "Licensed Content"), available to you (the "End User"). BY CLICKING THE "I ACCEPT" BUTTON AND/OR OPENING THIS PACKAGE, YOU ACKNOWLEDGE THAT YOU HAVE READ ALL OF THE TERMS AND CONDITIONS, AND THAT YOU AGREE TO BE BOUND BY ITS TERMS, CONDITIONS, AND ALL APPLICABLE LAWS AND REGULATIONS GOVERNING THE USE OF THE LICENSED CONTENT.

1.0 SCOPE OF LICENSE

1.1 Licensed Content. The Licensed Content may contain portions of modifiable content ("Modifiable Content") and content which may not be modified or otherwise altered by the End User ("Non-Modifiable Content"). For purposes of this Agreement, Modifiable Content and Non-Modifiable Content may be collectively referred to herein as the "Licensed Content." All Licensed Content shall be considered Non-Modifiable Content, unless such Licensed Content is presented to the End User in a modifiable format and it is clearly indicated that modification of the Licensed Content is permitted.

1.2 Subject to the End User's compliance with the terms and conditions of this Agreement, Cengage Learning hereby grants the End User, a nontransferable, nonexclusive, limited right to access and view a single copy of the Licensed Content on a single personal computer system for noncommercial, internal, personal use only. The End User shall not (i) reproduce, copy, modify (except in the case of Modifiable Content), distribute, display, transfer, sublicense, prepare derivative work(s) based on, sell, exchange, barter or transfer, rent, lease, loan, resell, or in any other manner exploit the Licensed Content; (ii) remove, obscure, or alter any notice of Cengage Learning's intellectual property rights present on or in the Licensed Content, including, but not limited to, copyright, trademark, and/or patent notices; or (iii) disassemble, decompile, translate, reverse engineer, or otherwise reduce the Licensed Content.

2.0 TERMINATION

2.1 Cengage Learning may at any time (without prejudice to its other rights or remedies) immediately terminate this Agreement and/or suspend access to some or all of the Licensed Content, in the event that the End User does not comply with any of the terms and conditions of this Agreement. In the event of such termination by Cengage Learning, the End User shall immediately return any and all copies of the Licensed Content to Cengage Learning.

3.0 PROPRIETARY RIGHTS

3.1 The End User acknowledges that Cengage Learning owns all rights, title and interest, including, but not limited to all copyright rights therein, in and to the Licensed Content, and that the End User shall not take any action inconsistent with such ownership. The Licensed Content is protected by U.S., Canadian and other applicable copyright laws and by international treaties, including the Berne Convention and the Universal Copyright Convention. Nothing contained in this Agreement shall be construed as granting the End User any ownership rights in or to the Licensed Content.

3.2 Cengage Learning reserves the right at any time to withdraw from the Licensed Content any item or part of an item for which it no longer retains the right to publish, or which it has reasonable grounds to believe infringes copyright or is defamatory, unlawful, or otherwise objectionable.

4.0 PROTECTION AND SECURITY

4.1 The End User shall use its best efforts and take all reasonable steps to safeguard its copy of the Licensed Content to ensure that no unauthorized reproduction, publication, disclosure, modification, or distribution of the Licensed Content, in whole or in part, is made. To the extent that the End User becomes aware of any such unauthorized use of the Licensed Content, the End User shall immediately notify Cengage Learning. Notification of such violations may be made by sending an e-mail to:
infringement@cengage.com

5.0 MISUSE OF THE LICENSED PRODUCT

5.1 In the event that the End User uses the Licensed Content in violation of this Agreement, Cengage Learning shall have the option of electing liquidated damages, which shall include all profits generated by the End User's use of the Licensed Content plus interest computed at the maximum rate permitted by law and all legal fees and other expenses incurred by Cengage Learning in enforcing its rights, plus penalties.

6.0 FEDERAL GOVERNMENT CLIENTS

6.1 Except as expressly authorized by Cengage Learning, Federal Government clients obtain only the rights specified in this Agreement and no other rights. The Government acknowledges that (i) all software and related documentation incorporated in the Licensed Content is existing commercial computer software within the meaning of FAR 27.405(b)(2); and (2) all other data delivered in whatever form, is limited rights data within the meaning of FAR 27.401. The restrictions in this section are acceptable as consistent with the Government's need for software and other data under this Agreement.

7.0 DISCLAIMER OF WARRANTIES AND LIABILITIES

7.1 Although Cengage Learning believes the Licensed Content to be reliable, Cengage Learning does not guarantee or warrant (i) any information or materials contained in or produced by the Licensed Content, (ii) the accuracy, completeness or reliability of the Licensed Content, or (iii) that the Licensed Content is free from errors or other material defects. THE LICENSED PRODUCT IS PROVIDED "AS IS," WITHOUT ANY WARRANTY OF ANY KIND AND CENGAGE LEARNING DISCLAIMS ANY AND ALL WARRANTIES, EXPRESSED OR IMPLIED, INCLUDING, WITHOUT LIMITATION, WARRANTIES OF MERCHANTABILITY OR FITNESS FOR A PARTICULAR PURPOSE. IN NO EVENT SHALL CENGAGE LEARNING BE LIABLE FOR: INDIRECT, SPECIAL, PUNITIVE OR CONSEQUENTIAL DAMAGES INCLUDING FOR LOST PROFITS, LOST DATA, OR OTHERWISE. IN NO EVENT SHALL CENGAGE LEARNING'S AGGREGATE LIABILITY HEREUNDER, WHETHER ARISING IN CONTRACT, TORT, STRICT LIABILITY OR OTHERWISE, EXCEED THE AMOUNT OF FEES PAID BY THE END USER HEREUNDER FOR THE LICENSE OF THE LICENSED CONTENT.

8.0 GENERAL

8.1 Entire Agreement. This Agreement shall constitute the entire Agreement between the Parties and supercedes all prior Agreements and understandings oral or written relating to the subject matter hereof.

8.2 Enhancements/Modifications of Licensed Content. From time to time, and in Cengage Learning's sole discretion, Cengage Learning may advise the End User of updates, upgrades, enhancements and/or improvements to the Licensed Content, and may permit the End User to access and use, subject to the terms and conditions of this Agreement, such modifications, upon payment of prices as may be established by Cengage Learning.

8.3 No Export. The End User shall use the Licensed Content solely in the United States and shall not transfer or export, directly or indirectly, the Licensed Content outside the United States.

8.4 Severability. If any provision of this Agreement is invalid, illegal, or unenforceable under any applicable statute or rule of law, the provision shall be deemed omitted to the extent that it is invalid, illegal, or unenforceable. In such a case, the remainder of the Agreement shall be construed in a manner as to give greatest effect to the original intention of the parties hereto.

8.5 Waiver. The waiver of any right or failure of either party to exercise in any respect any right provided in this Agreement in any instance shall not be deemed to be a waiver of such right in the future or a waiver of any other right under this Agreement.

8.6 Choice of Law/Venue. This Agreement shall be interpreted, construed, and governed by and in accordance with the laws of the State of New York, applicable to contracts executed and to be wholly preformed therein, without regard to its principles governing conflicts of law. Each party agrees that any proceeding arising out of or relating to this Agreement or the breach or threatened breach of this Agreement may be commenced and prosecuted in a court in the State and County of New York. Each party consents and submits to the nonexclusive personal jurisdiction of any court in the State and County of New York in respect of any such proceeding.

8.7 Acknowledgment. By opening this package and/or by accessing the Licensed Content on this Web site, THE END USER ACKNOWLEDGES THAT IT HAS READ THIS AGREEMENT, UNDERSTANDS IT, AND AGREES TO BE BOUND BY ITS TERMS AND CONDITIONS. IF YOU DO NOT ACCEPT THESE TERMS AND CONDITIONS, YOU MUST NOT ACCESS THE LICENSED CONTENT AND RETURN THE LICENSED PRODUCT TO CENGAGE LEARNING (WITHIN 30 CALENDAR DAYS OF THE END USER'S PURCHASE) WITH PROOF OF PAYMENT ACCEPTABLE TO CENGAGE LEARNING, FOR A CREDIT OR A REFUND. Should the End User have any questions/comments regarding this Agreement, please contact Cengage Learning at:
Delmar.help@cengage.com